For Dinah-Jane

GASTR

ONOMY

NICO LADENIS

with Alan Crompton-Batt

Photographs by Anthony Blake

EBURY PRESS LONDON

Published by Ebury Press
Division of The National Magazine Company Limited
Colquhoun House, 27-37 Broadwick Street, London W1V 1FR

First Impression 1987

ISBN 0 85223 682 4

Editor: Yvonne McFarlane
Art Director: Frank Phillips
Designer: Harry Green

Filmset by Advanced Filmsetters (Glasgow) Ltd
Printed and bound in Italy by New Interlitho, S.p.a., Milan

Contents

Foreword

My first visit Chez Nico (Battersea, 1980) is joined in my cast of sublime memories to the transcendental meals of my first visit to Alexandre Dumaine's Hôtel de la Côte d'Or in Saulieu in 1954 and of that to Chez-Garin in Paris, just after he opened in 1961. I had never heard of Nico until a few days earlier when Charles Florman, of whom Nico speaks in the book, told me that he considered Chez Nico to be the greatest restaurant in London. With apologies to Mr Florman and to Nico, I admit that I did not take this recommendation too seriously, simply because I have had too many mediocre meals in restaurants that are said to be the 'greatest'. But then, someone else told me that Nico was known for refusing to cook steak any way but rare. It may sound simple-minded but, for someone who has tried, unsuccessfully, over the years to create formulas for ordering a correctly cooked steak ('very, very rare' in America, only to receive a dried-out steak with hardly a blush of pink at the heart; 'saignant-à point' in France, for fear of receiving a blue steak, still chilled between the flash-seared surfaces), this seemed like a tremendous recommendation. The rest is past history – the steak was, of course, correctly cooked, its cèpes fumet a lovely complement, the mousseline of scallops was aerial, moist and velvety, the tulip of ice cream with its coulis of red fruits of a rare purity, and the wines – Champagne apéritif, Puligny-Montrachet 1974 and Hermitage 1962 – fell admirably into place (there may have been a moment

– hardly discernible – of consternation when I asked for the Hermitage to be splashily decanted to aerate it and put briefly into an ice bucket to cool its ardour) and I was in heaven.

Since that evening, a visit to London without a meal at Nico's is unthinkable. I cannot resist recalling a particular lunch, which Nico had accepted to serve on a closing day, simply because it made so many people happy. We were seventeen at table, the lunch was flawless and Dinah-Jane, Nico, the kitchen staff and the dining room staff were as delighted with the day, as euphoric after six hours of caring for us, as were my guests and I. This is what kept us busy:

DÉJEUNER DU 14 AVRIL 1984

apéritif: Champagne

·

Ballotine de Foie Gras avec sa Petite Salade d'Artichauts
Anjou (Coteaux du Layon) 1928

·

Délice de Barbue au Beurre de Morilles
Anjou 1928

·

Canette de Challans au Miel et au Poivre
avec sa Sauce au Fumet de Cèpes
Château Pichon-Longueville Comtesse de Lalande 1962

·

Plateau de Fromages
Château Rausan-Ségla 1928

·

Tartelette au Coulis de Pommes Caramélisées
Château Guiraud 1942

·

Café et Petits Fours

My Gastronomy is an autobiography and a book of meditations as well as a practical, exciting and unorthodox cookery book. Nico's gastronomic signature is too complex to analyse in detail for much of it lies in intuition, fingertips and the directives of his own palate; one should nonetheless take careful note of his very personal treatments of herbs, wines and honey in the kitchen.

At times the meditations well up and brim over in the form of outraged observations, as when Nico writes '... the gurgling and slopping many so-called wine connoisseurs indulge in quite honestly leaves me cold.' I have often suspected Nico of measuring his friends by a different yardstick than that which he applies to others, for he knows perfectly well that I, for instance, am an irredeemable slurper of wine (although, in public, and most particularly at Nico's, I try to slurp with discretion).

If Nico's observation about 'wine snobs' brought an affectionate smile, I confess to having howled with laughter when, a couple of pages after having related a scene during which he tore up an inadequate sum of money for a cheque given to unsatisfactory customers and flung it under the table, he writes, 'The picture of me as an ogre does not stand up....' Of course he is right – he is not an ogre but merely a lovable genius who does not mind sometimes upsetting people...

Nico is an incorrigible force of nature. You will have to accept him as he is, an explosion of incandescent passions, loyalties and prejudices, fierce dedication and occasional intolerance ... or get out of his way. If you accept him, the rewards are immense – and his food, the result of all that turbulance, is sober and harmonious, the presentations are ravishing in their simplicity and play of colour, the flavours are subtle, often surprising, and always signed 'Nico'; it is built on a solid classical foundation but there is no other food like it.

RICHARD OLNEY
Solliès-Toucas, 27 April 1987

Introduction

No-one can deny the unique contribution of Nico Ladenis in bringing good food to the attention of the public. Journalists and editors fall over themselves to interview the man who says that the customer is not always right, the man who tells the public what they should eat. His statements are given the force they carry both because of their controversial nature and because of his stature as one of Europe's leading chefs and restaurateurs. Nico has been critical of the 'food revolution' of recent years and has created a succession of fine restaurants, to fit his own personal vision and style. In the early Seventies, Chez Nico in Dulwich brought fine food to an area deprived of it before and since. Chez Nico, Battersea, which opened in 1980, was perhaps more classical, more confident and confirmed to many the true talent of the man. In 1985 he left London, his home and his natural audience, to open Chez Nico at Shinfield near Reading leaving Chez Nico, Battersea, in the capable hands of his young protegé, Philip Britten. Nico's team hit new heights at Shinfield and his presentation again broke new ground but his clients and he failed to find a true rapport. Within 12 months, he had sold up and quit the country and returned to a grateful London to create Simply Nico, a grand restaurant as busy as any the capital had ever seen.

A major inspiration even to those who would choose to follow a more orthodox path to success, he is always available to give help and advice to the many chefs who visit him, who eat at his restaurants and who write to him seeking answers to the inevitable problems of running a good restaurant in the late 1980s. His regular column in the trade paper, *Caterer and Hotelkeeper*, has been one of the few public outlets for the feelings of many British chefs in business on their own that the 'food revolution' does not show up in hard cash in their cash registers. Nico is an example to all of them, especially the young men in the small towns of rural England, that excellence and patience can produce success. Many of them treat him as a father confessor and seek reassurance or encouragement after a bleak day's business.

It is certainly an understatement to say that he is not one for joining clubs. The Académie Culinaire is an association of formally trained chefs which has its main branch in Paris. Based in the French tradition of the culinary arts and built on apprenticeships and techniques found particularly in the kitchens of hotels or grand establishments, there is no room in the Académie Culinaire for the self-taught (the great Raymond Blanc is merely an associate member). Nico makes no secret of his inability to compromise or to fit in, just as the Académie has made no attempt to invite him to harness his talent for their cause. Nico is by far the most eminent chef to have been excluded from the Académie Culinaire, something which does not bother him as he continues in a single-minded way.

Immediately it opened, his restaurant, Simply Nico, was the hottest ticket in town. It is probably the nearest thing to his ideal vision of a restaurant that he has yet created. There are no compromises in Rochester Row, and no vacancies either. Here he cooks a fixed price menu at lunchtime that brings to the business community excellent food at low prices. A great restaurant has its base in lunches and at night the food is perhaps more complex, for both the chef and the customer have more time. Nico's exemplary *confit de canard* is now a lunchtime favourite as are the leaf salad with grilled *crottin*, his famous fish soup and the roast rack of spring lamb with garlic sauce. In the evening he gives fuller rein to his talents, at least in terms of choice and also in the construction of certain more complex dishes, such as sweetbreads braised in a Madeira sauce, stuffed quails or duck breasts in a wild mushroom sauce. His major principles, good ingredients and simplicity, guide the menu.

I first met Nico in 1979 when I was dispatched by Egon Ronay to sample his then new restaurant in Battersea. As an anonymous inspector, I ate one of the finest meals of my life, including a sublime terrine of foie gras with Sauternes jelly and his famous or about to be *filet de boeuf au fumet de cèpes* and a *parfait à l'Armagnac* that was perfection. I was startled, as many others had been, to find such warmth and above all such talent in so quiet a street and behind a totally unassuming façade of wood with only the sign 'Chez Nico' visible as exterior decoration. His wife, Dinah-Jane, seemed to really care that both the food and the restaurant were seen at their best. I did not speak to Nico other than to say goodbye and yet when I returned a year later he immediately knew who I was. A memory which allows Nico to remember his experiences in such detail is a prominent part of his character. He is a man of his word. Keen on detail, honest, punctual and, of course, reliable. He finds it very hard to understand those who promise and then fail to deliver.

Nico and I have now worked together for some years and I have lost count of the number of times that people who have visited him with trepidation, expecting to find an ogre have subsequently been disarmed not just by his charm but by his honesty. This is, of course, his strength and his weakness. Honesty is, perhaps, unpopular in the 1980s and discretion is advised, particularly, in the so-called service industries. Nico, though, speaks his mind and is always ready to stand by his opinions and take the consequences. Many who agree with him in private would never dare admit it in public. No such scruples or self-interest affect Nico. It is this honesty that has led to controversy. Much of what Nico says has been echoed by chefs of his calibre – but in private and off the record and probably only to each other. However, many people now making a living from cooking and serving serious food must owe a debt to the man whose first act as a restaurateur was to erect a sign telling people what they could not have. It is as a restaurateur that Nico succeeds as much as he does as a chef. With Dinah-Jane he creates an ambience for his talent that eludes many chefs who can certainly cook but lack the magnetism or the nerve to be chef–patron or restaurateur.

When in 1974 he opened his first restaurant in Dulwich in outer London, England was yet to embark on its voyage of discovery through the virtues and excesses of *la nouvelle cuisine*. Dinner out was not a celebration of food but a social occasion, often a combination of both business and pleasure. Dulwich had no history of gastronomy and yet it was here that the intrepid Ladenis family, fresh from the ultimate tour of French restaurants, opened up shop for the first time. In an area chosen for obvious economic reasons, few have repeated the experience and none have repeated his success. Thirty-seven years old and self taught, Nico was as firm of purpose

Chez Nico

The cost of your starter is included in the price
of your main course.

La soupe aux amandes des 'Frères Troisgros'

Mousse de truite fumée aux petits légumes,
Chantilly au raifort

Terrine fondante de foies de canards avec sa
gelée au Sauternes

Salade tiède de petits légumes au beurre de truffes

Bouquet de petites langues de veau aux épinards

Les escalopes de saumon gratinées à la crème
de ciboulette

Les légumes sont dans le prix

Salade verte aux pignons   1.00

Le poisson du jour

Prices include VAT and Service and Cover Charge

Dinner
CHEZ NICO
Battersea, 1981

Chez Nico

Les escalopes de poulet 'en fricassée' à l'angevine   9.75

Carré d'agneau rôti, sauce béarnaise à la   10.85
menthe   (served pink)

Filet de boeuf grillé, beurre chateaubriand (served rare)   12.00

Ris de veau avec sa brioche et sa sauce   11.75
au fonds de carottes

Aiguillettes de canard aux kiwis, comme   11.00
à Valence   (served pink & for two)

Marquise à la mousse de Framboises avec son   1.75
coulis de Framboises

Mousse glacée au caramel, aux pétales de poires   1.85

Parfait à l'Armagnac à la purée de marrons glacés   1.70

Les sorbets   1.75

Petite salade d'oranges arrosée de liqueur   1.50
d'orange et de caramel

Notre assiette de fromages de France   2.00

Café   .75

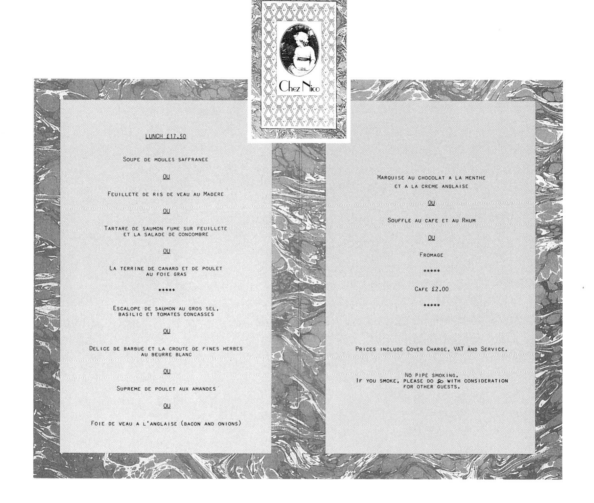

LUNCH £17.50

SOUPE DE MOULES SAFFRANEE

OU

FEUILLETE DE RIS DE VEAU AU MADERE

OU

TARTARE DE SAUMON FUME SUR FEUILLETE
ET LA SALADE DE CONCOMBRE

OU

LA TERRINE DE CANARD ET DE POULET
AU FOIE GRAS

*****

ESCALOPE DE SAUMON AU GROS SEL,
BASILIC ET TOMATES CONCASSES

OU

DELICE DE BARBUE ET LA CROUTE DE FINES HERBES
AU BEURRE BLANC

OU

SUPREME DE POULET AUX AMANDES

OU

FOIE DE VEAU A L'ANGLAISE (BACON AND ONIONS)

MARQUISE AU CHOCOLAT A LA MENTHE
ET A LA CREME ANGLAISE

OU

SOUFFLE AU CAFE ET AU RHUM

OU

FROMAGE

*****

CAFE £2.00

*****

PRICES INCLUDE COVER CHARGE, VAT AND SERVICE.

NO PIPE SMOKING.
IF YOU SMOKE, PLEASE DO SO WITH CONSIDERATION
FOR OTHER GUESTS.

Lunch
CHEZ NICO
Shinfield, 1986

THE PRICE OF YOUR MAIN COURSE
INCLUDES CHOICE OF STARTER

SOUPE DE ROUGETS,
SA ROUILLE ET SES CROUTONS

FEUILLETE DE PIGEON AUX ARTICHAUTS
ET AU BEURRE DE GIROLLES

MOUSSELINE DE SOLE AU CRABE,
SAUCE ROSE DE CRUSTACES

TIMBALE DE SAUMON FUME
A LA MOUSSE DE LANGOUSTINES
ET LA CHIFFONADE DE LAITUE

NOTRE TERRINE DE FOIE GRAS FAIT A LA MAISON,
LA SAVEUR DE POIREAUX, ET LA GELEE AU SAUTERNES

KALEIDOSCOPE DE NOIX DE ST JACQUES

CAILLE GRILLEE SUR LIT D'EPINARDS,
LA SAUCE AU CASSIS

*****

PAUPIETTES DE SOLE ET DE CRABE
AU FUMET DE LANGOUSTINES 24.00

LOUP DE MER ET LA CROUTE DE FINES HERBES
AU BEURRE BLANC 23.00

*****

SUPREME DE CANARD DU PAYS AU CALVADOS
ET LA PUREE DE POMMES (SERVED PINK) 25.50

AIGUILLETTES DE POULET AU CHAMPAGNE 22.50

FILET DE BOEUF AUX ECHALOTTES,
ACCOMPAGNE DE LA GALETTE DE POMMES DE TERRE AU FOIE GRAS
ET LA MOUSSE DE RAIFORT (SERVED RARE) 25.50

LES DEUX BROCHETTES DE FOIE ET DE ROGNONS DE VEAU
AU FUMET DE PORTO 23.00

LES DES DE RIS DE VEAU CROQUANTS SUR CANAPE DE BRIOCHE
ET LA SAUCE AUX CAROTTES 23.00

*****

Dinner
CHEZ NICO
Shinfield, 1986

Simply Nico

Simply Nico

LUNCH

Three courses
£16.50

including VAT, Service and Coffee

Smoking – Our only rule is: no pipes

SIMPLY NICO
Rochester Row, 1987

Simply Nico

Soupe de rougets avec sa rouille et ses croûtons
ou
Escalope tiède de saumon fumé et de concombre
croquant à la crème de ciboulette
ou
Salade aux fines herbes à l'huile de noisettes

Confit de cuisses de canard deglacé au vin rouge
ou
Tournedos de filet de veau rôti à la saveur de romarin
ou
Paupiettes de sole au beurre blanc

Mousse au chocolat avec son coulis léger de jus d'orange
ou
Sorbet à l'ananas et au kirsch
ou
Assiette de fromages

Café et petits fours

Simply Nico

Two courses
£26.00
including VAT and Service

Smoking – Our only rule is: no pipes

Dinner
SIMPLY NICO
Rochester Row, 1987

Soupe de Rougets

*Bonbonnière de coquilles St. Jacques
au beurre blanc*

Escalope de saumon au gingembre

Timbale de saumon fumé, sauce grelette

*Terrine de poireaux et de poissons à l'huile
de poireaux*

Salade de caille aux raisins

Foie gras chaud en salade d'haricots verts

Ballotine de foie gras avec sa gelée au Sauternes

·

Barbue en feuilleté au jus de homard

Escalope de saumon à la saveur de tomate

Loup de mer au fenouil au beurre blanc de pernod

Blanc de poulet au foie gras

Blanc de poulet farci de morilles

Suprême de canard rose au jus de cassis

Les deux cailles farcies au fumet de truffes

*Noix de ris de veau braisée au madère, au jus de
carottes et de Sauternes*

Carré d'agneau rose

Tournedos de boeuf au fumet de cèpes

Tous les plats sont garnis

then as he is now, perhaps even more so. He was certainly more volatile in those days and it is no surprise to read his reaction to his initial entry in the all-important *Good Food Guide*, when he refused to cooperate with them in year two because they failed to get their facts right in year one.

Since he began work as a professional chef, Nico has been at the heart of developments in the food world. Like everyone else, he, too, has developed over more than a decade, during which time good food and great chefs became big news and the restaurant world moved onto the front page of newspapers the world over.

Somehow, though, he is never a slave to fashion any more than he is to convention. Even the early menus were guided by his principles: 'To avoid misunderstanding we serve fillets of beef rare' proclaims one menu. The changes in Nico's menus come from his development and his ideas not from public opinion. As the public began to scoff at large *nouvelle cuisine* plates on which chefs artfully presented mere mouthfuls of food, Nico took them, circled them with vegetables in a way never seen before in England and gave them a new lease of life. The character of the man comes through whatever he serves: every salad, every *petit four* is as truly his as would have been a *mousse de foie de volaille aux amandes et aux raisins* in 1976. Probably only his fish soup remains in its entirety from his beginnings in Dulwich. However, the change has always been carefully thought out and each dish is researched and practised. At a time when chefs are saying that they cook what they can buy at the market, Nico has planned three months ahead. He knows exactly when the spring lamb, the wild salmon and the wild mushrooms will be available. He deals in quality not gimmicks. No 'first grouse in London' for Nico, who requires consistency from his suppliers, not party tricks.

Nico is, of course, a restaurateur not just a chef. As fashions have changed, his dishes have developed. It is one thing to be a chef or even a good chef but to be a restaurateur you must understand one essential demand of every customer – whether a regular eater-out or an occasional visitor – and that is consistency. People do not have to be surprised every time they eat out and at all Nico's restaurants you have known what to expect. His dishes do not change from day to day, nor do they change at the whim of a sous-chef who feels that he will slice the meat a different way. Nico's menus and his wine lists have been short but well constructed since the beginning. This natural sense of balance, his good taste in eating that has been praised as often as his cooking makes him unable to understand why some people order a meal which is unbalanced or awkwardly chosen.

To Nico, the whole experience of a lunch or dinner has a shape and form and it is his job to help create that framework for the customer.

People have a picture of Nico fretting endlessly about his customers, sweating over a hot stove and probably sleeping on a bed of nails. Of course, this is not so. Nico and his wife Dinah-Jane, who acts as his *maître d'*, feel a need to guide their customers towards the perfect meal, to advise and to coax them into selecting well-balanced dishes so they may derive an optimum amount of pleasure from eating their food. Often this is mistaken for 'bullying'. It is not; it is caring and being deeply concerned that a customer receives everything at its best.

The first journalist from a national newspaper to write a profile of Nico was amazed that he wanted to talk not about the texture of his mousses but about his beloved dogs. The stability of his family life with Dinah-Jane, Isabella and Natasha has certainly been the backbone to his progress in the restaurant world. There is no more volatile relationship than that between chef and *maître d'hôtel*. We have all heard stories of flying hatchets and torrents of abuse from kitchen to restaurant and vice versa. Yet Nico and Dinah-Jane have lived together and worked together for many years now. The Nico Ladenis I have seen surrounded by his family, ordering a never-ending stream of Chinese dishes on a Sunday afternoon and drinking a lager or even a 'diet coke' would come as a great surprise to those who have visited his restaurant expecting to meet an ogre who will deny them an ashtray. But you may smoke at his restaurants, though preferably not throughout the meal. Having outlawed pipe smoking, salt on tables and well-cooked meat many years ago, he finds himself now having been caught up by the fashionable restaurants of London, New York, and Paris.

Extracting this book from Nico has been a long process and a risky one! To spend hours with a perfectionist whose talent is to apply intense creativity to scientific principles can be a gruelling business. Getting him to rework the text or the same photograph a number of times can be a dangerous business. He has, however, written a book which, unlike so many cookery books, genuinely explains not only *how* to do it, but *why* to do it. As you read the book, you will see that Nico hides nothing, his recipes are as clear as his thinking and his principles are firmly gripped. I think he will be remembered as a great chef and a great inspiration.

ALAN CROMPTON-BATT
London 1987

'*I have always needed
a clear goal ahead of me, something to strive
for. My competitive spirit, my rich African
childhood and my French wife all conspired
to lead me to a career in food and, having
made my choice, I have to do better
than anyone else. Actors win Oscars,
politicians have their Honours List,
chefs get their Michelin stars.
For me, and for a handful
of my colleagues, the prize is
three Michelin stars.*'

CHAPTER ONE

Inspirations and influences

I spent part of my childhood in Paradise. I did not realise it then, but when I cast my mind back towards Africa, I see it all, now, clearly in my mind's eye, like a photograph. We lived on a sisal plantation in the central province of Tanzania, then called Tanganyika. Our house was located in the middle of five hectares of cornucopia surrounded by a vast sea of green spiky sisal plants. The plantation stretched for miles in every direction. The house itself was a very ordinary, square bungalow with a corrugated iron roof. It was surrounded by a wire netted verandah. The five hectares which surrounded it were a feast of colour over which my mother presided. We had incredible green lawns set in amongst which were dahlias and beds of roses, carnations and sweet peas. Nearer the house and surrounding it were Laurier roses, red, white and pink hibiscus, red and pink and purple bougainvillaea and dotted about the compound were jacaranda trees and an enormous creeper up one side of the house. Outside my window grew a lime tree and near the front door of the house, the deepest and most intensely scented plant of all – a gardenia.

I have an indelible image of my mother deeply imprinted on my mind. I picture her by our ancient, cast-iron wood-burning stove. Wooden spoon in hand, her apron covered in flour, she would move around the kitchen, tugging at the dough to make filo. And I remember the beautiful aroma of chicken stock made from whole chickens killed that very morning which wafted through the house. She cooked from a Greek translation of a battered French cookery book, though a sizeable part of her repertoire was authentically Greek or Turkish.

Our tropical garden

Amongst the small, European community dotted about the countryside over a vast area, my mother had a reputation for her gardens, her vegetables and her cooking. People noticed, too, the way she used to dress all us four children, which was held in great regard. She was a redoubtable, quintessential, Greek housewife. When anybody received an invitation to come to lunch with us, they quickly accepted knowing that they could expect a gastronomic experience, because my mother had golden hands. She tended a vegetable garden of such complexity and range, there was everything from avocados to tomatoes and French beans, from potatoes and sweet potatoes to carrots, kohlrabi, artichokes, aubergines, pumpkins and cucumbers. There were spring onions and parsley, marjoram and oregano, and bay trees grew everywhere in abundance. Red and green peppers grew to an enormous size.

The range of fruit was extraordinary. On the banks of the stream that flowed through the gardens there were no less than three distinct types of bananas. Then there were the enormous mango trees which again provided several varieties of the fruit. Pawpaw trees grew everywhere, hugging the more moist parts of the land. Pineapples grew virtually wild and we had to rescue them from their haphazard growth and tend them. There were passion fruits, limes, pomegranates, guavas, custard apples and, most incredible of all fruits, the extremely pungent sour sop.

My father lived a full life. The family name has origins in France, that much we have clearly established. He came originally from Constantinople and as a young man he emigrated to America with his elder brother. They settled in Kansas City and, before long, they owned and ran a string of restaurants. He was always reluctant to tell us much about his life in America, except to boast about the night he thrashed two incompetent gangsters who tried to commandeer his float from the till. Subsequently my father had returned to Europe, met my mother, and they had decided to emigrate to Africa and start a new life. They wanted a completely fresh start – and they were not disappointed.

He was a strict and severe man. My brother, two sisters and I were terrified of him. We had to behave ourselves when he was around and kept a keen lookout for the top of his hat, which was all we could see as he came back to the house through the fields at the end of a day's work. He had an obsession for cleanliness, and punctuality. Family meals were a very serious and solemn affair. Though we all instinctively adored my mother's cooking, mute appreciation and a very clean plate were the only ways to register our enormous satisfaction. My father insisted on silence at the table.

He, too, was a gifted cook. I have clear memories of the giant, American-style breakfasts he used to prepare for us: fried eggs, mountains of bacon, enormous, very aromatic, fried red bananas and huge waffles with my mother's homemade jam and the honey from the nearby beehive. A couple of fresh lamb's brains, fried in breadcrumbs and eaten with a generous squeeze of lemon juice, completed the menu. In the middle of the table, a row of homemade jams and jellies stood like a row of soldiers on parade. A bottle of Heinz tomato ketchup stood on one side and a bottle of Worcestershire sauce on the other. At weekends, he would sometimes roast suckling pig over an open fire in the garden. The surrounding land provided a supply of wild game birds and animals of such abundance that for us the rare treats were reserved for the days when we could obtain some fillet steak or a leg of lamb.

Wild guinea fowl, partridge and pigeon

Dotted about the compound there were clusters of maize and patches of millet, and when the chickens finished feeding, the guinea fowl and the partridges crept out of the thickets and polished off whatever grain was lying around. If we wanted to eat partridge or guinea fowl, my father would walk out of the front door with his shotgun at about 6.30 in the evening and shoot the birds as little as a hundred yards from our house. My African memories tell me that the meat of the guinea fowl over there was much darker and of a gamier flavour than its European cousin, although the flesh of the partridge was milder and whiter than the European variety, and the feet were bright red. Sometimes my father would hunt for gazelle and other times the Africans would deliver to us great hunks of wild boar which had been speared to death. Some of the most delicious memories of stews were associated with the way my mother used to cook wild boar.

There was one more special food memory from Africa, the pigeon. No one has experienced the deliciousness of pigeon whether from Bresse, from Norfolk, or from the woods of Europe, who has not eaten the most delicious bird of all – the green pigeon of East Africa. These birds, no more than the size of an ordinary, medium-sized European wood pigeon, perhaps a little smaller, would flock in particular in very tall trees that produced sweet red berries. Probably the single most lingering taste that persists in my memory is green pigeon roasted over an open fire. I will give you one thousand *pigeonneaux de Bresse* for just one of those freshly grilled green pigeons, brushed with melted butter and a squeeze of lemon from a fruit picked fresh from the tree.

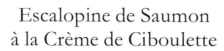

Escalopine de Saumon
à la Crème de Ciboulette

Escalopes of Fresh Salmon
in a Chive-flavoured Sauce

This is probably my favourite fish dish and
yet there is no mystique about it. Paper-thin slices
of the best fresh salmon are painted lightly
with olive oil and cooked briefly on the plate, in a
very hot oven. Served with my white wine fish
sauce and decorated with chives it looks sensational
and tastes delicious.

RECIPE ON PAGE 51

Terrine de Body

·

Veal and Bacon Terrine

*Another favourite of mine which is easy to
make. I'm always intrigued how the combination
of such simple basic ingredients — veal, bacon,
onions, herbs — can result in a dish whose
aroma and flavour are so authentically those of the
best French charcuterie. If you take time and
care when layering the ingredients, you will
also be rewarded by its beautiful appearance.
These days I serve this terrine with Cumberland
Sauce flavoured with green peppercorns.*

RECIPE ON PAGE 38

Exotic flavours

In our enormous paraffin-powered refrigerator there were always two large jugs, one with fresh lime juice sweetened with a lot of sugar and one containing fresh coconut water. The flavours of coconut, curry, cumin, Basmati rice and all the other spices of the East were part of my upbringing and my early education. The exotic flavours which only today are gradually creeping with great trepidation into the outer edges of *nouvelle* and modern French cuisine were flavours to which I needed no introduction.

Therein might lie the secret of my great affinity to Roger Vergé. He knows Africa – East Africa and North Africa as well as the Caribbean and South America. He has hunted big game in Kenya and his mind is open to spices and foods originating outside France, unlike so many of his peers. Only now are they beginning to look East.

When I left behind me this rich home life and went to school at the Prince of Wales in Nairobi and then on to university, the memories and the affinities of those early days began to fade.

My education in Africa had been as English as a red London bus. My university education should therefore be in England. I studied economics: naïvely believing that this would prepare me for a career in any business. In fact it seems to prepare you better for a life in research in a dusty library. My experience of business life certainly was not made easier by what they taught as economics at Hull. I threw myself into the world of commerce without any conspicuous success. Beautiful vegetable gardens, exotic fruit trees and the sweet smells of the kitchen became decidedly unimportant when I came face to face with the big wide world and the need to earn a living.

'Non-conformist, argumentative and unemployable'

I stumbled and fumbled and quarrelled and walked out of jobs and disagreed with managing directors, argued fiercely with superiors and refused to buckle down, to relax my sensibilities and allow my character to be moulded in the method and the tradition of the big corporations. My reintroduction to the pleasures of food came after my marriage to Dinah-Jane and around the same time I came to see that the big corporation was not for me and I was not for the big corporation. The point was driven home rather forcibly at an interview at 6 o'clock one evening in the London boardroom of the Shell Oil Company. This was the culmination of a whole day of aptitude tests. Appearing before the wise men I was told that I had not got the job with Shell Oil Brazil. What was more serious, I was advised not to seek further employment in the ranks of the big corporations because their tests had revealed to them that I was 'non-conformist, argumentative and unemployable'.

Discovering the food of France

I had to agree. Dinah-Jane and I left England to live in the south of France with her relatives. We took a sabbatical year and devoted it to exploring the countryside, visiting all the little villages in Provence, as well as Cannes, Nice Monte Carlo, St Tropez, Toulon, Marseilles and Avignon. All our savings went on food, restaurants, wine, Roquefort cheese, baguettes and lots of pâtisserie. All this time an idea was beginning to germinate in our minds and although we didn't quite know when, where, how or even what, we knew that we had to do something with food. Then certain important influences came onto the scene. We stopped one day at Pouilly-sur-Loire and had a meal at a small restaurant called Chez Mémère. Up to that time, the meals we had been eating in the tiny villages of Provence had been humble. This time we knew that we had finally come face to face with something special. The meal itself consisted of a terrine of duck, duck à l'orange and finally a soufflé au Grand Marnier. It was interminably long and it was our baptism. I remember with great clarity the flinty, woody, smoky taste of the local Pouilly Fumé wine. Later, we began to experiment with incorporating into recipes the red wines and eaux de vie we had discovered. The following recipe is a good example.

This dish tastes best made with a corn-fed poussin, or better still, you can make it with partridge. If you were having Egon Ronay to dinner, it would be a good way of winning his approval to serve him partridge – apparently it is his favourite dish. Garnish it with muscatel grapes, if you wish.

Poussins à l'Eau de Vie de Frontignan

Baby Chickens with Muscatel Grape Brandy

Illustrated on page 48

SERVES 2

2 medium-sized, plump, corn-fed poussins or partridges	150 ml (¼ pint) rich port
50 g (2 oz) butter	10 ml (2 tsp) tomato purée
pepper	10 ml (2 tsp) finely chopped fresh tarragon
6 rashers of bacon	salt
	30–60 ml (2–4 tbsp) eau de vie de Frontignan

Smear the poussins all over with butter and sprinkle with pepper. Wrap 3 rashers of bacon around each bird. Place them in a heavy cast iron pan and roast at 230°C (450°F) mark 8 for 20 minutes. Turn the oven down to 190°C (375°F) mark 5. Push the bacon rashers to the bottom of the pan and continue roasting and basting for a further 10 minutes. Remove the poussins from the pan, set aside and keep warm.

Now make the sauce. Discard the bacon and pour off the fat. Add the port to the pan, bring to the boil, add the tomato purée, stir well and simmer until the sauce reduces and becomes syrupy. Add the tarragon and season with pepper and salt; set the pan aside.

At this stage you can do one of three things. You can present the poussins whole, or you can remove the breasts and the legs and arrange the portions on plates, or you can split them open along the back bone. The last method is probably the best.

Now finish the sauce. Bring back to the boil, add the eau de vie de Frontignan, stir quickly and pour over the chicken. Serve with a fruity, medium-dry white such as a Riesling from Alsace or with a slightly chilled, young, fruity red, eg, a Cru Beaujolais.

Our continued trips to France, particularly to the South, brought us further important steps closer to real haute cuisine. One such unforgettable experience was a dinner at the Hôtel de la Poste in Montargis. I remember two courses of the meal, *ecrévisses à l'Américaine* and *coq au vin de Chinon*. There, too, we drank for the first time one of the special wines of France – a red Chinon. The restaurant had one star in *Michelin*. I was becoming aware of this great restaurant guide around this time. Instinctively, I was in awe of its mystery, its authority, its cursory pronouncements, its conclusions, its judgments, the rosette system and, not least, the respect it commanded. Something about it stirred in me and made my adrenalin race.

When we returned to England though, a chance encounter with a book called *Masterpieces of French Cuisine* by François Amunategui positively galvanised me. The colour pictures of food from one-, two- and three-star restaurants held me spellbound. Inspired by what I read, I began hunting for morel mushrooms and rang up wine merchants to look for Château-Châlon, a rich white *vin jaune* from the Jura. I became very excited and very impatient and I began to cook. We were at the same time, I might add, virtually penniless. For a short period of about 8 months, I helped my closest friend run his restaurant which mainly specialised in Greek food.

This is the first of a number of recipes which I have included here which have become part of my repertoire and which were originally inspired by *Masterpieces of French Cuisine*. It is a dish I have admired for years and even today it casts a peculiar spell over me. Its aroma is indescribable. The perfume which comes from a unique wine, fresh cream and the smell of freshly sautéed chicken add up, for me, to the greatest single individual taste I have

CINDERELLA
THE REAL TRUE STORY

BY CHERYL MOCH
MUSIC BY HOLLY GEWANDTER
FROM AN ORIGINAL IDEA BY HOLLY GEWANDTER & CHERYL MOCH
DIRECTED BY NONA SHEPPHARD
DESIGNED BY AMANDA FISK
LIGHTING DESIGN BY KATE OWEN

OVEMBER 26 – DECEMBER 19 • TUESDAY – SATURDAY 8PM

HE DRILL HALL ARTS CENTRE

6 CHENIES STREET • LONDON WC1 • 01-637 8270

Funded by Camden

LBGS

CINDERELLA
THE REAL TRUE STORY

THRILL
TO THE
ROYAL GOSSIP
YOU WOULD
**REALLY LOVE
TO HEAR**

'The story I want to tell you is about a time when the streams ran as clear as crystal and the sky was the colour of your dreams and the fish and the animals still spoke to us – oh, they can speak to us, they just don't want to anymore. Can you blame them? In any case, this is a story that is still being passed on, from parent to child, from generation to generation, but in the years of the telling, through the prism of prejudice, it's been altered. I want to set the record straight. I want to tell you the real true story of Cinderella . . . '

**PRINCESS
KISSES
GIRL**

**RUMPUS
AT
PALACE
OVER
ALL-GIRL
LOVE MATCH!**

the New York Critics said:
'AN ABSOLUTELY HILARIOUS SHOW'
'INSPIRED . . . SPECTACULAR'
*'FIZZING WITH ELECTRICITY BETWEEN
AUDIENCE AND PERFORMERS'*

**ARCHDUKE
IN
LOVE TANGLE
WITH
ARCHDUKE!**

with **KATE CORKERY, GILLIAN HANNA, NICOLA KATHRENS, BRYONY LAVERY, DALLAS LINGHAM, MARY McCUSKER, ADÈLE SALEEM, FAITH TINGLE**

Tickets:
Tuesday – Thursday £4.50
Friday & Saturday £5.00
Concessions (UNWAGED, CAMDEN RESIDENT, STUDENT, NURSE, SENIOR CITIZEN) £3.00
ONE FREE TICKET IN EVERY TEN BOOKED

Performances:
Thurs 26 Nov – Sat 28 Nov
Thurs 3 Dec – Sat 5 Dec
Tues   8 Dec – Sat 12 Dec
Tues 15 Dec – Sat 19 Dec

8PM

BAR & RESTAURANT · FREE CHILDMINDING FOR UNDER 5s on FRI & SAT EVES

THE DRILL HALL ARTS CENTRE · 16 CHENIES STREET · LONDON WC1E 7EX · 01 637 8270

Printed by Spider Web, 14-16 Sussex Way, London N7

INSPIRATIONS AND INFLUENCES

experienced in my 15 years of cooking. You must have morel mushrooms (*morilles*) and you must have *vin jaune*, preferably Château-Châlon. The chicken I prefer to use in this recipe is a plump, yellow, corn-fed chicken.

Poulet au Vin Jaune

Chicken with Vin Jaune

Illustrated on page 64

SERVES 4
36 plump dried morels
4 well-trimmed, yellow skinned, corn-fed
   chicken legs

flour seasoned with salt and pepper
225 g (8 oz) butter
300 ml (½ pint) vin jaune
600 ml (1 pint) double cream

Place the dried morels in a bowl and pour very hot water over them. Leave them to soak for 40 minutes, making sure all the sand and grit has settled on the bottom. Drain them and set aside, reserving a little of the soaking liquid.

Dust the chicken legs in a little seasoned flour. Melt the butter in a heavy, non-stick frying pan. When it begins to sizzle, place the chicken legs, skin-side down, in one layer in the pan and seal very lightly without browning. Turn the legs over and seal the other sides.

Remove from the pan. Arrange the chicken legs in an even layer in a roasting pan which has a lid. Pour over the buttery juices. Cover the dish and roast at 180°C (350°F) mark 4 for 20 minutes. Check that the legs are not browning halfway through.

When the chicken legs are cooked through, drain all the butter from the roasting pan. Place the pan with the chicken legs in over medium heat and add the morels and a little of the liquid in which they were soaked.

Pour over the *vin jaune*, immediately followed by the cream. Now the chicken will start to become infused with the aroma of the morels and the wine and the cream. This period is crucial: the sauce must not cook too fast and the chicken must both marinate and cook at the same time. But you must not cook it too slowly either, or the cream will become flecked with white specks.

Keep on tasting your sauce until the taste is right. Adjust the seasoning until the sauce is syrupy enough to coat the chicken.

To serve: Arrange the chicken legs on a beautiful platter. Remove the morels and put them on one side, keeping them warm. Pass the sauce through a stainless steel sieve or *chinois*, reheat it gently and spoon it over the chicken legs to coat them well. Arrange the morels in mounds on the top of each leg.

Do try some of the Jura wines – less difficult to find would be any fruity, medium-dry white such as a Gewürztraminer or a muscat from Alsace.

'Body' is an old French word for veal from the Berry area, south of Paris. This recipe is a perfect example of simplicity. If you were given equal portions of finely chopped onions and parsley, some fillets of veal and some green bacon, where on earth would you find the imagination to construct a terrine of such sharply clean taste, so beautiful to look at and so easy to make? Again, the inspiration for this recipe came from *Masterpieces of French Cuisine*. A special touch is the glass of white wine which you pour over the terrine just before baking it in the oven. It is also important to weight it down once it is cooked. You will need an enamelled 1.4 litre (2½ pint) cast-iron terrine with a heavy lid.

Served with a little salad, some gherkins and cocktail onions, this also makes a good main course salad.

Terrine de Body

Veal and Bacon Terrine

Illustrated on page 33

SERVES 12

60 ml (4 tbsp) clarified butter

1.4 kg (3 lb) best quality green bacon, rinded

3 large Spanish onions, very finely chopped

a very large bunch of parsley, very finely chopped

white pepper

4 well-trimmed veal fillets

150 ml (¼ pint) good quality dry white wine (preferably a Chablis)

2 bay leaves

To serve:

Some of the following: gherkins, Cumberland sauce, toasted brioche, sliced apples tossed in curry-flavoured cream

Brush the terrine with clarified butter. Line the terrine with overlapping bacon, leaving 5 cm (2 in) pieces dropping from the sides.

Mix the onions and parsley together in a bowl and season with 15 ml (1 tbsp) of freshly ground white pepper. Mix well together.

Slice the veal fillets lengthwise very, very thinly, then flatten them lightly with the palm of your hand until they are no more than 3 mm (⅛ in) thick.

Assemble the terrine as follows: Arrange slices of veal on the bottom and make sure they cover the entire area. Spoon in some onion and parsley mixture and spread it out evenly with a palette knife to cover the entire area. Then place a layer of bacon lengthwise along on top of the onion and parsley mixture, again making sure that you cover the entire area. Repeat layering the ingredients until you have a well-filled terrine, finishing off with a layer of veal.

Seal the terrine with the overlapping bacon slices. Pour over the white wine. Lay 2 bay leaves on the bacon, then close the lid.

Cook in a bain-marie in a 170°C (325°F) mark 3 oven for about 1½ hours or until cooked. Remove the terrine from the oven and set it aside to cool down. When it is completely cold, place it on a tray and weight it down hard. A lot of juices and jelly will come pouring out of the terrine. Refrigerate overnight and serve with chosen accompaniments and a glass of fragrant dry white wine such as a Chablis or a Ch. Carbonnieux which is quite rich and full.

It is a great pity that trout are no longer considered worthy enough to grace the tables of the best restaurants. I admit, too, that nowadays I do not serve trout. Farmed trout now grow to enormous sizes and are of a rather inferior flavour and quality to their wild brethren. To the purist, the only way to eat trout is to fish it out of a stream and rush it to the pan. In this way, the freshness and flavour of the fish is most fully appreciated. However, this recipe was one of the original ones that excited me when I first started to cook. It is one of the best ways to serve trout, and again it comes from Amunategui's book, which inspired me so much in the beginning.

Truite Nanno
Trout with Herbs

SERVES 2

2 fresh rainbow trout, each weighing about 250 g (9 oz), cleaned and boned (with the heads left on)
7.5 ml (1½ tsp) chopped sorrel
50 g (2 oz) spinach, finely chopped
5 ml (1 tsp) chopped fresh mint
15 ml (1 tbsp) each fresh finely chopped chives, tarragon and chervil, mixed together
salt and pepper
30 ml (2 tbsp) clarified butter (page 241)
15 ml (1 tbsp) chopped shallots

100 ml (4 fl oz) dry white wine
for the sauce:
30 ml (2 tbsp) unsalted butter
15 ml (1 tbsp) finely chopped shallots
7.5 ml (1½ tsp) chopped parsley
5 ml (1 tsp) each finely chopped fresh chervil, tarragon and chives
2.5 ml (½ tsp) chopped mint
salt and pepper
few drops of lemon juice
75 ml (5 tbsp) double cream
5 ml (1 tsp) Dijon mustard

Wash the cavities of the fish thoroughly and dry them very well.

Mix together the sorrel, spinach, herbs and salt and the pepper. Divide in 2 portions and use to stuff the trout.

Butter an ovenproof dish and lay the trout in it. Sprinkle with the shallots and pour the white wine over the fish. Bake at 190°C (375°F) mark 5 for 15 minutes or until the trout is cooked.

Meanwhile, make the sauce: in a non-stick frying pan, melt the butter, add the shallots, cook for a minute, then add the herbs, the salt, the pepper and the lemon juice. When the herbs have wilted, add the cream, bring to a boil and stir in the mustard.

Carefully skin the trout, arrange on two large warm plates and pour over the sauce.

We are particularly fond of fruity, medium-dry white Alsace wines and would probably choose one here.

From another original recipe in *Masterpieces of French Cuisine* this dish is named after a battleaxe of a woman who had a once famous restaurant in Normandy.

This is another of the first beacons whose light I discovered 15 years ago. It got me excited because the taste, perfume and appearance of the finished dish were new to me, and they aroused my curiosity. It subsequently became a regular dish on my menu.

Sole Mado
Sole with French Vermouth

FOR EACH SERVING

50 g (2 oz) unsalted butter

1 Dover sole (weighing about
   350 g/12 oz), skinned and well trimmed

salt and pepper

2 white button mushrooms, finely sliced

30 ml (2 tbsp) Noilly Prat or very dry
   French vermouth

45 ml (3 tbsp) double cream

Generously butter a dish which will hold the fish comfortably. Put the fish in it and season with salt and pepper.

Arrange 2 rows of overlapping finely-sliced mushrooms down the middle; pour over the Noilly Prat and place in the oven at 180°C (350°F) mark 4 for about 15 minutes or until the fish is cooked. If the fish flakes easily when pierced with a fork, it is ready.

Preheat the grill.

When the fish is cooked, pour the cream over it and place under the hot grill or salamander to lightly brown it. Serve at once. A good full-bodied white burgundy goes well with this dish. If you can still find a 1983, do try one.

By now, we were desperate to open our own restaurant. I put in unsuccessful planning applications for various shops in Chelsea and Holland Park, and because time and money were running out, I signed the lease of a shop in Lordship Lane, Dulwich. A French friend thought that Dulwich was a good area; I was convinced by the fact that my application was at last successful! At the critical moment when we were looking for the capital to open our first restaurant the right person came along to become a partner and thus enabled us to get off the ground. Colonel Aitken Lawrie was the antithesis of all that I was and am, but we had one thing in common: we had both spent long years in the colonies (he had been an Indian army colonel). It has been a very long, very fruitful, very interesting association and we remain to this day very close friends. In June 1973, Chez Nico was born. We opened our front door without ceremony and have never looked back.

Learning to cook, and to deal with bureaucrats

We soon found out that opening a restaurant is a complex business: the full force of bureaucracy is ranged against you. Health inspectors, fire officers, the licensing magistrates all have a view (not always the same view either). In few cases is their normally highly bureaucratic view one that assists a budding restaurateur to open his doors to the public.

At this time I was working hard developing several dishes from scratch. I was learning all the time and improving dishes from one day to the next. People are constantly asking how we dream up a recipe, and how does a dish develop? At that stage in my career there was a lot of physical trial and error and it was a time consuming and expensive though worthwhile process.

Developing the idea for a dish

Nowadays, the germ of an idea for a dish is often in one's subconscious. I might have a conversation with someone, a customer or the proprietor or chef of another restaurant. I might be browsing through a cookery book in a bookshop, reading an article on food, glancing through the *Good Food Guide* or the *Gault Millau* guide. I might be reading the speciality lists of the starred restaurants in the Michelin guide or someone might simply mention a word or a phrase – then the whole process begins. The idea takes hold in my mind. Then after a day or two it suddenly begins to bother me and becomes pleasantly irritating. I begin to feel a surge of excitement and become impatient. All of a sudden, I might realise that it is not worthwhile going on with the idea because of a major flaw. This is rarely the case. More often, I begin to think more seriously about it. Can I easily arrange the supply of a specific important ingredient? Would the idea be better using another type of meat or fish? How will the dish adapt to life in a restaurant kitchen? How many minutes or hours of staying power will it possess? Will it look good? Each question is wrestled with in turn. Then it may go out of my mind again. If the idea persists, and if it stays in my mind, it could very well become a full-blown recipe, but it is never developed into a dish until this long, tortuous journey, this continuous series of obstacles is finally overcome, and the dish has been cooked and recooked and arranged on the plate.

The process occurs first in the mind and then in practice. When all the pitfalls have been overcome, when the answers to each individual problem have been found, the recipe is put away. This process could take a few weeks, or it could take a few months. In the early days I physically went through the entire process, but these days much of the experimenting takes place in my mind. It is a very tough mental struggle for me, for each new recipe has been broken down into its component parts before it surrenders all its secrets. When the end comes I feel contented and I mentally file it away until one fine day, in a week or two, I might suddenly decide to put the whole thing together. It all happens in a flash. Of course, at this stage of my career, this kind of mental process is possible but it requires a number of years of cooking in a professional kitchen to reach this stage. In my early days, I wasted time and money, but it was all part of the training. I had to learn the rules. Are the ingredients within easy reach? Is it a worthwhile dish to develop? Would customers like it? Would they find it different? What is its nutritional value? Does it present well? Can it stand for some keeping time? Is it an economic proposition?

In 1973, when we first opened in Dulwich, several things were in demand and customers were regularly asking for rosé wine, German wine – particularly Piesporter – and even whole bottles of spirits. But we stuck firmly to our beliefs, though now I am surprised to see for how long chicken Kiev was a popular dish on our menu. Two years later, growing in confidence, bubbling with enthusiasm and feeling more and more assertive, we put our famous notice outside the front door instead of the menu. It read as follows:

'We have now been open for two years.

We do not feel we have to produce our menu

to show you how good we are. For your information, we do

not serve prawn cocktails or well-done steaks.

If you want to know more about us, you may look us up

in the Egon Ronay guide, or the other one which does not allow

the use of its name for promotional purposes.'

As a result, many rude letters were placed under the door and I became engaged in several heated telephone conversations. The *Daily Express* naturally came to hear about it, wrote a half page article, reproduced the whole text of my 'menu' and said rather kindly that they would not mention the name of the restaurant in case some group of 'enlightened patriots' from southeast London wrecked it.

In those early days a number of institutions and individuals influenced me. The greatest impact on my thinking and in my development at that time was the *Good Food Guide* under Christopher Driver. As Shakespeare wrote 'There is a tide in the affairs of men which, taken at the flood, leads on to fortune and . . . .' This tide in my affairs had arrived and came in the form of Aileen Hall, then chief inspector of the *Good Food Guide* and a cheerful, fiery, bubbling and very knowledgeable woman. She visited our restaurant on a number of occasions. We knew neither who she was nor what her job entailed. We found her formidable, but we liked her very much and, it seems, with the knowledge of hindsight, she took a liking to us.

One bitterly cold, late November Saturday evening, she came to dinner. In those days our most expensive bottle of wine, a London-bottled Château Giscours, was £4. Not until much later did we realise that she set a little trap just to see the kind of people we were. Dinah-Jane came into the kitchen to tell me that the lady sitting in the window was not quite sure whether to have Château Giscours or another more ordinary wine at half the price. What did we recommend? Since it was a very cold winter evening and the Château Giscours was also very cold, I told my wife to recommend the cheaper wine. We often think that this was the moment when Aileen Hall decided that we were people worth supporting. Because of her and the publicity generated from the *Good Food Guide*'s award of their highest distinction in 1976, everything began to take off for us. What we are today and where we are today, we owe to her, to Christopher Driver and to Sybil Eysenck, Professor Eysenck's wife, who was then the local inspector for the *G.F.G.* The scholarly brilliance of those key guide members of yesteryear is in direct contrast to the superficial, youthful hierarchy of today.

Influential cookery books

Apart from Amunategui's *Masterpieces of French Cuisine,* whose recipes I was now beginning to master, several cookery writers stand out in my mind. One very important early mentor was Elizabeth David and her *French Provincial Cooking.* She has since become a very regular and much valued customer. I grew to love this lady. Robert Carrier, too, was an influence, though less of an inspiration. Dinah-Jane had helped with the typing of some of the recipes from his *Great Dishes of the World* and soon all his recipes were splashed all over the glossy magazines. Recipes from recommended restaurants in the *Good Food Guide* were published in *The Good Food Guide Dinner Party Book* and some were really very inspiring: the taste of Margaret Costa's liver with Dubonnet and orange still lingers in my mouth.

This is the original Margaret Costa recipe. It was very clever of her to marry the flavour of the slightly bitter Dubonnet with the perfume and tanginess of the orange. When I first started cooking, this was one of my early formative recipes and it made calves' liver taste so incredibly good that I very quickly adapted it for my menu. What's more, it was a very popular item. When there is an argument about what is original and what is not, this great recipe must be an example of what is definitely a true original. Just as I associate Pierre Koffman with pig's trotter stuffed with morels, or Paul Bocuse with his truffle soup, so I associate Margaret Costa with this recipe.

Foie de Veau au Dubonnet

Calves' Liver with Orange and Dubonnet

SERVES 2

65 g (2½ oz) butter
30 ml (2 tbsp) olive oil
2 small shallots, very finely chopped
1 garlic clove, finely chopped
60 ml (4 tbsp) flour
salt and pepper

two 175 g (6 oz) 1 cm (½ inch) thick slices
  of calves' liver
30 ml (2 tbsp) orange juice
120 ml (8 tbsp) red Dubonnet
5 ml (1 tsp) finely grated orange rind
5 ml (1 tsp) very finely grated lemon rind
30 ml (2 tbsp) finely chopped parsley

In a heavy cast iron pan, melt 50 g (2 oz) of the butter, add the olive oil and very carefully fry the shallots and garlic until soft and transparent (do not allow them to colour or crisp up). Set aside.

Sprinkle the flour on a wooden board and season with salt and pepper. Turn the liver in this mixture.

Slightly increase the heat of the pan and fry the liver, taking care not to burn the shallots and garlic. Turn the liver over and with the tip of your finger, test it to see whether it is done. Cook it as much, or as little as you like. Remove the liver from the pan and set aside on 2 warm serving plates.

Add the orange juice and the Dubonnet to the same pan and reduce, stirring well. Add the orange and lemon rinds, plus the remaining butter and sprinkle over the parsley.

Arrange the liver on the plates and pour over the sauce. Serve with a good full-bodied red wine such as a Château Rayas from Châteauneuf-du-Pape.

In later years, the book I consider to be of outstanding importance to me is Michel Guérard's *Cuisine Gourmande* given to me by Nico Kairis. If I had to part with my entire library of cookery books and could plead that I would be spared only three – *Masterpieces of French Cuisine, Cuisine Gourmande* and Elizabeth David's *French Provincial Cookery* would be the ones I would choose.

This was the first sorbet I ever made. It was during the early Seventies when Michel Guérard's book first appeared on the scene, that, dotted here and there, fresh, shiny, green limes appeared in some greengrocers' shops. In those days my sorbetière was a very weak and feeble little mechanism with plastic paddles which you had to put in the freezing compartment of a refrigerator. Nevertheless, it did provide my introduction to the world of sorbets. (I go into more detail about making sorbets, and give more recipes, in chapter five.) Try to find African (especially Kenyan) or Brazilian limes for this recipe.

There are two accompaniments for this sorbet. You can either serve it in a large glass with ice-cold champagne poured over and a sprig of fresh mint, or you could arrange it on an attractive display of pawpaw. But since I have never yet tasted a pawpaw outside Africa which tastes of pawpaw, perhaps it is best to avoid this combination. If, however, you come across a pawpaw which is as big as a long water melon, that is the time to marry the two great flavours of lime and pawpaw. In East Africa we used to avoid all small pawpaws like the plague. They were insipid, had no perfume, and no colour.

Sorbet au Citron Vert

Fresh Lime Sorbet

Illustrated on page 209

SERVES 8
8 very fresh, very shiny, green limes
600 ml (1 pint) sugar syrup (page 158)

With a zester, remove the rind from the limes and add to the sugar syrup. Bring to the boil and simmer for 45 minutes. Allow to cool completely.

Meanwhile squeeze the juice from 4 of the limes.

Strain the syrup and lime juice through a tammy-cloth or fine sieve. Pour into the sorbetière and freeze for about 10 minutes.

Encouragement from friends

Individuals gave us a lot of encouragement and, among many others, Clive Barda was a major ally in those early years. A brilliant photographer in his own right, he is also a great gourmet, very fastidious and very sensitive to taste, colour and texture. He spurred me on a great deal and I found his company fascinating. Out of his chaotic kitchen came some truly sensational food.

One day, Bertrand Tavernier, the great French film director, walked into our restaurant, ordered Poulet au Vin Jaune, drank two bottles of Jura wine and exchanged all this for a subscription to *Gault Millau* magazine! As a result we subsequently visited a restaurant in Paris called Les Semailles. It was Christmas Eve, 1977, and this was our first introduction to nouvelle cuisine. At the time we were impressed, though I look back on the meal with mixed feelings. One member of the family party of five had smoked salmon mousse. It was just a plain, neat, square slice of salmon and crème fraîche. I mentioned to Jean-Jacques Jouteaux, the owner and chef, that I, too, made this dish, but that I put a layer of caviar in the middle and another on top. A few months later I saw a photograph of smoked salmon mousse by Jean-Jacques Jouteaux with a layer of caviar in the middle and a thin layer of caviar on top.

By now, I was learning all the time. I had discovered *Great Chefs of France* by Quentin Crewe and photographer Anthony Blake. I read the book again and again, spellbound by the magic of three-star restaurants and impressed particularly by the personality of one man, Roger Vergé. Now fate stepped in. Chef and cookery writer Michael Smith, who was then cooking in a regular daytime television series called 'Pebble Mill', surprised us by including Chez Nico in his list of featured restaurants for a special series called 'Posh Nosh'. We had great fun filming the programmes and at the launch for the book of the series in 1979, we first met Michel Roux. I casually mentioned to him that it was my dream to work one day in the kitchens of Roger Vergé. Within 10 days he had arranged for me to spend a short period at Vergé's famous Moulin de Mougins restaurant near Cannes.

The formative meeting with Roger Vergé

We went to France to meet the great man and to make the arrangements. Surrounded by flowers and exotic plants, it was 11.30 one morning and we were seated in the garden awaiting our introduction to Roger Vergé. He appeared in the sunlight in immaculate whites, white hair, white beard, white moustache, his hand extended and his eyes twinkling with warmth and pleasure. We arranged that I should go to his kitchens that Christmas. He sat with us for a few minutes, asked the head waiter to escort us to another table and told us that he would arrange lunch himself. This was our first experience of three-star food. It was unforgettable, it was a landmark, perhaps the greatest of all watersheds. The menu was as follows:

Salade tiède de langoustines au beurre de truffe

• ● •

Escalope de saumon à la crème de ciboulette

• ● •

Aiguillettes d'agneau de Sisteron à la purée d'ail doux

• ● •

The meal ended with vanilla ice cream presented in a tulip case on a bed of raspberry coulis. It was the most sensational vanilla ice cream I had ever eaten and it was flecked with the tiny black seeds of the vanilla pods.

I returned to Mougins before Christmas 1979 to see and work for the first time in a three-star kitchen. On many occasions thereafter people have asked me repeatedly what I saw, what I learned. The truth of the matter is that I was totally transformed, inspired, electrified. My memories of Vergé's kitchen were as follows. Great order, great organisation, cleanliness, professionalism, dedication and very hard work from all 20 members of the brigade.

On my first day I was given two crates of *salade de mâche* to pick over and piles of glistening langoustines to sort out. The second day I was asked to empty 52 litres of local red wine into a pot so large that it required two men to lift it. The carcases of a large variety of game birds came next, then a mixture of vegetables. This stock was being prepared to form the basis of a sauce to accompany wild duck for a party of 80 who were coming to lunch next day.

During my time in Vergé's kitchen, I worked in all sections and remember being staggered by seeing a new way of making fish stock by roasting fish carcases in the oven with shallots and Noilly Prat, that very dry French vermouth which I have come to use a great deal in my cooking. Here, too, I became an expert in segmenting oranges. Oranges went everywhere with everything and the whole kitchen smelt of them, for they were his favourite fruit. I saw, too, the arrival of the pink grapefruits which were then turned into the delicious *granite de pamplemousse rose* which I had eaten between the courses of that first meal with Vergé.

Vergé was not like the other French chefs of the time and I felt a great rapport with him. I responded to his breadth of vision, his liberal, open mind, the total respect he commanded from his brigade. His connection with Africa had resulted in an enthusiasm for exotic spices, avocados, limes, beans, curry powder, coconut and cumin, all of which were, of course, familiar to me.

Vergé is not afraid of new equipment and when I was there I saw a microwave oven. He thought it could be useful. He was right. Freshly 'turned' carrots took only a few minutes to cook in the microwave and he made good use of it. There for the first time too I saw a large commercial steamer which was used mostly for scallops. Laid out on a stainless steel tray they cooked in a few seconds. I was surprised to see so few copper pans in such a great kitchen, but Vergé is a modern man who is unafraid to break with tradition. His *sautoires* and *sauteuses* were made of stainless steel with copper bottoms. My time with Vergé gave me much to think about.

When I close my eyes and think back over the years, my mind clicks back to the first time I saw this salad on a clear sunny day in July at Mougins. The bright setting was punctured by the spindly shadows of Roger Vergé's green paradise. I now know that this was a turning point in my life.

The palette of colours – yellow, red, black, white, mauve, light green, dark green – which makes up this dish inspired me to learn to be a master in the preparation of salads. Here, at last, was a departure from the vinaigrette dressing syndrome which has accompanied salads from time immemorial.

Poussin à l'Eau
de Vie de Frontignan

Baby Chicken with Muscatel Grape Brandy

This is one of the original dishes from our very early days. It is ideal for making at home, though you have to finish off the sauce at the last minute. It is a good way of cooking corn-fed poussins or partridges. The grapy, aromatic flavour of the eau de vie de Frontignan is distinctive and delicious.

RECIPE ON PAGE 35

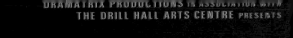

CINDERELLA
THE REAL TRUE STORY

BY CHERYL MOCH
MUSIC BY HOLLY GEWANDTER
FROM AN ORIGINAL IDEA BY HOLLY GEWANDTER & CHERYL MOCH
DIRECTED BY NONA SHEPPHARD
DESIGNED BY AMANDA FISK
LIGHTING DESIGN BY KATE OWEN

NOVEMBER 26 – DECEMBER 19 • TUESDAY – SATURDAY 8PM

THE DRILL HALL ARTS CENTRE

5 CHENIES STREET • LONDON WC1 • 01-637 8270

Funded by Camden   LBGS

THE REAL TRUE STORY

THRILL TO THE ROYAL GOSSIP YOU WOULD REALLY LOVE TO HEAR

'The story I want to tell you is about a time when the streams ran as clear as crystal and the sky was the colour of your dreams and the fish and the animals still spoke to us – oh, they can speak to us, they just don't want to anymore. Can you blame them? In any case, this is a story that is still being passed on, from parent to child, from generation to generation, but in the years of the telling, through the prism of prejudice, it's been altered. I want to set the record straight. I want to tell you the real true story of Cinderella . . . '

PRINCES KISSES GIRL

RUMPUS AT PALACE OVER ALL-GIRL LOVE MATCH!

the New York Critics said:
'AN ABSOLUTELY HILARIOUS SHOW'
'INSPIRED . . . SPECTACULAR'
'FIZZING WITH ELECTRICITY BETWEEN AUDIENCE AND PERFORMERS'

ARCHDUKE IN LOVE TANGLE WITH ARCHDUKE!

with **KATE CORKERY, GILLIAN HANNA, NICOLA KATHRENS, BRYONY LAVERY, DALLAS LINGHAM, MARY McCUSKER, ADÈLE SALEEM, FAITH TINGLE**

Tickets:
Tuesday – Thursday £4.50
Friday & Saturday £5.00
Concessions (UNWAGED, CAMDEN RESIDENT, STUDENT, NURSE, SENIOR CITIZEN) £3.00
ONE FREE TICKET IN EVERY TEN BOOKED

Performances:
Thurs 26 Nov – Sat 28 Nov
Thurs 3 Dec – Sat 5 Dec
Tues   8 Dec – Sat 12 Dec
Tues 15 Dec – Sat 19 Dec

8PM

BAR & RESTAURANT · FREE CHILDMINDING FOR UNDER 5s on FRI & SAT EVES

THE DRILL HALL ARTS CENTRE · 16 CHENIES STREET · LONDON WC1E 7EX · 01 637 8270

Printed by Spider Web, 14-16 Sussex Way, London N7

Salade Tiède de Homard
au Beurre de Truffes

Lobster Salad with Truffle Butter Sauce

I first saw a salad like this at Roger Vergé's green paradise at Mougins in the South of France (his was made with langoustines). The combination of colours, flavours and textures is sensational and here I have married slices of lobster, avocado, orange, grapefruit and Jerusalem artichoke with leaves of mâche and oak leaf lettuce. I like a little sweetness in a salad and here the fruit, and in this case the orange-flavoured beurre blanc (as a change from truffle butter sauce) picks up that touch of sweetness.

RECIPE ON PAGE 50

Salade Tiède de Homard au Beurre de Truffes

Lobster Salad with Truffle Butter Sauce

Illustrated on page 49

SERVES 4

truffle butter dressing:
truffle peelings
150 ml (¼ pint) Noilly Prat
juice of 1 lemon
30 ml (2 tbsp) double cream
225 g (8 oz) good quality, unsalted butter
salt
salad:
hazelnut oil
12 orange segments
2 large, round, red tomatoes, cut into 8 petals
4 large, perfect champignons de Paris, sliced into rounds

1 avocado, sliced into 8 pieces
4 'turned' carrots
2 artichokes, sliced into halves and opened out
8 frisée or curly endive leaves
4 radicchio leaves
16–20 mâche (lamb's lettuce or corn salad) leaves
4 oak leaf lettuce leaves
1 cooked lobster weighing about 900 g (2 lb)
4 asparagus tips
1 large fresh truffle, brushed clean of any earth and sliced into 8 pieces

First make the truffle butter dressing: finely chop the truffle peelings and place in a copper sauté pan. Pour over the Noilly Prat and reduce to 15 ml (1 tbsp) of liquid. Squeeze in some lemon juice. Add the cream. Chop up the butter and add a little at a time, just as you would when making a beurre blanc. Whip to amalgamate, adjust the salt and add a little more lemon juice, leaving a little for the salad.

Make the vinaigrette with the hazelnut oil, a little salt and lemon juice.

Arrange the following ingredients round the outer edge of the well of a plate, leaving the middle free for the arrangement of the salad leaves and the lobster. Keep the plate on a warm surface while you compose the salad.

On each plate, arrange 3 segments of orange, 1 next to the other, followed by 2 tomato petals, slightly overlapping, the sliced mushroom, 2 slices of avocado, a 'turned' carrot and half an artichoke. Dress the salad leaves with the vinaigrette and then place 2 small leaves of frisée, a radicchio leaf, 4 or 5 mâche leaves and an oak leaf lettuce leaf in the middle of the plate. Slice the lobster down the middle, lengthwise, and slice the halves again, taking care not to break the flesh. Remove the meat from the claws (keeping the shape of the claw). Allow one claw per portion and half of the body meat per portion.

Your final arrangement then is this: lean an asparagus tip against the salad leaves. Arrange the lobster slices partly on the salad leaves and partly on the orange segments. Place 2 slices of truffle on the top of the mound of leaves. All this time, your plate with all the ingredients should be resting on a warm surface. Now spoon the truffle-flecked dressing over all the outer ingredients and let a little of it dribble on to the warm lobster. Serve at once with a good, full-bodied dry white wine such as Auxey-Duresses or the quite rich dry Château Ygrec from Château d'Yquem.

I ate this dish for the first time when we made our first visit to Roger Vergé in Provence. It was so delicate and so perfectly flavoured that I shall remember it always. I recall the extreme thinness of the salmon and my visions of horror when I imagined the work which goes into slicing and cooking such a fragile, paper-thin escalope of salmon. As I later found out when I went to work in Vergé's kitchen, the process was indeed simple. You have to slice the fresh salmon using the same technique and to the same thickness as if you were slicing smoked salmon.

Escalopine de Saumon à la Crème de Ciboulette

Escalopes of Fresh Salmon in a Chive-flavoured Sauce

Illustrated on page 32

SERVES 2

2 very thinly sliced escalopes of fresh salmon, weighing about 100 g (4 oz) each

15 ml (1 tbsp) well-flavoured olive oil

salt

cayenne pepper

100 ml (6½ tbsp) Sauce Crème de Ciboulette (page 235)

15 ml (1 tbsp) chopped fresh chives

Put the salmon escalopes in the centre of two good-quality porcelain plates which will withstand heat.

Brush the escalopes with olive oil and arrange them in an untidy manner (allow some edges to fold under).

Dust very lightly with salt and cayenne pepper. Surround with Sauce Crème de Ciboulette. Sprinkle the chives onto the sauce and place in a very hot 240°C (475°F) mark 9 oven. Cook fast for about 3–5 minutes. Do not allow the salmon to be overcooked and dry.

Serve with a good dry white burgundy such as St Aubin.

Escalope de Saumon Fumé à la Crème de Ciboulette

Variation

Salmon is now beginning to be treated in many different ways. At first, as a change from fresh salmon, we had smoked salmon and that was all we knew. Then came the Scandinavian gravad lax, pickled salmon flavoured with dill, and this was then followed by a wide proliferation of different types of marinated fish. Fresh salmon is very versatile and adapts well to being pickled using flavourings such as fresh ginger or red peppercorns. Smoked salmon, too, has joined in the revolution and the biggest change in its treatment is that it is no longer only served cold with black pepper and lemon juice. As a variation on the previous recipe for fresh salmon, you can use smoked salmon in equal amounts and cook it in exactly the same way. The only difference is that in the process of smoking it will have lost a lot of natural moisture, and you should therefore be very careful to cook it even more lightly; you may not need to add salt.

I could not possibly forget to mention one particular meal we had in the summer of 1978. As a family we usually travelled to the South of France for holidays via the Autoroute du Soleil, but on this occasion we decided that we wanted to have a look at the Périgord. We made an overnight stop at the Château de Castel Novel (once the house of Colette, the French novelist), a two-star Michelin château at Brive-la-Gaillard, in the heart of the walnut growing area. That evening we had an incredible meal which combined the finest smoked salmon I have ever tasted and the best starter I have eaten anywhere: warm veal tongues, beautifully cooked, served with warm boiled potatoes, sprinkled with capers and dressed with tarragon and walnut oil. It was this experience that somehow, through a tortuous journey, led me to develop this recipe.

Like strawberries with cream or tomatoes with basil, veal tongues and Madeira are one of those culinary marriages that seem to have been blessed in heaven.

Bouquet de Langues de Veau aux Epinards à la Sauce Madère

Veal Tongues with Spinach and Madeira Sauce

SERVES 4 AS A STARTER OR 2 AS A MAIN COURSE

for the bouillon:
1 large onion, spiked with 1 clove
1 large carrot, peeled
3 bay leaves
pinch of thyme
peppercorns
parsley sprig

150 ml (¼ pint) white wine vinegar
2 veal tongues
450 g (1 lb) young spinach leaves, cleaned
75 ml (5 tbsp) clarified garlic butter
   (page 242)
juice of 1 lemon
300 ml (½ pint) Demi-Glace (page 228)
Madeira

Make a bouillon with 3.4 litres (6 pints) of water, the onion, carrot, bay leaves, thyme, a few peppercorns, a sprig of parsley and the vinegar. Bring to the boil and remove any scum that comes to the surface. Simmer for 2 hours.

Add the veal tongues, cover and cook over a low heat for 2 hours, or until done. Let them rest for 1 hour or until cool. Remove them from the bouillon and peel off their skins, using a sharp knife.

In another pan, heat some water to boiling point, add the spinach, cook for 30 seconds, strain and drain well. Place in a non-stick pan with the clarified garlic butter and season with salt, pepper and some lemon juice. Fry lightly to warm up. Turn out on to absorbent kitchen paper and pat gently to remove any excess butter and juices.

In the middle of each plate place an egg poaching ring, tip some spinach into it and arrange in a tidy mound. Slice each tongue diagonally across to make 8 'petals'. Arrange those round the spinach.

Heat up the demi-glace, sprinkle over a few drops of Madeira and add a little lemon juice. Pour carefully over the tongue petals and if you are feeling adventurous try a glass of Condrieu, a distinctive white wine from the Rhone.

One of the great influences on the world of British gastronomy over the last 30 years is Egon Ronay. His team of inspectors have, aided by his flair for publicity, attracted much attention to standards of food in the UK. When we began at Dulwich, he helped us get off to a flying start. His article in *The Evening News* headed 'The Secret of Lordship Lane' predicted that one day people would travel a long way to eat our food.

Then came the Battersea years, the period with which I associate our great leap forward. One day, an immaculately dressed Swedish gentleman came to dinner. His name was Charles Florman and he turned out to be a great gastronome who had eaten in every 3 star restaurant in Europe, including, at the time of writing, over 45 visits to Frédy Girardet alone. Another regular customer was Johnny Apple of the *New York Times*, a very knowledgeable writer on food and restaurants. Charles Florman and Johnny Apple were both close friends of Egon Ronay and between them they were responsible for gradually and painstakingly bridging the wide chasm that had developed between Egon and me. Eventually, Chez Nico was chosen as the venue of the inaugural lunch of the British Academy of Gastronomes, of which Egon Ronay is President.

Two stars from Michelin

However, I felt in Battersea that the greatest honour was yet to come. I began to sense that the *Guide Michelin* was watching my restaurant and paying it great attention. I was becoming tired of working in the kitchen with only one assistant and I began to have butterflies in my stomach. I felt that my second *Michelin* star was getting close. I found a young man, Phillip Britten, and explained to him the great things that were around the corner. Phillip responded immediately to the challenge. In time, we received our second *Michelin* star. All my influences have combined to create for me one summit of excellence – three *Michelin* stars. The great restaurants are held together by this terrifying symbol of excellence. I wanted to join that rare group, I wanted to belong. The great ascent had begun.

'*Precision. Restraint.
Simplicity. And the perfect sauce. These are my
guidelines. A perfect piece of meat can stand
on its own without too much fuss.
If it could speak, it would shoo away
a scallop, a crab or a lobster
sharing its plate.
All it might need is a
shiny, glistening robe
of sauce to cover it.*'

CHAPTER TWO

My philosophy on food

A bove all, I believe in simplicity of approach followed by the use of perfect ingredients with good taste and restraint in presentation. A simple dish consists of perfect ingredients simply cooked. When we opened our first restaurant in Dulwich, we bought a random selection of old prints, among them a picture of a shy, demure young girl which was a print of 'Simplicity', a famous picture by Sir Joshua Reynolds. We were both fascinated by this picture and decided that it had a story to tell and a principle to establish. Simplicity became our theme, and this young girl now appears on all our menus and literature.

I would like to lay down unequivocally certain principles. To achieve simplicity in food and constant perfection, there should be no marriage between two meats, or between a meat and shellfish or a shellfish and fruit. If a fruit such as a mango is cooked its texture and taste is altered. A piece of good quality meat perfectly cooked can, if need be, stand on its own without a complementary sauce. What it certainly does not need is shellfish of any kind to accompany it.

Nouvelle cuisine arrives

From the late Sixties to the early Eighties, the world of cooking underwent a revolution: a new era in cooking. Two clever French journalists, Henri Gault and Christian Millau, took a good look around them and identified something dramatic that was taking place in French kitchens. They christened it *la nouvelle cuisine* and won themselves fame and fortune. These two chroniclers who were interested in food did not, of course, invent this new style of cooking but they will be forever part of that culinary revolution.

This made everybody sit up and think. It made all the chefs want to emulate, develop and practise the new style. At the same time the writings of Messrs Gault et Millau, through their successful guide book and their magazine, reached millions of Frenchmen. The bandwagon was under way. With every new idea, the converts, the honest and the idealists become the fellow travellers of the charlatans and the cowboys. Those who did not understand what this new movement was all about suddenly deified the kiwi fruit, the raspberry vinegar and the pink peppercorn. They became excited, got out of control, and the movement was in danger of losing all credibility. Critics appeared from everywhere. Small portions, raw meat, raw fish, tepid food, high prices became the justified criticisms levelled at many who claimed to embrace the movement. *La nouvelle cuisine* had become a gimmick. I was on a radio show with Christian Millau who illustrated perfectly what I mean by a dislike of too many marriages in *la nouvelle cuisine*. He talked of a dish of kidneys, mushrooms and foie gras. His impression was that although each one of these individual ingredients were good in themselves, the mixture was rather a failure. He would have preferred the dish to be more simple.

Simple dishes cooked perfectly

It is very unfortunate that aspiring young chefs now begin to judge the brilliance of an established chef in the way he combines his ingredients. The ever-present desire to create more and more unlikely liaisons throws up some bizarre marriages. Duck and lobster, duck and pawpaw, lobster and mango. These are the mistakes and the pitfalls. Young people who misguidedly develop a passion for unlikely marriages must be taught and shown that there is only one thing that makes a chef a good chef. It is the ability to create a simple dish perfectly. To be able to make a perfect vanilla ice cream, to be able to grill a good steak perfectly, this is good cooking, even to be able to fry an egg is good cooking. To be able to stuff a duck breast with mango can never be good cooking. Here are some examples of good simple dishes.

I always think the mark of a good vanilla ice cream is seeing the little black specks from the vanilla pod embedded inside. My method of making ice cream is more in the classical tradition than just the churning of a *crème anglaise* and I always, therefore, make my vanilla ice cream with a sugar syrup. Egon Ronay goes into ecstasies every time he has it and says it reminds him of Vienna.

Glace à la Vanille

Vanilla Ice Cream

Illustrated on page 192

SERVES 12
900 ml (1½ pints) milk
600 ml (1 pint) double cream
1 whole vanilla pod

Sugar syrup (made with 600 ml/1 pint
water and 400 g/14 oz sugar), boiled
down until thickish (page 158)
18 egg yolks

Mix the milk and the cream together. Split the vanilla pod and scrape out the seeds. Add both the empty pod and the seeds to the cream and milk. Bring to the boil then set aside to infuse for 30 minutes.

Bring the sugar syrup to the boil. Put the egg yolks into a blender or food processor and with the motor running, add the hot syrup to the eggs. Mix together well until the eggs fluff up to the top of the bowl.

Turn the egg mixture out into a large bowl and add the milk and cream. Remove the vanilla pod and allow to cool.

Turn into an ice cream machine and freeze for 15 minutes.

Perfecting sauces

The only 'confusion' which I introduce to a dish is to sometimes use two different sauces for fish. Sauce making is the most fertile area in cooking. It is here where the imagination, properly controlled, can really reach new heights and it is within a particular sauce that improvements can be made and remade and continuously perfected. If you grill a steak, fry a kidney or steam a fillet of fish, the processes of grilling, frying or steaming cannot be perfected beyond a certain point. However, a sauce *can* be improved, its taste enhanced, its texture further polished, its lightness accentuated and its colour made more vivid. This is the area where the improvement can take place and where the mind is dominated, where the chemical, scientific and artistic battle takes place. It is the battle of the sauce. Sauces are a series of battles towards the general winning of the war of perfect cookery.

This is quite an extraordinary dish – offal at its supreme best. The pungent aroma that escapes from the plate is difficult to describe, the sauce is strong, dark and glistening. It is an audacious recipe which has brought us many compliments from our customers.

There seems to be some controversy about bay leaves and some people believe that eating too many bay leaves may cause a toxic reaction. But they have been used in cooking for many hundreds of years and have been an essential flavouring for stock, soups, terrines, pâtés and bouillons.

Rognons de Veau aux Feuilles de Laurier

Veal Kidneys flavoured with Bay Leaves

SERVES 2

150 ml (¼ pint) Demi-Glace (page 228)
75 ml (5 tbsp) port
1 good sized veal kidney

25 g (1 oz) butter
10 bay leaves
salt and pepper
15 ml (1 tbsp) freshly chopped chives

First make the sauce: in a saucepan over medium heat, reduce the demi-glace and the port to a thick syrup. (The sauce needs to be very thick, because after you add the kidney to it, the juices released will thin it down.) Set aside and keep warm.

Clean the kidney in the following way. Remove any fat, then blanch for 20 seconds in boiling water and immediately afterwards run under a cold tap. With a very sharp small knife, remove each lobe individually discarding gristle and fat. If the lobes are very large, cut them in half. The lobes should be about 2.5 cm (1 inch) in diameter.

Dry the kidney thoroughly. Melt the butter in a heavy cast iron pan and let it sizzle. Add the kidney and the bay leaves and sauté very rapidly for 1 minute only, shaking the pan vigorously.

Remove the pan from the heat and drain the kidney and bay leaves in a sieve for 15–20 seconds to allow any excess juices to run away.

Tip the bay leaves and the kidneys into the sauce. Stir thoroughly, add salt and plenty of black pepper and dish up on 2 warm serving plates. Sprinkle with the chives and serve with a rich, earthy red Pomerol.

Personal masterpieces

Gastronomy, famous restaurants and great chefs are all linked by a common theme. Since the early days when I started cooking, I have always believed that to become a good chef, to have a good restaurant or to aspire to greatness, you must be engaged in the perfection of a handful of your own undisguised creations. By this I mean that all the great restaurants in France have become praised on the strength of a handful of their main dishes. The late Fernand Point at La Pyramide restaurant in Vienne had certain famous dishes which he perfected over the years and which people from all over the world came to eat. His *poulet en vessie* or his *terrine de foie gras* encased in brioche were examples. People travel from all over the world to visit Paul Bocuse in Lyon and eat his famous truffle soup, or his *loup de mer en croûte sauce choron* which is stuffed with a mousseline of lobster. You go to the L'Ousteau de Beaumanière for baby lamb stuffed with its kidneys and morel mushrooms, or you go to the Tour d'Argent just across from Nôtre Dame in Paris, for the famous pressed duck. While I would never aspire to be on equal terms with these famous personalities of French gastronomy, I nevertheless seriously attempted always to seek to perfect, to improve and to search for a new detail.

For some reason or another, this is one soup of mine which has become a personal classic. The aroma of the clear mushroom and Madeira essence is quite haunting and the sharp, fresh taste of the coriander leaves make a perfect contrast. When it is correctly made, the colour, clarity and sparkle of the golden soup against a shiny silver spoon are stunning. Elizabeth David loves this soup and frequently asks for second helpings.

Consommé de Champignons au Madère Aromatisé aux Feuilles de Coriandre

Mushroom Consommé with Madeira, flavoured with Fresh Coriander Leaves

SERVES 6–8

40 g (1½ oz) fresh foie gras
100 g (4 oz) onion, very finely chopped
15 ml (1 tbsp) tomato purée
2.25 litres (3½ pints) Fond de Volaille
  (page 229)
450 g (1 lb) button mushrooms, very
  finely chopped
75 ml (3 fl oz) Madeira
5 egg whites
salt
whole coriander leaves, stalks removed

Melt the foie gras in a large saucepan, add the onion and sauté in its own fat until transparent.

Add the tomato purée, chicken stock and mushrooms and cook, covered, for 1 hour. Just before removing from the heat, add 50 ml (2 fl oz) of Madeira.

Strain the mushroom mixture through a fine sieve, pressing the mushrooms through, until they release their juices into a clean saucepan. Don't try to force them through the sieve.

Allow the mixture to cool. Whisk the egg whites until frothy then, still using the whisk, gradually add to the mushroom mixture. Continue whisking until the egg whites have been well amalgamated.

Place the soup on a very low heat, bring to simmering point and cook, uncovered, for 30–45 minutes to clarify.

Strain the liquid through 2 or 3 layers of muslin until completely clear.

Add the remaining Madeira and salt to taste. Test the seasoning and if necessary reduce again until taste and colour are correct.

Serve in individual bowls and decorate with fresh coriander leaves floating on top. If you must drink, try a glass of Madeira or sherry.

This is more than an ordinary terrine of duck and three vital ingredients make it special: foie gras, very bright green fresh (unsalted) pistachios and rich meat jelly. It is a time-consuming and somewhat laborious dish to make, but then all beautiful and well-flavoured meat terrines are.

In France, the preparation of pâtés and terrines is almost an art and there, the charcutier is a very important person. He usually works independently in his own little shop, whether in a village or in a town.

You need a 1.4 litre (2½ pint) Le Creuset terrine with lid for this dish. A note of caution. You will lose the pinkness of the farce if you add too much alcohol and too much jelly.

Terrine de Canard

Terrine of Duck and Foie Gras with Pistachio Nuts

Illustrated on page 97

SERVES 15

150 ml (¼ pint) cognac
150 ml (¼ pint) Gelée (page 229)
1 clove garlic, finely diced
1 shallot, finely diced
1 bay leaf
sprig of thyme
sprig of tarragon
16 black peppercorns
275 g (10 oz) lean duck meat (from the breast or leg), diced in small cubes
150 g (5 oz) lean pork, diced
150 g (5 oz) lean veal, diced
150 g (5 oz) pork fat, diced
75 ml (5 tbsp) Madeira

3 cloves garlic, crushed
8 crushed juniper berries
5 ml (1 tsp) ground Jamaica Allspice
1.25 ml (¼ tsp) quatre épices
salt
black pepper
150 g (5 oz) fresh pork fat, cut in tiny dice, blanched
150 g (5 oz) foie gras, diced
150 g (5 oz) bright green pistachios, shelled, blanched and skinned
clarified butter (page 241)
675 g (1½ lb) pork fat cut in thin strips, diced
3 bay leaves

Mix together well 75 ml (3 fl oz) cognac with the meat jelly, the diced garlic, the diced shallot, bay leaf, thyme, tarragon, black peppercorns and diced duck. Cover and marinate in the refrigerator for 24 hours.

Strain the liquid through a muslin cloth and discard all the flavourings, reserving the duck. Bring the marinade to the boil and cook for 5 minutes. The blood from the duck will coagulate and trap all the impurities. Allow the liquid to cool and you will have left some very clear, very bright meat jelly.

Mince the diced pork, veal and pork fat using the medium-sized blades of the mincer. Add the Madeira and remaining cognac, the crushed garlic, crushed juniper berries, the allspice and quatre épices. Season with salt and plenty of freshly milled black pepper.

Fold in the blanched diced pork fat. Add the reserved diced duck, diced foie gras, the pistachios and the jelly. Mix together well.

Brush the bottom and sides of the terrine with clarified butter. Line the terrine with pork fat, then pack it well with the farce. Knock the terrine on the table several times to ensure the mixture is evenly spread in the terrine. Fold over the fat towards the centre and place 3 bay leaves on top.

Cover with several layers of kitchen foil and press the lid on top. Put in a bain-marie filled with 5 cm (2 inches) of boiling water and cook in a cool 150°C (300°F) mark 2 oven for 1½ hours.

Remove from the water bath, let it cool slightly and place it in a tray. Remove the lid and replace it with a wooden plank and a heavy weight. Chill in the refrigerator overnight. Allow this terrine to mature from two to four days before slicing.

Serve with brioche and, perhaps, a glass of Chignin Bergeron, a delicious white wine from the Savoie.

My philosophy can be summarised another way as a constant avoidance of being 'a Jack of all trades'. This chap spoils his chances and can only be a good cook, not a great chef. Many young chefs with their menus changing daily or even twice daily are really cooks. They devise a dish and try it out on their customers. If it reappears a week or so later it may be quite a different dish. The aim of a chef is to seek perfection of one dish over a long period: to amend it little by little, to 'finely tune' it. A great chef cannot create a dozen new dishes a day, if he has any intention of creating perfection. He must stick to his principles of simplicity which apply to the home cook too. Paul Bocuse has been quoted as saying that if in a lifetime a chef has genuinely invented just one dish, only then is he considered a great chef.

Cèpes sauce and this recipe for duck have come to be associated with me and my cooking for the last seven or eight years. This recipe has evolved over the years and has finally come to rest as a very simple affair. I find the flavours of creamed leeks, pink duck, slightly crisp skin and the essence of wild mushrooms all together add up to a sensational combination of tastes.

Suprême de Canard au Fumet de Cèpes

Breast of Duck with Wild Mushroom Sauce

Illustrated on page 80

SERVES 2
45 ml (3 tbsp) chopped leeks (white part)
15 ml (1 tbsp) clarified butter (page 241)
1 × 3.6 kg (8 lb) duck, breasts removed
salt and pepper

25 ml (1½ tbsp) reduced Fond de Volaille (page 229)
25 g (1 oz) butter
100 ml (4 fl oz) double cream
150 ml (¼ pint) Fumet de Cèpes (page 232)

First blanch the leeks very briefly, dry thoroughly on absorbent kitchen paper and set aside.

In a heavy griddle pan, bring the clarified butter to smoking point and grill the duck breasts, skin down, for 10 minutes. Turn over and cook for 3 minutes only on the flesh side, then return again for a further 10 minutes to cook, skin-side down. Sprinkle with salt and pepper and keep warm. The skin should now be crisp and charred.

Put the chicken stock and a knob of butter into a small stainless steel pan and reduce to a syrup. Add the blanched leeks and the cream and cook down until you have a nice purée. Do not overcook the leeks, or else you will lose their attractive pale green.

Divide the purée of leeks between two warm plates, pat down lightly and spread evenly all over the surface.

With a very sharp knife, slice the duck breasts into thin escalopes and open out in a straight line across the plate. If any blood escapes, dab with a piece of absorbent kitchen paper, then place, skin side up, on the leeks.

Warm the mushroom sauce and pour over the duck. Let the sauce run into the purée and do not worry much about the slight mess. It will taste delicious. Serve with a good full-bodied red wine such as a burgundy. One of my favourite clarets was a 1975 Cru Bourgeois, Ch. Latour St Bonnet.

This fish soup came into my repertoire very early on in my cooking career. Over the years, it developed as a wider variety of fish became more readily available and as I ate more and more fish soups all over France. Crushed shellfish shells add that extra authentic taste, so in future when you eat prawns, crabs, lobster or any other similar seafood, don't discard the shells – keep them in the freezer for making fish soup. Making this soup is a time consuming and elaborate process, but if you follow the recipe and make this large quantity, you can always freeze some of it and serve it on another occasion.

Soupe de Poisson
Mediterranean Fish Soup

SERVES 8–10

75 ml (5 tbsp) good olive oil

25 ml (1½ tbsp) clarified butter (page 241)

6 garlic cloves

75 g (3 oz) each fennel, carrots, onions, leeks and celery, diced

25 g (1 oz) chopped shallot

300 ml (½ pint) white wine

150 ml (¼ pint) red wine

120 ml (4 fl oz) ruby port

50 ml (2 fl oz) brandy

225 g (8 oz) tinned Italian tomatoes

150 g (5 oz) tomato purée

1 strip of orange rind

15 ml (1 tbsp) fresh or dried savory

9 fresh basil leaves

15 ml (1 tbsp) crushed fennel seeds

7.5 ml (1½ tsp) ground star anise

15 ml (1 tbsp) fresh tarragon

15 ml (1 tbsp) fresh thyme

15 ml (1 tbsp) fresh parsley

2 bay leaves

15 ml (1 tbsp) mixed dried Provençale herbs

1 kg (2¼ lb) Mediterranean fish (red mullet, grondin, rascasse, weaver fish, conger eel, sea bass), cleaned

about 2 litres (3½ pints) of Fond de Poisson (page 230) made with the addition of 225 g (8 oz) crushed lobster, crab, prawn or langoustine shells

45 ml (3 tbsp) pastis (eg Pernod or Ricard)

5 ml (1 tsp) ground saffron

salt

cayenne pepper

Aïoli (page 238) and fresh croûtons, to serve

Heat the olive oil and clarified butter in a large pan. Halve 3 cloves of garlic and fry gently for about 10 minutes with the diced vegetables and chopped shallot, until golden. Deglaze the pan by stirring in the white wine.

Add the red wine, port and brandy. Cook for a few minutes to allow the alcohol to evaporate, then add the tomatoes, tomato purée, orange rind, savory, 3 basil leaves, fennel seeds, star anise, tarragon, thyme, parsley, bay leaves and mixed herbs.

Cut the fish into small pieces and add to the pan. Cook for 5 minutes over a moderate heat and then add the stock almost to the top of the pan. Simmer the soup for one hour, uncovered.

Finely slice the last 3 cloves of garlic and add with the remaining basil leaves and the pastis. Cook for a further 20 minutes and 5 minutes before the end, add the saffron.

Remove any large bones, liquidise the soup in batches in a blender and pass it through a sieve, squeezing out all the liquid.

Sieve the soup a second time into a clean pan. Reheat and season with salt and just enough cayenne pepper to feel the heat on your tongue.

Serve at once with Aïoli and freshly made croûtons.

Serve with a full-bodied white wine or even with a robust red wine.

This is one of my favourite fish dishes. Not only does a herby, golden and very aromatic crust look extremely appetising, but it is also easy to make. Apart from the cleaning of the fish (and sea bass is a messy fish to clean), there is only a little work involved in the preparation of the herb crust, for which you need very fine brioche crumbs, and dried Provençal herbs, very, very finely chopped. The end result is spectacular.

Escalope de Loup de Mer en Croûte aux Fines Herbes

Escalope of Sea Bass with a Herb Crust

Illustrated on page 81

SERVES 8

120 ml (8 tbsp) clarified butter (page 241)
1 sea bass, about 1.8 kg (4 lb) in weight, skinned and filleted in 8 pieces of about 150 g (5 oz) each
juice of 1 lemon
275 g (10 oz) fine brioche crumbs

175 g (6 oz) very dry, very finely chopped mixed Provençal herbs
30 ml (2 tbsp) very, very finely chopped parsley
salt and pepper
450 ml ($\frac{3}{4}$ pint) Beurre Blanc (page 234)

Brush clarified butter over the fillets, add a squeeze of lemon and set aside.

Mix together the brioche crumbs, the dried herbs, the parsley, salt and pepper to taste. Mix very well to amalgamate completely. Preheat the grill.

Arrange the fillets of sea bass on a baking tray and grill on high heat for 3 minutes on each side or until cooked, basting with the mixture of clarified butter and lemon. When the fish is just cooked, set aside to rest in a warm place for 10 minutes.

Spread a spoonful of the brioche herb mixture all over the fish and pat gently with a palette knife to completely cover the top of each fillet.

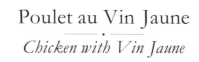

Poulet au Vin Jaune

Chicken with Vin Jaune

*Another recipe from my early repertoire
which even today casts a spell over me. The aroma
of freshly sautéed chicken, morel mushrooms
and a scented, creamy wine sauce is indescribable.
You need very plump chicken legs and you
must be generous with the mushrooms — there's
no substitute for them or for vin jaune, that
delicious golden wine from the Jura.*

RECIPE ON PAGE 37

Paupiettes de Sole au Crabe

Paupiettes of Sole stuffed with Crab

*The colours, flavours and textures of
this dish go well together. Fillets of lemon sole
are wrapped around a simple stuffing of white
crabmeat flavoured, oriental-style, with fresh
ginger. Spinach goes well with fish and here I have
placed the sole on a bed of spinach and served
with it a well-flavoured langoustine sauce.*

RECIPE ON PAGE 152

Place the beurre blanc on 8 warm plates.

Flash the fillets back under the hot grill again and cook for a few seconds until the topping is golden. With a palette knife, place the fillets in the centre of the pools of beurre blanc on each plate. Serve at once.

Serve with a good light or full-bodied dry white wine such as a Meursault.

The total experience

The subject of gastronomy, the enjoyment of the table, the philosophy of food and the heightening of the experience has another very important corollary – the setting. For me the setting is very important. I like to keep an immaculate table. Food is a total experience. It is the feasting of the eye and the satisfaction of the taste and the smell. I always ensure that beautiful food is placed on beautiful plates on clean white tablecloths. I like the use of heavy, white tablecloths without ridges or folds, two or three simple, very fine sparkling clean glasses arranged in clusters, fine cutlery and lovely flowers on the table. Flowers, their arrangement and presentation in good restaurants are a matter of very great importance. I seem to associate memorable occasions with lots of flowers on the table, arranged in beautiful bouquets, or sitting by a window with a breath-taking view of olive trees, pine trees, mimosa and other wild flowers reaching to find their way through the opening. And while I'm on the subject, there is one flower I heartily dislike: that is a flower made from the skins of tomatoes. I admire the skill involved, but frankly I cannot find it acceptable on the grounds that it is inedible and anything inedible is unnecessary on a plate. We spend our lives and our skills trying to dislodge the skin off the tomato to throw it away, and yet some people still try to make it into a flower!

Cooking: art or science?

For some time now, the chef has been portrayed as an artist and has himself portrayed his trade in an artistic form. One era is suddenly passing and another is about to begin. Harold McGee's book *On Food and Cooking* is the major force which I have awaited for some considerable time. The book which this young American professor from Yale has written on the science of the kitchen will in due course become more important than Escoffier's work, and as important as the writings of Brillat-Savarin in the nineteenth century. During the making of a television series 'Take Another Six Cooks', I became involved in a debate with Raymond Blanc on the subject of whether cooking is a science or an art. For me, cooking has always been a battle against the elements. You are constantly exposing different textures, consistencies, different liquids, different fats and vegetables to the energy of heat. To know how to proceed in order to achieve certain results means that you are constantly engaged in chemical reaction. When you have tiptoed through the chemical minefield, encountering all sorts of scientific rules, methods and processes on the way, you are then ready to exercise the natural artistic talent inherent in you to put the final dish together and make it look attractive. Chemistry and biology are involved here, and only when the various laws are unlocked in order to find an answer does art take a hand. While not really an argument about whether cooking is a science or an art, it is more a debate about where one ends and the other begins. Is it the knowledge of the rules of chemistry or biology that enable a chef to cook a piece of meat or a vegetable perfectly? There can only be one answer. It is certainly not the rules of art, whose main rule is that there are no rules.

The chroniclers on the subject of food over the ages have often pronounced their opinion on the philosophy of the table in various historical contexts and reflecting the climate of the time. It is not a strange phenomenon that those chroniclers whose work stands out more than others are those who have applied philosophy and scientific deduction and thought to the subject of food. I have in mind the man who is always quoted as the definitive guru on the science of gastronomy and cooking, Brillat-Savarin. I would like to draw the attention of the cook to a short pronouncement from *La Physiologie du Goût* which for me summarises eternally my deep conviction that cooking is a science and presentation is an art: 'The professor to his cook: "You are a little opinionated and I have had some trouble in making you understand that the phenomena which take place in your laboratory are nothing other than the execution of the laws of nature, and that certain things which you do without thinking, and only because you have seen others doing them, derive nonetheless from the highest scientific principles."'

Harold McGee devotes seven hundred pages in plain, simple language to tell us all about science in the kitchen. The best investment any young aspiring cook can make is to buy his book, read it well, and thoroughly understand it. Without knowing it, this young professor has probably turned everything on its head. Never mind the wonderful recipes from Michel Guérard, Joël Robuchon or Roger Vergé. Knowledge of the contents of this book should precede anything else.

I have observed a habit which I find unnecessary and futile. A lot of pretentious local restaurants introduce a sorbet or a granité in between the starter and the main course. I really do not see the point of it, other than to lull the customer into a false sense of getting something for nothing – a ploy which succeeds brilliantly in the country.

It is a very rare occasion indeed to see the offer of a little glass of very

chilled Sauternes, Barsac or Frontignan with a starter of foie gras. I like this practice immensely. The sweet wine goes beautifully with goose or duck liver. This habit which we have had for many years now caused one of the most hilarious incidents of my career. At Chez Nico in Battersea we used to serve a *mousse de foie de volaille*. It was creamy and very rich and we used to serve it with a little glass of Sauternes. This is not a joke about Irishmen, but I have to be truthful and say that the customers concerned were three very well-dressed Irishmen. One of them ordered the chicken liver mousse and it duly arrived with the obligatory glass of Sauternes by the side. This baffled him, he looked at the pâté, then at the Sauternes, then at his colleagues, reached for the glass, held it in his hand and proceeded to pour it all over the chicken liver mousse!

This particular dish has brought to us more compliments, more enjoyment and more praise than any other single dish we have served on our menu. The evolution of this recipe was quite tortuous and many-sided. It was originally based on the world-famous chicken liver mousse from the Auberge du Père Bise, the 3-star restaurant in Talloires on Lake Annecy. It evolved via Michel Guérard's famous *terrine fondant de foie de volaille* and was adapted by me on many different occasions. It has finally ended up in a period of great stability where the recipe is executed faithfully to the last little milligram of each ingredient concerned. The end product is such a fragile and delicately smooth mousse, there is extraordinary tension in the kitchen each time an order for it comes in. It has been called the definitive version of a chicken liver mousse.

I use a 1.1 litre (2 pint) duralex terrine for this recipe. Glass terrines do not retain fierce heat for any length of time, and more importantly, you can see through the glass whether you have ruined the livers by overcooking them (in which case they will be slightly cracked and separating) or whether they're still pink and smooth and correctly cooked.

Mousse de Foie de Volaille
Mousse of Chicken Livers

SERVES 12

15 ml (1 tbsp) clarified butter (page 241)
450 g (1 lb) fresh or frozen chicken livers
   (as pale in colour as possible)
150 ml ($\frac{1}{4}$ pint) ruby port
120 ml (8 tbsp) cognac
yolks of 8 eggs

150 g (5 oz) melted butter
150 g (5 oz) melted fat from foie gras
150 g (5 oz) melted pork fat
450 ml ($\frac{3}{4}$ pint) double cream
salt
finely ground white or cayenne pepper
pinch of nutmeg

Paint the bottom and sides of a glass terrine with clarified butter.

Clean each chicken liver individually removing all bile, sinews and veins. Wash very well, dry very well on absorbent kitchen paper and marinate in the port for 24 hours. Remove from the marinade, or strain through a sieve and dry thoroughly.

In an electric blender place the cognac, eggs, chicken livers, melted butter, foie gras fat and pork fat and blend together thoroughly. Pour the cream into the mixture at the last moment and blend again briefly. Pass everything through a fine wire sieve. Adjust the seasoning, and pour into the terrine.

Cover with a double layer of kitchen foil and seal tightly all around. Cook in a bain-marie in 5 cm (2 inches) of water for 20 minutes in a cool 150°C (300°F) mark 2 oven.

From this point on, you will have to play it very much by ear. If the chicken liver mousse is still very wobbly, you will have to decide either to leave it in the oven for a few more minutes, or to let it cool in the hot water until it is set. It is very easy to check and keep on checking merely by shaking the glass terrine periodically. A very light wobble and a smooth, leather-like appearance on the surface means that it is correctly cooked and it should be cooled down fast.

When the terrine is cold, cover again with foil and leave to set in the refrigerator until the following day. Serve with toast and a glass of good-quality dessert wine.

I concede that other people have their own philosophy of food too! For example, the occasion was unforgettable when, serving three immaculately cooked spears of bright green asparagus, the plate came back with the stalks devoured and three bright, green, perfectly formed heads pushed to the side. This gentleman obviously had his likes and dislikes and philosophies as well. Or perhaps he had never seen asparagus in his life before.

I have never been afraid to break certain rules. For example, the practice of serving home made bread, or home made brioche because it is made on the premises, for me, is not the indelible mark of a good restaurant. If I cannot make bread which is as good as some of the bread which is available and which comes frozen, half-cooked, from France, then I will not do so and would prefer to buy it from outside. The same applies for brioche. My rule, therefore, is this: if you cannot cook something better than you can buy it there is no point in cooking it simply to be able to say that it is home made.

It is worth remembering that it is imperfect cooking and poor ingredients that have produced 'bad' food. There is nothing wrong with the freshest, the best prawn cocktail you can possibly make. I have no quarrel whatsoever with the prawn cocktail as a dish in itself. I have, however, a serious quarrel with all those purveyors of the travesties served as the prawn cocktail. A tomato soup is surely one of the greatest soups in French cuisine, or any other cuisine, if made properly. Too many tomato soups one encounters are either red dishwater, or thick, sweet purées more reminiscent of the all-conquering tinned variety. If I put a tomato soup on my menu, it would be made freshly and well. If I had a smoked fish, it would be a spanking fresh smoked trout with a whipped, fluffy, horseradish sauce. Who knows, one day I might serve a beautiful Dover sole, either grilled, or meunière. I may serve a proper *sole bonne femme* and I would restore to my favourite composer Gioacchino Rossini the respect he deserves as a truly great gastronome by rendering for his memory an impeccable version of his favourite dish, tournedos Rossini. I would not turn my nose up at a good sherry trifle and I would concoct a gooey, fresh version of a Black Forest Gâteau to remind everybody what a non-plastic version of the famous confection should be. These dishes have sadly been tainted by poor imitations passing into daily use.

There are certain foods that go extremely well together. Fish with mushrooms is one of the great marriages in general, and mushrooms with sole, in particular, make a good combination. I often use puff pastry cases lined with a soft purée or *duxelles* of mushrooms and shallots to accompany my fish dishes.

This dish is slightly difficult to execute because it entails the boning of a sole. The bone should be removed from the side of the fish with black skin — the fish is fleshier here and the meat is thicker. The first time you do it, this will probably seem an enormous task, but the more you try, the easier it gets. The best way is to use good kitchen scissors and a pair of tweezers and remove the bone a little at a time in small sections. Do take care not to damage the flesh.

Sole Fourée à la Mousse de Champignons
Sole Stuffed with a Purée of Mushrooms

SERVES 2

100 g (4 oz) butter
10 ml (2 tsp) very finely chopped shallots
12 well trimmed, white button mushrooms, very finely chopped
few drops of dry white wine
salt
cayenne pepper
30 ml (2 tbsp) double cream
10 ml (2 tsp) finely chopped parsley

5 ml (1 tsp) very finely chopped tarragon
2 × 350 g (12 oz) Dover sole, skinned and well trimmed
butter
30 ml (2 tbsp) very finely chopped shallots
120 ml (8 tbsp) sliced mushrooms
300 ml ($\frac{1}{2}$ pint) Noilly Prat (very dry French vermouth)
lemon juice
30 ml (2 tbsp) double cream

First make the *duxelles*: in a non-stick pan melt 50 g (2 oz) of the butter, add the shallots and the chopped mushrooms. Sprinkle over a few drops of wine, add salt and pepper to release the juices and for seasoning. Cook down for 8–10 minutes. Add the double cream, parsley and tarragon, cook together and process well in a blender to make a smooth purée. Set aside.

Next bone the sole: take a small, flexible, very sharp pointed knife and run the blade down the middle of the fleshy part of each of the fish, then slide the knife on either side at an angle from head to tail. With scissors, clip the backbone in 8 or 9 sections, and one by one, lift off the bone with tweezers. Check to see you have not left any bones, sprinkle with a little salt and a squeeze of lemon and stuff the cavities with the *duxelles*.

Butter an ovenproof dish using 25 g (1 oz) of butter, sprinkle with shallots, add the sliced mushrooms and the Noilly Prat and place the sole on top, stuffed sides up. Cover with kitchen foil and place in a fairly hot 190°C (375°F) mark 5 oven for about 20 minutes or until cooked.

When the fish is ready, lift off with a fish slice, pat dry on absorbent kitchen paper and keep warm.

Strain the juices, pour into a pan and reduce by half. Add a squeeze of lemon, the double cream, the remaining butter, salt and cayenne pepper and simmer until thickened. Lay the fish, stuffed side down, on warm plates and pour the sauce over.

Serve with a full-flavoured dry white wine such as a Puligny-Montrachet.

Marriages made in heaven

My very strong convictions cannot allow me to finish off my philosophy on food without a look at the tastes and the marriages of such tastes which make the practice of fine cuisine such an intensely enjoyable subject. I list below for discussion, titillation and experiment what I call 'marriages made in heaven'.

Strawberries and cream
Coffee and rum
Steak and chips
Scallops and garlic
Madeira and tongue
Duck and orange
Tomatoes and basil
Foie Gras and Sauternes
Chicken and morels
Chicken and Château-Chalon
Salmon and sorrel
Turbot and lobster sauce
Caviar and vodka
Melon and port

White truffles and pasta
Basmati rice and chicken tikka
Lamb and garlic
Provençal fish soup with rouille
Port with cheese
Fried eggs and bacon
Calves' kidneys and mustard
Armagnac ice cream with
marrons glacés
Pears with chocolate
Caramelised apples
with puff pastry
Chicken with tarragon
Cold lobster with mayonnaise

Perfection is the result of simplicity. That is my philosophy: to be restrained in presentation, to produce every dish consistently and always approaching the ideal.

'My ideal menu
might begin with a small clear soup, it
may be followed by a salad including shellfish
or foie gras, it may lead to an exquisite, lightly
sauced fish dish, ungarnished, to be followed
by the meat course and end with
a pudding ideally composed of
a spotty vanilla ice cream,
perfumed exotic fruit,
a little pastry and a vivid
coulis of some very
aromatic fruit.'

CHAPTER THREE

Planning menus and choosing wines

*P*lanning your menu is an essential part of eating well and deciding what to drink with the food you choose is just as important. Professional chefs plan their menus carefully, bearing in mind the tastes, and these days the health, of their customers. With the help of the waiter, who knows the dishes on the menu, restaurant customers need to learn how to choose from the selection of dishes provided by the chef. Home cooks, too, must plan what to serve family or friends, knowing their personal limitations of time, budget and practicality. Whether at home or in a restaurant the 'meal experience' begins with the aperitif. Choose carefully. Marry the wines to the dishes with care: a well planned combination of wines and food will always be greater than the sum of its parts.

The guiding principles

The chef has several criteria to bear in mind: the availability of ingredients, balance of sauces with the different courses, temperature and texture of the ingredients and so on. The seasons have always dictated to and inspired the cook, and while availability of produce was once strictly seasonal, today this fundamental principle no longer applies to the same degree. Rapid communication and fast transportation, together with advances in refrigeration are increasingly making the world an all-year-round feast. When it is freezing in northern Europe or on America's east coast, countries in the southern hemisphere are in the grip of a steamy summer. In recent years there has been a dramatic change in the availability of fresh, raw materials from all over the world. Only a few stubborn ingredients adhere to the essential elements of the four seasons.

Seasonal availability of ingredients

A few essential main ingredients play a very important role for me as a professional chef and are crucial to my decisions when it comes to the planning of my menus. Wild salmon, spring lamb, fresh wild mushrooms, grouse and game birds in the autumn – these are my guidelines, my beacons. Of secondary importance to me are the fresh lychees in December and January, the Alphonso mango from India in April and May, early white asparagus from France, again in April or May, fresh chestnuts in December and January, fresh walnuts and big juicy figs from Italy and France in October. Gone are the days when an 'r' in the month denoted the availability of mussels and when scallops were unavailable during the spring and summer months – shellfish farms have changed all that.

The clues to balancing a menu are right there among the various ingredients – the fish, the meat, the poultry and game birds, the vegetables and the exotic fruits – it is from these that you make a choice and compose your ideal menu. Use sauces as a guiding principle: there must be no clash of similar types, whether brown sauces or cream sauces.

The sauces

Both the professional and the home cook must consider very carefully the kind of sauce which goes with each course. If you have a mousseline of sole as a starter, and you are serving it with a fish cream sauce flavoured with Sauternes, you should not follow it, for example, with a veal or chicken dish with another cream sauce. There is nothing to beat the rich velvety texture, flavour and look of a beautiful cream sauce, but too much of it can lead to indigestion, not to say overweight.

Usually, when you plan a menu for a dinner party at home, or when you are steered through a restaurant menu by a competent *maître d'*, you tend to combine a fish starter, maybe in a cream sauce, or a butter sauce, with a main course of meat in a brown sauce – that is you marry the fish with the meat and this is a sensible balance. So it is vitally important to balance and trade off one sauce with another. This applies even to superbly executed flour-free brown sauces. For example, one of our very popular starters is sautéed goose liver on toasted brioche. We offset the richness of the dish and balance the flavour by serving with it some caramelised orange segments and a few leaves of *salade de mâche* tossed in lemon juice and hazelnut oil. The foie gras is dressed with a very light reduction of veal stock. Such a starter, though a heavenly concoction of tastes, flavours and textures, may cause you problems when it comes to choosing the main course. To avoid a clash of sauces, even within the brown sauce range, you may wish to have another offal dish and have calves' kidneys with very light cream mustard sauce, or a sweetbread made crisp in hot clarified butter, lightly glazed with a Madeira and truffle reduction and served on a sauce based on the juices of carrots and a little cream. Although you may be choosing two offal dishes, this would be a sensible balance because you are avoiding following a starter with a rich brown sauce with a main course with a similar rich brown sauce. The hot foie gras has a light reduction and the kidneys or sweetbreads are served in very light coatings of mustard and cream on one hand and a reduction of Madeira and truffle juice on the other.

Texture

The next important principle to think about is texture. Too many mousses on a carefully planned menu are self-defeating. If you eat a mousse of lobster in a rich champagne sauce as a starter, you should certainly not choose a main course consisting of a whole fish which has been stuffed with another fish mousse – in any case both would be served either with butter or cream sauce and they would therefore clash.

We have so far identified the key points as follows: main ingredients in season; sauces; balancing fish and meat; the texture of the chosen ingredients, both within one course and between different courses. We now must come to what I consider are five further very important principles which apply to the home cook as much as the restaurant chef: temperature, vegetables and fruit, pastry, colour and, finally, the actual cooking process. Let us look at all these individually.

Hot versus cold

If you decide to give a cold buffet, you do not have a problem with temperature because the entire meal is cold. But if you are planning a menu for a dinner party or are eating out in a restaurant then you have to take into account whether your starter will be a cold one or a hot one. If it is a hot one, be careful, because you can't eat or serve a hot starter, a hot main course and hot pudding. Paul Bocuse quite categorically states that one hot course in any meal is quite enough. This maxim is, of course, a godsend to the home cook who works during the day and has a dinner party to prepare. The opportunity for early preparation of a cold starter and cold pudding allow you to concentrate on the main course on the night.

Vegetables and fruit

Vegetables and fruit are important elements in any meal. A dish which is very rich, even if it has been offset by a simpler starter, can have its richness cut by the introduction of certain vegetables of such humble origin as to bring it down to size in a jiffy. Broccoli, cauliflower, cabbage, all are wonderful neutralisers. It is probably the reason why a side salad, lightly dressed and spiked with vinegar or lemon juice, is sometimes served automatically as an accompaniment to a main course. In the same way a grapefruit, an orange, a lemon or a lime segment will counterbalance a rich sauce admirably.

Pastry

Pastry is a very important element in balancing menus and its over use, or under use, can cause trouble. A puff pastry case filled with asparagus and served with a *beurre blanc* should not be followed by a shortcrust pastry case containing kidneys or some other meat. Desserts are often made with pastry so it may be sensible to concede to this course your preference for pastry – and remember when coffee time comes around, there could very easily be yet more pastry there, too, in the form of *petits fours*. If you plan to make a sensational pastry main course for a dinner party and you also wish to have a pastry for pudding, then you must demote its importance in the latter – a very light tulip case containing either fruit, ice cream or sorbet will be sufficient.

Colour

At every good dinner party there will be beautiful flowers on the table. The question of colour, therefore, must also be taken into account. Seek out colour and use it as much as possible. This is where vegetables and fruit come into their own. Use the bright colour of an orange or a carrot, the strong red of a tomato, the vivid green of broccoli, the golds and the browns of potatoes and, if you can afford it, the pitch black of the glorious truffle.

Methods of cooking

Menu planning and composition should always take a very serious account of the way in which the various courses have been cooked. Basically, the major methods of cooking are grilling or griddling, boiling or poaching, frying, steaming, roasting and baking. A fried starter, followed by a fried main course, followed by a fried pudding is obviously very bad for the health and does not say very much for the cook or the guest – it is out-and-out gastronomic sabotage. Similarly, a boiled starter, followed by a boiled main course, followed by a boiled pudding, could end up being a boiled bore. Everything is wrong in these two extreme examples: nutrition, temperature, colour, texture.

If you are serving fried scallops as a starter, follow them with a grilled or roast main course and finish with a cold pudding. In other words, combine a roast dish with a steamed one, a cold dish and a poached one; alternate hot with cold and bear in mind all the other variables to achieve a good balance.

Sorbets and granités

For some reason or another, sorbets and granités seem to have become almost commonplace on restaurant menus, especially in the provinces. Somebody must have told somebody else that to serve a sorbet in the middle of a dinner is the mark of elegance, is good for the digestion, it shows that you know how to eat and that you are part of the modern scene. It is nothing of the sort. It is a well flogged, twisted and abused sensible practice when the occasion arises and when the menu cries for it. The occasions arose and menus cried for it in the days, 30, 40, 50, 60 years ago, when dinners were composed of upwards of five courses. The confusion was perpetuated when so-called *nouvelle cuisine*, with its many little courses, came on the scene again. But the modern practice of the *menu dégustation* finds with me very little favour and even less flavour. Invariably, experiences like these leave you over indulged, over fed, bloated, uncomfortable and, frequently, wanting to vomit. The most I would go to is a five course, very well planned, very carefully sauced and multi-vegetable structured menu. On an occasion like this, the *granité de Beaujolais* of Paul Bocuse, or the *granité de pamplemousse rose* of Roger Vergé are apt and perfectly matched. Making sorbets of sage, peppercorns or thyme is abhorrent to me.

Trust the waiter

Most of us at some time or other eat out in a good restaurant. We hope that the chef has planned the menu carefully so we may make a balanced choice. It is time to make our selection. I must insist: trust the *maître d'* or the waiter. He knows the chef, the food, the secrets which may not be immediately apparent from the menu. Be guided by him: his interest and that of the chef, is best served by your enjoyment. Following the principles we have already discussed, he will help you avoid ordering dishes that are too similar, too rich or dishes which simply do not complement one another. Do not resist. Do not say 'Whose party is this? I'll have what I like'. You are both on the same side. I am always pleased to be guided through a strange menu by a polite, skilful waiter or *maître d'*.

The best aperitifs

There is one other significant area to exercise your skill as a menu planner. Whether at home or in the restaurant once you have chosen your food, the

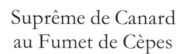

Suprême de Canard
au Fumet de Cèpes

*Breast of Duck with
a Wild Mushroom Sauce*

*Simply cooked duck breasts are served here
with one of my favourite wild mushroom sauces.
The accompanying vegetables, steamed kohlrabi,
confit of shallots, gratin dauphinois and leek
purée served in a tartelette case are a perfect foil
for the richness of the dish.*

RECIPE ON PAGE 61

Escalope de Loup de Mer
en Croûte aux Fines Herbes

Escalope of Sea Bass with a Herb Crust

*I use this herby crust for both lamb
and fish and in spite of its being considered
delicately flavoured, bass can stand up well to the
robust flavours of Provence. Beurre blanc is
a traditional sauce for serving with bass and the
clean flavours of simply cooked mangetout,
asparagus, spinach and potatoes make this a
simple yet elegant dish.*

RECIPE ON PAGE 63

wine must follow. But let's go back a stage: your meal will probably begin with an aperitif. A gin and tonic is no way to prepare the palate for a good dinner. No harsh spirit is suitable for this purpose: these days, the restaurant bar begins to resemble the pub.

Both Dinah-Jane and I are non-drinkers, or nearly so, and never have understood the pub attitude where you go to a place to get systematically intoxicated. The idea of a bar is to us out of place when it comes to the running of a good restaurant. We have never wanted to get involved with complicated cocktails or have a barman and so we decided very early on to have a short spirit list which was different from most others, reasonably comprehensive, and which was designed to provide a list of aperitifs in the strictest sense of the word. Aperitifs should whet your appetite, rather than dull it, they are drinks which open the proceedings, they help you to choose your food and stimulate your appetite. We have always believed in serving what we like, or more precisely something which would appeal to us and to our palate. A glass of champagne or white wine, a glass of sherry or a very nice light vermouth, this is how we like to start.

The only restaurant we ever had a bar in was in the country, at Shinfield (and what problems that created), but in the end we were forced to close down the smoke-filled room. In provincial England we discovered that the bar room was more important than the dining room. But good food is not an afterthought – it is a carefully thought out programme. Each individual taste all along the line is designed to heighten the experience. I can quite understand that a string of gin and tonics consumed while propping up a bar in an East African gymkhana club, or a New Delhi officers' mess could well be followed by a hearty Vindaloo or a Madras curry, lots of papadams, mountains of rice and two or three beers. But I don't quite see how a gin and tonic could ever complement a terrine of foie gras. In my mind, the grape and the rare fruits of the earth were intended for betrothal. Ice cold vodka with a first-rate Sevruga are the exception. Better in my view to stick with sherry or vermouth. Champagne is, of course, a wonderful aperitif as is Château-Châlon *vin jaune* (an intense yellow wine from the Jura area of France which tastes similar to sherry) or a light fresh glass of Savennières from the Loire. All fruity white wines make good aperitifs. Syrups of *cassis*, *framboise* or *mûre* added to white wine or, better still, to champagne, also make excellent summertime aperitifs – but be mean with the syrup or it will become oversweet.

Red wine

But then what do you drink with the meal itself? To begin with, there is a paramount requirement which we always looked to satisfy, which is that wines, however great, however humble, whatever their origin, should be enjoyed in spite of ceremony, rather than because of it. As a blanket rule, we feel that all red wines should be served at cellar temperature, which means straight from the cellar, or if you are not lucky enough to have one, very slightly cool. By this, I don't just believe that all light, young red wines such as Beaujolais should be served cold, but that all red wines should be served slightly cool. Unfortunately a lot of nonsense prevails on the subject of wine. One such outdated idea is that all red wines should be served at room temperature, which means that an inferior wine thus served will probably taste very coarse, very acid and flat. Served cool, or indeed cold, its acidity will be arrested, and its near absent fruit will almost come from nothing. As a general rule, red wines are served too warm. Richard Olney, an American greatly respected in France for his knowledge, his opinions, and his in-depth research of revered châteaux, has tried over the years to persuade us that since we insist that a beautiful Scotch fillet should be served rare and have established that principle, we should, at the same time, adopt a similar attitude on the serving of red wines and say that we serve them cool, at cellar temperature.

Wine snobs

It is a fact that the English have always prided themselves on their love and knowledge of wines. Indeed, many English wine lovers most probably know more than the average Frenchman who is quite content most of the time to drink nothing more than *vin du pays*. The French certainly look with great amusement at the antics across the Channel and across the Atlantic. They don't have Masters of Wine and wine snobbery there is a recent phenomenon, I'm afraid. Because the subject of wine is of great interest, is widely discussed and written about, it also leads to the most awful posturing. I look at the whole subject of wine in England as an iron curtain dividing two classes, two cultures, and two nations. You are led to believe that there are the beer bellies of the north or the east, or of the south, or of anywhere on one side, and on the other, you have the tall, slim, pinstripe public school stockbroker type who 'knows his wine'.

When a person's knowledge of a subject is slight and they attempt to know more about something because it is fashionable or because it has snob value, then it becomes dangerous. A little knowledge, as the saying goes, is a dangerous thing. We very rarely get involved with customers when they complain about wine. We simply provide a new bottle and send the offending one to our wine merchant. Invariably, the answer comes back that there is nothing wrong with the wine, there is something wrong with the customer! The whole point is that when a customer, in our experience, normally complains about the quality of the wine, he is not really saying that the wine itself is at fault. All he is really saying is that it is not to his taste, which is what he should have said in the first place and is a very different thing. In point of fact, it is not very difficult, usually, to detect from the smell and colour of the cork whether all is well with a wine. The elaborate ceremony, the gurgling and slopping many so-called wine connoisseurs indulge in quite honestly leaves me cold. We had such a recent occasion to observe a pompous wine snob in full flight – it was hilarious. The noise and movements he made swilling the wine around in his mouth, the expression on his face and the final remarks he made were comical. He was a perfect example of pomposity, ignorance and a desire to show off his spurious knowledge to his guests.

The wine list

One must never forget that the whole object of wine is that it is there to be drunk, to be enjoyed, to accompany food and not to be drooled over. I have never been able to understand why people go into rapture and ecstasy over the wine list of a restaurant which is pages long. In the last 20 years, the surge of great food and great restaurants has been accompanied by the phenomenon of the short menu. Short menus made it possible for a chef to cook well and to concentrate on a handful of spectacular dishes. Why should this not apply to wine as well? Why not a short, well-thought-out wine list? After all, in the final analysis, when you sit down and have a meal you are likely to be able to drink only one or possibly two bottles. In our Battersea days we overheard someone saying we had a bad wine list. When the subject was raised later, this charming know-all admitted that what he meant really was that it was a short wine list, not that the wines listed were bad.

Decanters are another area of great controversy. In France, they don't go in for decanting red wine as a matter of course. For the record, I firmly believe that you shouldn't decant any bottle of wine that costs less than a (non-crystal) decanter. We have now decided to decant without argument for anybody who wants his wine decanted, whatever it is. It really saves a lot of trouble. People quite often show their ignorance by that request and how much they wish to show off, but that is their privilege. It is also my privilege to find these antics hilarious except that the typical show-off wouldn't really understand it.

One very clear preference both Dinah and I have is for younger wines. We especially like French regional wines which are often overlooked – from the Jura, from Savoie and from Provence. We are increasingly impressed by the wines from California, Australia and New Zealand, which are beginning to rival traditional French wines in both price and quality. We also find it exciting not to hold fast on such rules as white wines for fish and shellfish, and various red wines with game or roast beef. If somebody wishes to drink a heavy red with fillet of sole in a white wine sauce, that is a matter for him, the sole and for the red wine. We should really go on as a natural corollary of this to acquiesce with some people's desire to drink a bottle of Suduiraut with their grilled fillet steak. Though we might comply with such a request, we would make it our duty to tell the customer that the dessert wine he has ordered might go better with a delectable ice cream with fruit than a grilled fillet steak. In Dulwich we came across a Cockney millionaire who had in his cellar 27 cases of Château Yquem 1947 and drank it with everything, even kippers or bangers and mash. Most people enjoy a more conventional combination of wines and food. Some great marriages include Sauternes with foie gras, poached fresh salmon with a rich St-Emilion or drinking sweet wine with cheese. Conversely, avoid wine with smoked salmon and beware of chocolate with any wine, however sweet. When it comes to accompaniments for sorbets and ice creams, I recommend a dessert wine such as Sauternes, Barsac or Muscat de Frontignan or a spicy Gewürztraminer or even an Italian sweet sparkling Moscato Asti Spumanti or an Australian liqueur muscat.

Wine is one of the most pleasurable things in life and should be enjoyed simply. The glasses should be quite fine and reasonably large. They should not be filled more than halfway, and although our wine waiter has strict instructions to keep an eye on all glasses and top them up as necessary, I personally become incensed when I detect an over-zealous wine waiter. On one occasion when I found that my wine glass was being topped up after every single sip, I simply took the bottle away, hid it under the table and told the wine waiter that that is where I wanted it left. Unfortunately if in our restaurant we don't keep customers' wine glasses filled, we are accused of giving inferior wine service. We call this service 'over service'. Some customers refuse to pour their own wine and call you over to ask that their glasses be refilled. At Paul Bocuse's restaurant in France we were particularly struck when dining there on one occasion by his unpompous, unpretentious and down-to-earth approach – from the great slab of butter served in its own paper to the same-size plain glasses which we used for nearly all wines. You could tell the place was owned and run by a simple man. As it happens, we also decided it was the most unpretentious three-star restaurant we had experienced, and one of the nicest.

White wines

White wines should be served distinctly cold; for example, this includes the lighter styles such as all muscadets, Sancerres and Loire wines in general. On the other hand, the more important white wines such as the great white burgundies, or the perfumed, noble Alsace wines, should not be served so cold as to suppress their incredible taste and flavour. Champagnes and the great sweet wines of Bordeaux should be served very cold.

These days, many people take mineral water alongside their wine. In France 85 per cent of all mineral waters are non-fizzy, such as Evian and Vittel. Of the bubbly variety, Badoit and Perrier are the most popular, though Perrier is usually drunk as an aperitif, but not as an accompaniment to a meal. My preference is decidedly for Evian or Vittel.

Digestifs

Digestifs are always extremely popular. Of the sweet liqueurs I enjoy Benédictine, Grand Marnier, Cointreau and yellow and green Chartreuse. Then of course there is port, that wonderful drink made by English families who settled in Oporto many years ago. Vintage port (a vintage is declared probably three times a decade) is a wonderful drink. A glass of 1963 port, a piece of Roquefort and a few ice cold Muscatel grapes is another 'marriage made in heaven'. We offer a good selection of cognac and Armagnac. With cognac seek out a vintage if you can and try to avoid the obvious 'blends'. Armagnac has a more rustic feel. Vintages are not hard to find. We also keep *marc*, a spirit which is made in every wine growing district in the world from all the skins, pips and other detritus left after pressing. My favourites are from Frontignan or Gewürztraminer from Alsace. *Fine de Bourgogne*, a brandy made from grapes from the burgundy region, is a superb digestif. *Eaux de vie* are clean spirits distilled from fruits; notable ones are poire William, mirabelle, kirsch, framboise and gvetsch. Calvados is basically an *eau de vie* made from apples; try to find a smooth one – some can be very rough indeed. Malt whisky is a much overlooked digestif and a very enjoyable one. Malts vary greatly in both character and quality.

To sum up, I feel that the balancing of the menu is the critical choice which governs the enjoyment of a meal. Then the wines can be added in. And above all, drink what you enjoy.

Here are seven different menus composed of dishes which we have served in our restaurants and which appear in this book. They give a clear illustration of what a well balanced menu is all about and, hopefully, will also stimulate discussion. All the wines, aperitifs and digestifs are chosen with a *style* in mind. For the most part, we do not recommend vintages, as this is a very personal choice and also dependent on cost. Lucky the person with such a rich cellar!

Menu One

·

The way not to begin this meal is with a pink gin! You start the proceedings with a glass of Taittinger Comtes de Champagne Blanc de Blanc, accompanied by a tiny lobster quiche. With the consommé you drink nothing, you merely finish your champagne. With the terrine of foie gras, you drink a glass of sweet dessert wine such as Muscat de Frontignan. With the mullet, a glass of meursault. With the duck, you drink a stylish claret such as Pichon Lalande or a Château La Lagune. You finish the red wine, or you might wish to have a glass of 1963 vintage Taylors port, or if you are eating the Roquefort only, a very chilled dessert wine such as Sauternes, which can follow on into the pudding. How about a Château d'Yquem 1967.

This is a supreme example of a fairly elaborate meal, and one for a very special occasion only. It goes without saying that you couldn't make a meal like this at home under any circumstances, *unless* . . . no, there is no *unless*!

Consommé de champignons au madère
aromatisé aux feuilles de coriandre
(*page 59*)

·

Terrine de foie gras avec sa gelée au sauternes
(*page 175*)

·

Rouget au beurre de romarin
(*page 123*)

·

Sorbet aux pamplemousses roses
(*page 162*)

·

Suprême de canard au
fumet de cèpes
(*page 61*)

·

Assiette de fromages aux raisins muscatelles
(*Selected cheeses and muscatel grapes*)

·

Tulipe aux fruits frais assortis et
au coulis de framboises
(*pages 165 and 244*)

·

Café et petits fours
(*pages 197–9*)

Menu Two

———— • ————

This is an example of a more straightforward simpler gastronomic occasion. With the Provençal fish soup you could choose a light, medium-dry white such as Pouilly-Fumé or an Australian Petaluma, for a change. With the tournedos you drink a light, elegant red burgundy such as Santenay or a Morey-St-Denis and with the marquise au chocolat, you may sip a very cold eau de vie de poire.

Soupe de poisson
(*page 62*)

———— • ————

Tournedos aux échalotes confites
(*page 98*)

———— • ————

Marquise au chocolat sauce
crème anglaise orangée
(*pages 195 and 245*)

———— • ————

Café et petits fours
(*pages 197–8*)

Menu Three

———— • ————

Since the garnish is a good dollop of caviar, you may wish to drink a glass of chilled vodka with the smoked salmon. With your lamb you should drink a very young, chilled light dry red such as a Cru Beaujolais or a youngish St-Emilion. And with the exquisite apple tart, chilled Calvados.

Timbale de saumon fumé à la mousse
de langoustines
(*page 179*)

———— • ————

Carré d'agneau rose en croûte de fines herbes
aux légumes confits et à la purée d'ail doux
(*pages 101, 142 and 240*)

———— • ————

Tartes fines aux pommes
à la sauce caramel
(*pages 197 and 245*)

———— • ————

Café et petits fours
(*pages 197–8*)

Menu Four

·

Accompany your salad with a glass of Tokay d'Alsac such as Meursault. With your main course you could drink a rich red such as Côte Rôtie. With your dessert, a glass of good-quality dessert wine – Château Doisy-Daëne would be ideal.

La salade de caille
au beurre de cèpes
(*page 106*)

·

Noix de ris de veau au jus de carottes et de Sauternes
(*page 171*)

·

Sorbets au syrop aux citrons verts
(*pages 158–163 and 244*)

·

Café et petits fours
(*pages 197–8*)

Menu Five

·

As an aperitif have a glass of dry white Chambéry vermouth with a slice of lime, and throughout the fish courses, either a bottle of strong, fruity, sharp white such as Coulée de Serrant, or a more fragrant white wine such as Pouilly-Fumé Baron de L. You might like to accompany your parfait with a glass of luscious, fruity dessert wine such as 1976 Gewürztraminer either Schlumberger's Cuvée Christine or Hugel's Sélection des Grains Nobles.

Bonbonnière de coquilles St Jacques au beurre blanc
pointillé de poivrons rouges
(*page 124*)

·

Feuilleté de turbot au coulis de langoustines
(*page 183*)

·

Parfait à l'armagnac aux
marrons glacés
(*page 164*)

·

Café et petits fours
(*pages 197–8*)

Menu Six

Champagne is a wonderful aperitif. Try Canard Duchêne, which you continue to drink with the mousseline. With the main course, choose a fruity, dryish white Riesling from Alsace. Drink nothing with the salad. A glass of Château de Malle, or a glass of Muscat de Frontignan go well with the dessert.

Mousseline de sole et de crabe
à la sauce de langoustines
(*page 118*)

Poussins à l'eau de vie de Frontignan
(*page 35*)

Salade aux Fines Herbes
(*page 127*)

Tulipe aux fruits rouges
à la sauce crème anglaise orangée
(*pages 167 and 245*)

Café et petits fours
(*pages 197–8*)

Menu Seven

·

Begin this menu with a glass of champagne framboise, Dinah-Jane's favourite aperitif. A dry white wine from Bordeaux such as Château Carbonnieux would be very nice to drink throughout, for a change, and then treat yourself to a wonderfully old dessert wine, a Barsac such as a 1955 Château Coutet with your pudding.

Terrine de body
(*page 38*)

·

Escalope de saumon au spaghetti de concombre
(*page 182*)

·

Tulipe à la glace au caramel
(*pages 167 and 166*)

·

Café et petits fours
(*pages 197–8*)

'*A good chef could create an acceptable dish from poor ingredients, but first class ingredients in the hands of a cowboy stand a very good chance of being ruined. It is more important for a chef to find a good supplier upon whom he can rely and to be able to recognise good ingredients in a box on the kitchen floor, than to create the myth of daily negotiation with traders in wholesale markets at 4 o'clock in the morning.*'

CHAPTER FOUR

The raw materials

We are fortunate that the 'foodie' movement, the personality cult of the chef and the rise of the food writer have caused an explosion in the availability of good, fresh produce everywhere. Meat, game, fish and shellfish, fruit, vegetables, herbs and spices are more generally available in greater abundance than ever before. Progressive supermarket chains and some inspired individualists among the food merchants give us the opportunity to obtain fine ingredients from all over the world. Freshness, health, authenticity and the move away from additives in food and chemicals in the rearing of animals have brought about great changes. To understand how to select and use fine produce is to understand the basis of good cooking.

Dairy products

In true gastronomy, dairy produce can be divided into the ingredients such as cream or butter, which a chef uses in the preparation of his dishes and his sauces, and cheeses, which are a very important element in the pleasure of the table. In the West, we are very lucky in that science and technology have played a very large part in the kind of milk and cream we have available. Some prefer the less purified, more rustic dairy produce of France and praise to the skies the slightly acidic taste of *crème fraîche*, though I have come across many French chefs in this country who prefer to use ordinary English double cream for the kitchen. And for the ordinary consumer in search of a cool glass of milk straight from the fridge, the English variety is infinitely more palatable than its very smelly French counterpart. Unfortunately, the reverse is the case with butter. There can be few more intense pleasures than eating a hot crusty loaf smothered with a top-quality French butter. It is said that the best butters and dairy products come from Normandy, but I think that the Charentes region produces a higher quality. For our restaurants, we import direct from France the very highest quality butter in small, individual tubs. Echiré is a small town in the Charentes from which comes the best butter I have ever tasted. The dairy industry in this region is very highly specialised and the *bovin* is a type of beef specially reared for this purpose. Lescure, another butter from the same region, is the one we use for making *pâte feuilleté* because of its particular purity. In the kitchen we basically use two types of cream. Single cream for coffee at table, and double cream for pâtisserie and sauces. The quality of the cream is obviously fundamental to the quality of the end product.

The cheese board

Cheeses are a pillar of French gastronomy and there has been a trend towards ever more elaborate cheese boards, but there is no need to import cheeses from Boulogne or from a *maître fromagier*, nor a need to have more than two or three goat's cheeses on a cheese board at one time. Fourteen years ago when we were still in Dulwich, I took the decision that I did not want to proffer a smelly tray of different cheeses like everyone else. We decided instead that we would make a feature of our cheeses and serve them with a big bunch of grapes, neatly cut and freshly arranged on a plate. Over the years we received a lot of criticism and a lot of praise. I have stuck to my guns unflinchingly and I am beginning to notice that the practice is creeping steadily into the repertoire and presentation of cheese everywhere. For many years we bought direct from Harrods, but we eventually discovered that the main supplier of these cheeses was located no more than 400 yards away from our restaurant in Battersea, so we switched allegiance, and saved ourselves some money.

Most restaurants have a cellar which is the perfect place to keep cheese at the right temperature and consequently in good condition. Our cheeses come fresh twice a week but they can be kept in good condition without the benefit of a cellar. Keep them tightly sealed in aluminium foil in the refrigerator. Remove them an hour or two before you need them and they will be fine. I totally disagree that a refrigerator spoils the texture or flavour of cheese. But what cheese to choose?

I prefer Roquefort to the best Stilton. Of the English cheeses I find some of the Caerphillies, the Cheddars and the lesser known Isle of Avalon of very good quality. The French cheeses we have a preference for and which we have always attempted to serve include Roquefort, Coulommiers, Reblochon, Explorateur, Pont l'Evèque, Epoisses, Chèvre à la Sariette, Chèvre Bûche, Pavé Jacquin, Magnum, Brillat-Savarin, Saint-Marcellin, Pipò Crème and Fourme d'Ambert. Over the years, these cheeses have proved themselves to us.

One great omission from the list is Brie. Everyone knows what a great prince of cheeses it is. But we also know how cantankerous and how temperamental it can be. You serve an excellent Brie when it is ready to be served, not a moment sooner nor a minute later. Unfortunately, in a restaurant, the time at which it might be ready may be 11 o'clock in the morning or at 4 o'clock in the afternoon. For this reason, we offer neither Brie nor Camembert. I eat cheese with grapes and bread or biscuits, as the mood takes me. I also confess a preference for eating sweet biscuits with cheese – this is a particularly English habit, I think.

I regularly use three particular cheeses in the kitchen, Gruyère, Feta and Roquefort. I make little *tartelettes* of Feta and serve them with very thinly sliced courgettes with Provençal herbs, as an accompaniment for my lamb dish; and a chilled Roquefort mousse in a *feuilleté* of pastry with a creamy chive sauce is another cheese-based favourite which I serve as a starter. I make no mention of cheese sauces, for I find béchamel or flour-based sauces thick and bland and a cheese sauce can only be made this way.

Beef

And so to beef. The cut of beef I have always used and preferred is fillet. I have found no convincing evidence to persuade me that entrecôte or rump has more flavour than the fillet. If I was offering a simple, plainly grilled piece of beef with no garnish or sauce, without any fuss or sense of presentation, I might plump for rump, or I might choose entrecôte. I could not be convinced, however, that either has better flavour, nor are they as tender as the fillet. Both entrecôte and rump might be better treated served medium rare, for when a rump or an entrecôte is served rare, I have always encountered a messy, tough, inedible piece of meat. I'm afraid that I must say that I prefer fillet any day.

I have always had a fillet of beef dish on my menu – I somehow prefer the taste and flavour of fillet to any other cut of beef. It is very rare nowadays to find that very dry, marbled Scotch beef. Commercial pressures are forcing growers, wholesalers and retailers to hang meat less and less and to produce ever leaner meat. Still, in this practice we are becoming more and more attuned with the French who hardly hang beef at all. The next recipe is simply cooked beef fillet at its best.

Les Cailles Farcies
au Fumet de Truffes

Stuffed Quails with a Brown Truffle Sauce

*I am very fond of this dish. It is based on
a traditional French regional recipe and produces
a heavenly, elusive aroma. It is traditional
to serve something crisp with roast birds and here
I have chosen to serve the quails on a galette
of potatoes (a variation on game chips)
with sweet and sour red cabbage and some simply
cooked carrots and white asparagus.*

RECIPE ON PAGE 172

Terrine de Canard

Terrine of Duck and Foie Gras with Pistachio Nuts

*You can make this terrine look and taste
very like something made in a French charcuterie.
Bright green pistachios, foie gras and rich
meat jelly are the key ingredients and the secret is
to marinate the meat in Madeira and cognac
and to leave the finished dish to mature for a
couple of days in the refrigerator before serving.
A few leaves of mâche or oak leaf lettuce
are all that are needed for a garnish.*

RECIPE ON PAGE 60

Tournedos
aux Echalotes Confites

Fillet of Beef with Caramelised Shallots
in a Red Wine Sauce

Illustrated on page 113

SERVES 4

4 × 175 g (6 oz)/5 cm (2 inch) thick fillets
   of beef, well trimmed
150 g (5 oz) butter
juice of 2 lemons

salt and pepper
100 ml (4 fl oz) red wine
30 ml (2 tbsp) Confiture d'Echalotes au
   Cassis et au Vin Rouge (page 151)
300 ml (½ pint) Demi-Glace (page 228)

In a large, heavy cast iron pan, melt 125 g (4 oz) of the butter. Let it sizzle then brown each steak on both sides, including the edges. Cooking time depends on how you like your steak, how high the heat is, the type of pan you are using, etc. I cannot be specific on this matter. Remove from the pan and keep the steaks warm. Squeeze over a little lemon juice and season with salt and pepper.

Meanwhile, in a small stainless steel pan, cook the red wine, the shallots and the demi-glace. Reduce and thicken with the remaining butter. The sauce should reach a glossy, syrupy, dark red consistency.

Place each fillet on a warm plate and pour the sauce over. Serve with a mature red claret such as Château Chasse Spleen or burgundy such as a 1978 Auxey-Duresses.

My kind of food always involves beef with a glorious sauce so if there is any lack of flavour in the meat, compensation will be found in the sauce accompanying it. A fillet steak is also more presentable. There is one exception to the rule. I find a good rib of beef takes a lot of beating when it comes to roasting. For grilling in the French *côte de boeuf* style, I always serve only the first 4 or 5 ribs (the second half of the rib is probably better for roasting). Rib of beef is a fine example where the meat will benefit considerably from a long rest of at least 45 minutes in a warm place before carving.

So much advice is given on the qualities to look for in beef. Gone are the days when you could buy a whole fillet and could pull off the fat and the sinews around it with your bare hands. In those days, meat was hung for 12–14 days at a temperature of 2–4°C (34–36°F). Today, commercial pressures are forcing meat producers to shorten the hanging period and save money. I wonder how many of today's young chefs will ever experience the pleasures I found in peeling off fat from a really dry, well-hung fillet. As a result of this corner cutting and the prevalence of vacuum packing today's meat is becoming more and more wet and flabby and is certainly more bloody than I can remember 12 years ago. As a result of demands from a health-conscious public it is becoming unusual, too, to find that the marbling of fat in the meat once intrinsic to good Scotch beef is becoming a thing of the past. The meat is certainly leaner, but it is also correspondingly drier and less succulent, and less flavoursome than years ago. I should say here too that I find the much-praised American meat tasteless and undoubtedly inferior to Scotch beef.

Lamb

Though I like lamb a great deal, it provides more cuts that are better suited to the domestic kitchen than to the professional. Having said this, however, a very amusing incident springs to mind. I had to select three members of my brigade to take part in a competition for a television programme called 'In at the Deep End'. Paul Heiney, a television personality, was given the task of becoming a great chef in a very short period of time. He did his training at the three-star Waterside Inn under Michel Roux. He was to enter a competition against my brigade and those of two other top-class British restaurants, Le Manoir aux Quat' Saisons and Sharrow Bay. All we knew in advance was that a shoulder of new season's lamb and a full hamper of ingredients were to be provided at eight o'clock in the morning and that we had to prepare a three-course meal for eight people. I asked my butcher to supply me with a shoulder of lamb. His reaction was very interesting and he asked me how I planned to serve it, because all of a sudden, Raymond Blanc of Le Manoir had also ordered the same cut from him. He found this strange because shoulder of lamb is not a cut which is normally found on the menus of great restaurants. I realised that Raymond was practising hard and was already way ahead in his thinking. I told my brigade that I was sure that most of our rivals would bone and stuff it. I was equally convinced that if we were to win, we had to do something different. As night follows day, I told my team, we would win if we prepared the following dish: we would bone the shoulder, discard all fat and sinews, cut the meat into one inch cubes, sauté it very lightly, place it in a puff pastry case and top it with a béarnaise sauce. From the bones we would make a lamb stock and reduce it with rosemary and Madeira to make a lovely sauce to pour round the meat. With some 'turned' vegetables, it would look a picture. Sure enough, two out of four competitors turned out the kind of dish I expected and we won hands down. This is, I think, a good illustration of how to utilise a prime ingredient and make it work for you to show itself at its best. However, it does not alter my conviction that boned shoulder of lamb, beautiful garlic-scented roasted leg of lamb, crown roast of lamb, chump chops (which for me have more flavour than almost any other part of the lamb) are cuts which should be served at home. In my restaurant, two cuts only have provided the lamb dishes I have on the menu – noisettes and best end.

Noisettes are small, thick slices cut from the loin or from the best end of lamb. They are boned, shaped into rounds and tied with a band of fat (though I do not usually bother adding this). I trim each noisette as much as possible into a round shape and then cook them on my griddle. I then make a reduction of port, *demi-glace* and dried herbs and serve them dressed with this glistening robe of sauce.

This is a dish with strong flavours. The veal stock reduction, the heavy flavour of port and the pungent aroma of Provençal herbs, make it a dish with a lot of power. I have always found the aroma of port and herbs irresistible and it is a combination which goes well with grilled veal kidneys.

Noisettes d'Agneau au Porto
Noisettes of Lamb glazed with Port and Provençal Herbs

SERVES 2

2 slices of white bread	pepper
15 ml (1 tbsp) clarified butter (page 241)	squeeze of lemon
salt	150 ml ($\frac{1}{4}$ pint) Demi-Glace (page 228)
1 best end of lamb	75 ml (3 fl oz) port
50 g (2 oz) butter	5 ml (1 tsp) dried Provençal herbs

Cut 6 croûtons from the bread with a round pastry cutter. Brush with clarified butter, sprinkle with salt and toast in the oven. Keep warm.

This time there is no need to clean the best end. With a very sharp knife detach the round fillet from the bones (you will be left with a rounded fillet about 23 cm/9 inches long). Slice the meat into 6 noisettes. Trim them really thoroughly and make them as round as possible.

Melt the butter in a heavy cast iron pan and bring it to a sizzle. Cook the noisettes very rapidly on either side; do not turn more than once. Remove from the pan and keep warm. Sprinkle with salt, pepper and a little lemon.

In a small heavy stainless steel pan, simmer the demi-glace, port and herbs. Season with salt and pepper. When the liquid has reached coating consistency, pour it on to a plate and roll the noisettes over and over in this to coat them. Place 3 croûtons on each plate, sit the noisettes on them and spoon any extra sauce on top. Serve with a full, fruity red such as Réserve de la Comtesse, the second wine of Château Pichon Lalande.

My favourite cut of lamb is best end of neck which I roast in the following way. The first four cutlets are first cleaned and trimmed all in one piece and the bones are scraped clean of all fat and gristle. I make a mixture of very fine brioche crumbs with finely chopped parsley, dried savory, dried thyme and dried rosemary and then throw in finely chopped garlic and season it well with salt and pepper. This mixture coats the lamb and is patted on with great care. Roasted in a hot oven for a few minutes only and then allowed to rest in a warm place for half an hour, this makes a superb dish.

It is, without doubt, one of the very best lamb dishes I have tasted – it probably equals the gigolette (leg of milk-fed lamb) at Raymond Thulier's restaurant L'Ousteau de Beaumanières in Provence. I remember a very sad occasion at Les Beaux, when a party of English people at a neighbouring table took one look at the pink and red juices which oozed from the slices of pastry-covered milk-fed lamb which had just been served to them, looked at each other and sent the whole thing back to the kitchen. If you want to prevent a lot of juices pouring out of any roasted meat, you must let it rest for a good long time. This allows the meat to develop a pinkness and a rosiness which is so inviting and so mouth watering that it will be impossible for anyone to refuse.

Carré d'Agneau Rose en Croûte de Fines Herbes

·

Best End of Lamb with a Brioche and Herb Crust

Illustrated on page 144

SERVES 2

1 best end of lamb with 8 perfect cutlets
60 ml (4 tbsp) extra-fine brioche crumbs
5 ml (1 tsp) very finely chopped dried
   Provençal herbs
15 ml (1 tbsp) very finely chopped parsley
2.5 ml (½ tsp) salt
2 garlic cloves, chopped into tiny cubes
pepper
60 ml (4 tbsp) clarified butter (page 241)

Clean the lamb well and trim. Scrape off the sinews from the bone and leave about 7.5 cm (3 inches) of cleaned bone. Trim off all the excess fat.

Mix together the crumbs, herbs, parsley, salt, garlic and pepper. Make sure that the mixture is really well blended and put it on a flat tray or large plate.

Brush the lamb with clarified butter and, before it hardens, apply the herb mixture as follows: press the best end of lamb on to the herb mixture, applying some pressure and rolling slightly so that it covers the entire area. Pat again, lightly shake off any loose crumbs and leave for 20 minutes at room temperature.

Place the lamb on a rack over a roasting pan and roast for 20–25 minutes at 200°C (400°F) mark 6. Leave to rest in a warm place for another 20 minutes. Carefully carve the cutlets, taking care not to detach any crust with the knife. Serve with a youngish, smooth red St-Emilion such as the little known Château Canon La Gaffelière.

Lamb varies according to the age and the breed of the animal. Most lambs are slaughtered when they are between three and 12 months old, after that, the meat enters the mutton stage and this older meat is rarely used in top kitchens. Of all the ingredients which nature surrenders each year, the most eagerly anticipated arrival for me is new season's lamb.

The age-old argument between the French and the English about lamb is won by the English and the Welsh. I am afraid I far prefer English lamb to French (including the much vaunted *pre salé* lamb from Normandy). I find English lamb less aggressive in flavour and more tender. The only French lamb that comes anywhere near the quality of English and Welsh lamb is the young lamb from the hills of Sisteron in the south of France. No-one who has eaten the baby lamb at L'Ousteau de Beaumanières makes it easy for themselves when it comes to judging between the English and the French varieties.

The same considerations apply to the hanging of lamb as for beef. A reasonable amount of hanging time will always improve the quality, but again, commercial pressures and the loss of weight incurred in hanging are cutting the process to a minimum. If you add the problems of storage to the problems of weight loss, there is a great incentive for meat producers to send their lamb to market as quickly as possible.

For me, lamb does not yield great riches by way of offal. Probably the only succulent and nourishing part is the kidney. Less of an aristocrat than the veal kidney it can nevertheless be made into a great dish. I always blanch lamb's kidneys to eliminate all unwelcome odours and tastes before I cook them.

Veal

Veal is an enigma. I get more excited by seeing bright, glistening, veal bones, and I find much more pleasure in the taste, flavour and the natural gelatine which these bones will finally yield, than in the tasteless and dry veal meat itself. A knuckle of veal, for me, is the true taste and flavour of veal. I love to use the knuckle to make small quantities of pure, sparkling, intensely flavoured veal stock. I then purify the stock to make a jelly and eat the tender morsels of meat left round the knuckle separately with a herby vinaigrette.

Veal is a very difficult meat to cook. It must not be overcooked or it will dry up and it requires supreme expertise and attention to make sure that it is cooked well and remains juicy. The danger is to be tempted to leave the meat slightly undercooked. This is not a good thing. On its own, veal tends to be bland and sauces, stuffings and seasonings are often used to provide additional flavour. Roast fillet of veal makes an ideal light luncheon dish and I stuff the middle of the fillet with dried Provençal herbs, brioche crumbs, chopped parsley and very fine garlic. Then roast it in aluminium foil in the oven. I then brown it under the grill, let it rest for 45 minutes before slicing and serving it with a brown Madeira-and-rosemary-flavoured sauce.

Veal is not a particularly exciting meat to cook with (though I make an exception with a great dish such as Blanquette de Veau) for the taste of the actual meat itself is so mellow as to be bland. All the flavour, the power and the goodness of veal is in the glorious jellies which can be made from the bones, for it is these bones and knuckles of veal that enable a good chef to create lovely sauces for myriad other dishes. This dish has a very strongly flavoured stuffing which helps counteract the neutral flavour of the meat.

Filet de Veau Farci
à la Sauce de Romarin
Stuffed Fillet of Veal with Brown Rosemary Sauce

SERVES 2

4 garlic cloves
3 fresh rosemary sprigs
150 ml (¼ pint) Demi-Glace (page 228)
Madeira
40 g (1½ oz) butter
salt
1 fillet of veal weighing 400 g (14 oz) after it has been completely trimmed and cleaned

2 whole eggs, beaten
90 ml (6 tbsp) brioche crumbs
15 ml (1 tbsp) Provençal herbs
15 ml (1 tbsp) very finely chopped parsley
pepper
12 green peppercorns
1 bay leaf
juice of ½ lemon

First make the sauce: thinly slice 2 cloves of garlic and add to the rosemary, demi-glace and 100 ml (4 fl oz) of Madeira. Simmer very carefully, covered, for 30 minutes. Remove the rosemary, reduce by half, thicken with 25 g (1 oz) of the butter and strain through a wet muslin cloth. Season to taste with salt and keep warm.

Make an incision horizontally down the length of the veal fillet to reach halfway in to the centre. Open out the meat and beat it down slightly.

Add the beaten eggs to the brioche crumbs, herbs and parsley. Finely chop 1 clove of garlic and add to this mixture with 20 ml (4 tsp) Madeira. Season with salt, pepper and green peppercorns. Mix everything into a paste and spread with a palette knife over the veal, allowing 2.5 cm (1 inch) clear at each edge. Roll it tight lengthways and secure with string at 3 points. Season with salt and pepper and add the rest of the butter. Slice the remaining garlic clove in half, then rub the veal with the garlic, put a bay leaf in the centre and wrap tightly with foil.

Roast at 180°C (350°F) mark 4 for 30–40 minutes, turning the meat in its foil over and over again, every 10 minutes or so.

Remove from the oven and allow the veal to rest in a warm place for 30 minutes, still sealed. Meanwhile, reheat the sauce and add the lemon juice.

Unwrap the meat carefully and slice into 6 slices. Pour the sauce on to 2 serving plates and arrange 3 slices of veal on each plate.

Serve with a robust red wine such as a Crozes-Hermitage.

I personally find the offal from a young calf far more interesting. Sweetbreads, kidneys, liver, these are some of the great delicacies of French haute cuisine, treasures to be prepared simply in some classic way.

Poultry and game

Let's begin with the humble chicken. From the old days, when chickens were part and parcel of the domestic scene, to the present-day plethora of scientifically reared birds, the leap has been spectacular. Unfortunately, in between came the twentieth century. Conveyor-belt battery production and feeding with fish meal have brought prices down and quality and nourishment even lower. Fifteen years ago, I could virtually use my chicken stock as a dual purpose stock – for both the chicken stock and fish stock tasted the same – you couldn't tell the difference. It is quite incredible how fishy, how flaccid and insipid a chicken becomes when exposed to fish meal feed and freezing. Thank goodness, that era is almost gone. We have to thank our friends across the Channel for forcing this change, and for reminding us what a proper chicken should taste like. I think the onslaught began with the introduction to England of plump, yellow, corn-fed Brittany chickens. Once the door opened, the other regions of France began to send their specialities. There followed the *poulet fermier* from the Landes and the aristocrat of all chickens, the *poulet de Bresse*. Restaurants and the public began to see and to feel what a chicken should look like. To the touch, the flesh should feel firm and to the eye, it should be plump with a yellow tinge. It became exciting once again to experience the proper flavour of a roast chicken.

Almost at once, our native producers rose to the challenge and now I prefer the flesh, flavour and texture of a chicken reared here in the traditional way or of a Brittany chicken to the flavour and texture of the more expensive *poulet fermier* or indeed to the *poulet de Bresse*. All over England, independent producers are increasingly finding favour with the good local restaurants in their regions, and, consequently, with the public. Long may it continue.

Chicken has a lot of potential for enthusiastic cooks. From the moment when you make the chicken stock to the time, probably three or four days later, when you eat a chicken sandwich smothered in honeyed jelly, the variety of ways of cooking chicken is extraordinary. In many restaurants, however, breast is the joint which attracts most of the attention. There are two ways I personally prefer eating chicken: poached in *Soupe aux Amandes* (opposite) or *Poulet au Vin Jaune* (page 37).

This is more than a soup. It is more like a full meal (but a light one, nevertheless) in which whole breasts of roast chicken are served in a lovely rich almondy broth. Roast chicken has a natural affinity with freshly roasted almonds and with the beautiful aromatic flavour of Basmati rice. If you want to serve it purely as a soup, then do not bother to roast the breasts separately.

Soupe aux Amandes

Almond Soup with Freshly Roasted Chicken

SERVES 2

1 free-range 1.6 kg (3½ lb) maize-fed
   chicken
1 medium carrot, pared and cut
   lengthwise in 4
1 medium onion, skinned and stuck with
   2 or 3 cloves
1 celery stick
1 small leek split down the middle, green
   part entirely discarded

bouquet garni
black peppercorns
150 ml (¼ pint) dry white wine
30 ml (2 tbsp) Basmati rice
knob of butter
225 g (8 oz) flaked almonds
15 ml (1 tbsp) clear honey
coarse salt
200 ml (7 fl oz) double cream

Remove the legs from the chicken and chop them in small pieces.

Simmer for 1½ hours with the carrot, onion, celery, leek, bouquet garni, a few peppercorns and 600 ml (1 pint) of water. Strain and slowly reduce by half. Add the wine and set aside. Meanwhile, boil the rice for about 10 minutes, drain, rinse and leave on one side.

Place a large knob of butter in the middle of a baking sheet. When it has melted, add the almonds, coat them in butter and leave for about 10 minutes until golden brown.

Brush the breast part of the chicken with honey, sprinkle over some salt and a few crushed black peppercorns and roast in the oven at 180°C (350°F) mark 4 for 40 minutes until cooked and crisp, but not dry. Remove the chicken and allow it to rest in a warm place.

Liquidise the chicken stock, almonds and double cream until smooth. Tip the stock into a clean pan, add the rice and cook together for about 10 minutes. Season and pour into individual soup plates.

With a small, sharp knife remove each breast and place on top of the soup. Sprinkle with freshly ground black pepper.

Guinea fowl

Other types of poultry and game are also increasingly popular. Guinea fowl, for example, has now followed much the same course: the French showed the way and now the home growers are meeting the demands of the market. This, however, is one bird I have never enjoyed. The meat is very much like chicken – the difference is minimal unless it is hung for a period of time – and does not compensate for the bird's smaller size and scrawnier, slightly tougher appearance. A true guinea fowl is the guinea fowl of Africa. Its flesh is dark and gamey, quite unlike a chicken's. If you do cook guinea fowl, though, and wish to overcome its toughness, roast it very slowly and carefully, then switch off your oven, leave it to rest, in the oven, for $1\frac{1}{2}$ hours – then eat it. A method of roasting which I love, whether for a chicken or a guinea fowl, is to combine bacon, honey and crushed black peppercorns and coat the skin thoroughly, then cook it in the oven, carefully basting it to keep it moist. Remember to let it rest for at least 30 minutes in a warm place before bringing it to the table.

Quail

One of my favourite little birds is the quail. These are now farmed on a large scale both here and in France. I prefer the English quail which is usually a little bit bigger than its French counterpart.

Quails have provided inspiration for two favourite dishes of mine – a warm salad with a dressing made of cèpes butter sauce, the other – stuffed quails (see page 172), with chicken livers, pistachios, Jamaica allspice and juniper berries – to name only a few of the ingredients for the stuffing. Eaten on a bed of finely shredded cabbage cooked in cider and dressed with a sauce of truffles and Madeira, this is an extraordinary dish. When we serve it in our restaurant, the whole dining room is enveloped in heavenly aromas (the smell of this dish and that of *Poulet au Vin Jaune* are my two favourite aromas).

Quail can be a little tricky to cook. It should be left slightly under cooked, but in order to get the colour on the skin of the bird, I usually paint it with a very thin layer of honey. When the blow torch is applied, the browning effect becomes dramatic. At home you can achieve almost the same effect by cooking the bird in a hot oven and basting it thoroughly.

This salad is so colourful and the range and variety of tastes so wide, the end result is quite stunning, both to the eye and to the palate. Fresh citrus fruit combines very successfully with salad leaves, the lovely flavour of the butter sauce and the glazed quail topped with truffles. It is our most successful salad in the restaurant, but it is the devil of a job to put together. One evening we sold nineteen of these individually constructed salads!

La Salade de Cailles au Beurre de Cèpes
Quail Salad with Wild Mushroom Butter Sauce

SERVES 4
for the wild mushroom butter sauce:
250 g (9 oz) butter

15 ml (1 tbsp) finely chopped shallots
175 g (6 oz) dried cèpes, finely chopped
5 ml (1 tsp) mignonette pepper

THE RAW MATERIALS

15 ml (1 tbsp) chopped chives
200 ml (7 fl oz) dry white wine
100 ml (4 fl oz) chicken stock
100 ml (4 fl oz) double cream
salt
squeeze of lemon
50 ml (2 fl oz) milk
for the salad:
4 quails, cleaned and ready for roasting
30 ml (2 tbsp) clarified butter (page 241)
15 ml (1 tbsp) honey
8 truffle slices, grilled
100 ml (4 fl oz) Demi-Glace (page 228)
  and 100 ml (4 fl oz) port mixed together
  and reduced to a coating consistency
a few radicchio leaves
a few frisée leaves
a few oak leaf lettuce leaves
a few salade de mâche leaves

a few curly batavia leaves
15 ml (1 tbsp) hazelnut oil
salt
squeeze of lemon
a few fresh tarragon sprigs
a few chives, chopped into 2.5 cm (1 inch)
  lengths
4 cooked artichoke hearts, sliced into 12
  rounds
2 oranges, cleaned and segmented into 12
  perfect segments
2 pink grapefruits, cleaned and segmented
  into 12 perfect segments
1 avocado, cut into 12 petals (shaped like
  an orange segment)
4 tomatoes, shaped into 16 individual
  tomato petals
30 ml (2 tbsp) finely diced red pepper

First make the wild mushroom butter sauce as follows: In a copper *sautoire* melt 200 g (7 oz) of the butter. Put in the shallots and fry until transparent. Add the mushrooms, mignonette pepper and chopped chives. Cook together well and deglaze with white wine and chicken stock. Reduce carefully by two thirds, then add the double cream and the remaining butter, chopped into small pieces, slowly. Cook a little to obtain a thick coating consistency, then strain through a triple layer of muslin, making sure that all the fine sand and dust from the dried cèpes is left behind. Add salt, a squeeze of lemon and the milk. Stir with a whisk and keep warm.

Roast the quails by brushing the birds all over with butter and honey. Roast in a very hot oven at 230°C (450°F) mark 8 for 10 minutes. Remove and brown under the grill. Cut the legs off and detach the breasts. Reshape each quail by placing the legs side by side and the breasts on top. Place a freshly grilled truffle slice on each breast and pour the reduced demi-glace and port over each of the 4 quails.

To make the salad, place an egg poaching ring in the centre of 4 clean plates. Cut the salad leaves to about 6.5 cm (2½ inch) lengths and use the most colourful parts.

Place the hazelnut oil in a clean bowl, add salt and a little squeeze of lemon, the tarragon leaves and the chives. Add the salad leaves and turn over and over lightly with your hand, being very careful not to bruise them. Divide in 4 and place inside the egg poaching rings.

Place a quail on each warm plate, then on the opposite side of the plates arrange 3 discs of artichoke, overlapping each other. Put 3 orange segments and 3 grapefruit segments on another side of the plates, and 3 avocado slices and 4 tomato petals on the opposite side.

Very carefully, pour the wild mushroom butter sauce over the artichokes, orange, grapefruit, avocado and tomato segments, over half the area only, letting the other

107

halves display their colour. Place 3 small portions of diced red pepper on 3 different parts of each plate.

Remove the egg poaching ring and serve.

A firm white *pinot gris* wine such as a Tokay from Alsace goes well with this salad.

VARIATION
Illustrated on page 161

Caille Rôtie au Madère et Sa Galette de Pommes de Terre
Roast Quail with Madeira Sauce and Shredded Crisp Potato Cake

This is a variation on my quail salad recipe in which I roast the quails as described above, and then remove the breasts and legs. These are then arrayed, breasts on top of the legs, on a potato galette (see page 186) which in its turn sits on a bed of sweet and sour red cabbage.

Pigeon

I am obviously not going to cover the entire range of poultry and will confine myself to those birds which I have cooked with, whose taste, consistency and flavour I enjoy. I cook the poultry I like to eat, in the way I like to cook it. That really leaves us with pigeons and ducks.

How can I get enthusiastic about pigeons in Europe, when the memory of the sweet green pigeons of Africa is still so markedly imprinted on my mind? I know the accepted way of cooking a *pigeonneau de Bresse*, for example, is to leave the breasts rosy red. I personally don't enjoy that. I would much prefer a pigeon stew with lots of port and button onions. Pigeons, too, are now becoming more plentiful, better fed, more plump and with better flavour.

Duck

There are two main differences between French and English ducks. French ducks have a thinner layer of fat and, consequently, a higher proportion of meat. The colour of their flesh is darker and the flavour is slightly more gamey. To the connoisseur of ducks, all these characteristics are important. To me, however, English ducks, especially those from Norfolk and Suffolk, are more to my liking. If I am looking for gaminess in the flavour of duck, then I can always find it in wild duck. From Challans in France comes a cross-bred duck, between domestic and wild, called a *canette de Challans*. In the early days I used to cook this duck often. We painted the skin with honey, sprinkled it with coarse salt and crushed black peppercorns, roasted it well and then left it to rest for a long time. The skin became very thin and crisp and the meat was gamey and dark. Duck roasted this way was a very popular choice and was one of renowned gastronome Egon Ronay's favourite dishes.

The area around Challans in the Vendée is famous for the quality of its ducks. In due course, perhaps our duck farmers may get around to breeding ducks with a high meat content and very thin skin, like the ones they rear in France. To achieve best results you need a thin-skinned duck for this recipe and it is undoubtedly more successful when I make it with the famous *canette de Challans*.

This is one of the finest duck dishes I have ever come across. It involves roasting the whole bird but only the breasts are eaten – this way they remain succulent. (You can make a beautiful meal of the legs if you roast them a while longer than the breasts, remove them, let them rest a while, and then eat them cold with a salad.) Encrusted with rock salt, crunchy pepper and sweet honey the crackling, crispy skin is very flavoursome. No red, blue, or pink duck here. The meat comes out well cooked and it tastes of real duck. It is a recipe more in tune with the up-and-coming 'cuisine de la grande-mère', the rustic cooking of our grandmothers' days. Gone are the chic pink birds of *nouvelle cuisine*.

Canette de Challans au Miel

Crisp Breasts of Duck with Honey and Peppercorns

SERVES 2
1 × 1.8 kg (4 lb) duck
30 ml (2 tbsp) clear honey
15 ml (1 tbsp) rock salt

30 ml (2 tbsp) pepper
150 ml ($\frac{1}{4}$ pint) Demi-Glace (page 228)
25 ml (1$\frac{1}{2}$ tbsp) cognac
25 g (1 oz) butter

Paint the duck all over with honey. Be liberal with its use and apply it everywhere. Sprinkle over the coarse salt and black pepper. Pat well all over with a palette knife and roast at 200°C (400°F) mark 6 for 25 minutes. Turn off the oven and leave the duck inside for a further 45 minutes.

Remove from the oven and very carefully, with a sharp knife, remove both whole breasts; set aside.

Over medium heat, simmer the demi-glace and cognac together and reduce to a syrupy consistency. Add the butter to thicken and stir together. Spoon the sauce out onto 2 warm plates, place the breasts in the centre of the pools of sauce and serve at once.

A robust red such as a Côte Rôtie or a Châteauneuf-du-Pape from the Rhône goes well with this dish.

Game birds

Three favourites of mine in the game bird range are pheasant, grouse and partridge. The disappearance of wild salmon in September is partially compensated for by the arrival of grouse first of all and later on by the arrival of partridges and pheasants towards the end of the year. I love grouse. I can quite understand why the English are so fond of it and I am pleased in many ways that probably the greatest of all game birds does not find itself in the repertoire that the great chefs of France know and use. Grouse is a truly British phenomenon. It must be one of the most fleshy game birds and its flavour and taste are very pronounced. Here lies one of the greatest contradictions. Game birds like grouse are preferred cooked rare, sometimes very well hung and quite strong in flavour. But when it comes to beef and to lamb, the preference for rare meat doesn't necessarily prevail. I find this a great mystery. Personally, I like grouse roasted to the point of pale pinkness. One of the great sauces I have used to accompany grouse is a vivid dark, purplish red sauce made with a blackcurrant liqueur and whole fresh blackcurrants.

Since quails no longer count as game, the only true game bird I really adore is grouse. Grouse is something special. The flesh on the breast is so abundant, the texture of the meat so fine and smooth, the flavour so well pronounced, that it makes a truly special feast. It is fascinating to note that the French, who profess to be such great gastronomes, have nothing really to compare with this wonderful bird. They give it odd names such as *coq de la bruyère*. Unfortunately, in Britain grouse has definite connotations because of its associations with the landed gentry and grouse shooting folk. But this is not a book on sociology, and in my mind, grouse is the King of them all. I personally do not like it to taste very gamey – two to three days' hanging is sufficient for grouse.

Rouge d'Ecosse à la Sauce Groseille
Roast Grouse with Redcurrant Sauce

SERVES 2

2 grouse, cleaned and well trimmed
30 ml (2 tbsp) clarified butter (page 241)
salt and pepper

4 rashers bacon
200 ml (7 fl oz) Demi-Glace (page 228)
45 ml (3 tbsp) liqueur crème de cassis
45 ml (3 tbsp) redcurrants

Paint the birds all over with clarified butter and sprinkle with salt and pepper. Cover with the bacon and roast in a medium 180°C (350°F) mark 4 oven for 20–30 minutes. Remove from the oven and allow to rest in a warm place for 15 minutes.

Meanwhile, over medium heat, reduce the demi-glace with the crème de cassis. When syrupy, add the redcurrants. Season with salt and pepper, set aside and keep warm.

To serve, remove the breasts from the grouse, or carve it on the bone. Pass the sauce separately.

Serve with a good, full-bodied red wine such as a burgundy.

I find pheasant equally interesting though the flesh is naturally dry and it is a very difficult bird to roast correctly. I personally do not like the *nouvelle cuisine* practice of removing the breasts and sautéeing them. This way, you lose what little natural moisture the meat has, and frankly, the taste is so elusive, you could be eating anything. The best way to eat prime pheasant is to roast it, basting it continuously, until the flesh is a very pale pink colour. The bird is then allowed to relax and when the whole breast is subsequently removed, most of the moisture will have been preserved. The legs, incidentally, will make the basis of an excellent terrine. I personally like to use pheasant in the preparation of game terrines with fresh pistachios, foie gras and black truffles.

The European partridge is another bird which bears no resemblance to the ones tasted and eaten as a young boy in East Africa, and though I personally am not over enthusiastic about either the English grey-legged bird or the French red-legged one, when I look back to 1985, the partridges we roasted and cooked in the restaurant were of a very high quality and flavour. The greatest treatment for partridge is to cook it as we do with muscatel grapes and the fiery, pungent, aromatic eau de vie de Frontignan made from the unique sweet grapes of the region. A pinkly roasted partridge with a sauce made of port, tomato purée, lots of tarragon, pepper and, at the final moment, generous quantities of eau de vie de Frontignan, is a dish and an experience which you come across very rarely.

I am often asked about how I choose what goes on my menus. Why do I not have rabbit on the menu? Why no venison? The inevitable answer must be that, frankly, I just don't like them! This may be a relic of my youth. There was an abundance of game all around us all the time. Beef and lamb were the rarities then. Pork, too, I ignore in all forms except bacon and for moistening my terrines. I use fillet of pork and pork fat for my terrines, but I'm afraid apart from that I find pork meat very dry (I might be persuaded to eat a roasted suckling pig in the open air, but that's another story).

Offal

Offal has a special place in my mind. Why? My introduction to offal goes back to the giant breakfasts my father used to cook for us in Tanzania. One of the essential elements of a hearty Sunday breakfast was a dish composed of lamb's brains fried in breadcrumbs and sprinkled with generous quantities of lemon juice. Since then I have loved all types of offal, from the humblest to the aristocrat of them all, foie gras (fattened duck or goose liver).

My love of offal is dominated by the veal calf (that is not to forget the lovely flavour of lambs' tongues or the texture of the pink pickled ox tongue — particularly if it is accompanied by buttery spinach and a Madeira sauce) which

Mousseline de Sole et de Crabe au Beurre Blanc

A Mousse of Sole and Crab with a Butter Sauce

Decorated with lumpfish roe, diced courgettes and carrots this dish makes a stunning looking starter with contrasting flavours and textures. It is a long-term favourite of mine and I have modified the presentation in any number of ways. Here, for example, it is actually served with a beurre blanc as a change from the usual langoustine sauce, and I sometimes stuff it with diced langoustines instead of crab meat. I use lemon sole for this dish, it has softer flesh and is more workable than Dover sole.

RECIPE ON PAGE 118

Tournedos
aux Echalotes Confites

*Fillet of Beef with Caramelised Shallots
in a Red Wine Sauce*

*I always have beef fillet on the menu. Here
it is cooked in butter until it is crisp on the outside
and moist and rare inside. There is no secret
to cooking meat like this. Have a very hot
cast-iron pan, and allow the meat to relax for 10
minutes or so before you serve it. The sauce of
shallots cooked in cassis gives a wonderful flavour
(it also goes well with simply cooked duck
breasts). Root vegetables are a traditional
accompaniment to beef and here we have prettily
presented roast parsnips, carrots glazed with
honey, diced celeriac and gratin dauphinois plus a
simply grilled brochette of mushrooms.*

RECIPE ON PAGE 98

gives the rich variety of offal dishes in the great restaurants. A dish which helped enforce my reputation in the early years was veal tongues with spinach and Madeira sauce (page 52). This has its origins in the tongue dishes with caper sauce which my mother used to cook, and more directly in the brilliant cooking our whole family encountered at the Château de Castel Novel at Brive which I discuss in more detail in chapter two.

Veal kidneys, veal sweetbreads and calves' liver are three raw ingredients which give me a great deal of pleasure in cooking. When it comes to kidneys, always look for the kidneys with the bigger lobes, for better texture. I always blanch the entire kidney in boiling water for 30 seconds. This way, you remove traces of odour and taste that should not interfere with the actual flavour of the kidney. I usually separate each lobe and remove the white fat and sinews from inside the kidney. There is a great variety of sauces that go with kidney. Its greatest natural companions are mustard and pastry.

Veal kidneys and mustard sauce is a traditional way for serving kidneys. How good the end dish will be depends on the quality of your kidneys, the way you slice them, the way you cook them, the calibre of your sauce and the way you present them. Because kidneys go terribly well with pastry, I serve this dish in a pastry case.

The mystery in the title of the dish is easily explained. When you slice the individual lobes of a veal kidney into little escalopes, they tend to look like sliced mushrooms. To add more mischief to the punning title, and because kidneys go very well with mushrooms, I also add a tablespoon of sliced, perfectly white, button mushrooms. The kidney has to be marinated for 24 hours, so begin this recipe a day ahead.

Champignons de Rognons de Veau à la Moutarde

Finely Sliced Kidneys with Mustard Sauce

SERVES 2

1 kidney, well cleaned, blanched and trimmed
75 ml (5 tbsp) Madeira
for the sauce:
50 g (2 oz) butter
15 ml (1 tbsp) very finely chopped shallots
75 ml (5 tbsp) dry white wine
150 ml (¼ pint) double cream
25 ml (1½ tbsp) cognac

2.5 ml (½ tsp) finely diced tarragon
2.5 ml (½ tsp) finely chopped parsley
2.5 ml (½ tsp) finely chopped chives
salt and pepper
2 × 10 cm (4 inch) pastry cases (made with pâte brisée, page 246)
15 ml (1 tbsp) finely sliced white button mushrooms, wiped clean
15 ml (1 tbsp) Moutarde de Meaux

Slice each lobe of the kidney into 5 escalopes, about 0.5 cm ($\frac{1}{4}$ inch) thick. Marinate these little slices in Madeira for 24 hours in the refrigerator.

Next make the sauce: in a heavy stainless steel pan, melt 25 g (1 oz) of the butter and fry the shallots carefully for about 5 minutes until transparent. Deglaze with the white wine, cook down and reduce to a thin syrup. Add the cream and boil down until the sauce is thick. Add 15 ml (1 tbsp) cognac, boil down again and thicken. Add the tarragon, parsley and chives and set aside. Season with salt and pepper.

Heat the pastry cases in the oven and keep them warm. Set aside.

In a heavy cast iron pan bring the remaining butter to a strong sizzle and add the kidneys. Toss and stir and cook very quickly and very lightly. Add the mushrooms and stir well together. Sprinkle over the remaining cognac and set alight. Tip into a sieve to strain well.

Stir the mustard into the sauce, warm up very rapidly, add the kidneys and the mushrooms. Turn and stir the kidneys into the sauce thoroughly, scoop into the 2 tartelettes and serve with a full-bodied wine such as a burgundy, red Auxey-Duresses, or a red Meursault.

Sweetbreads are the pancreas and thymus glands, one located in the chest cavity and one in the throat. The two are invariably sold together and they provide a big problem for the supplier of meat to the restaurateur. The better of the two, unquestionably, is the bread that is located near the heart. It is rounder, flatter, whiter and of a more delicate flavour and of better texture than the bread located in the throat. One is always in demand and the other is always discarded — at least by the better restaurants. The availability of good sweetbreads is limited. The way to eat sweetbreads is to cook them in clarified butter over fierce heat in order to achieve a crisp, golden brown, outer skin. They go very well with morel mushrooms, freshly roasted pine kernels and grapes. We serve them with a brown sherry-based sauce, or a carrot and Sauternes sauce. I find sweetbreads are very rich; a cream sauce would be gilding the lily. Classic French cuisine marries sweetbreads with crayfish and lobster, but I do not find much merit in these combinations.

I find a very dark liver too strong in flavour. Calves' liver should be pale in colour, as pale as you can find it. The best calves' liver is a pale milky brown in colour and soft to the touch. My first introduction to the cooking of liver came by way of Margaret Costa's famous recipe of calves' liver with Dubonnet and orange (page 44). It was a good introduction and still is one of the best ways to enjoy it. Remember, when cooking liver, that it doesn't take long to cook and from liver being too underdone to going over the top is a very short journey indeed. Liver should be pink inside but by no means should it be eaten bloody. Ingredients that go well with it are bacon, a hint of garlic, parsley, lemon, pepper, dried Provençal herbs and port.

Fish and shellfish

For me the subject of fish and shellfish is one full of contradictions. The biggest problem with fish is freshness. How and where do you get really fresh fish? What is a fresh fish? When does a fish stop being fresh? At its height, the hysterical interest which *nouvelle cuisine* created made a lot of food critics and chefs look foolish. So much emphasis was being placed on freshness that a lot of people forgot that fish has to be caught by fishermen or by trawlers. It has to be landed on the quay. It has to be temporarily stored, then transported long distances by road or rail before it reaches the market. The wholesaler will receive it, grade it, store it, and then put it out on display in his market stall. Any time from 24 hours to a week could easily have elapsed from the time it takes to land the fish to the moment when it appears on a customer's plate.

Skate is one fish which you should avoid using unless it is absolutely spanking fresh. At the very most, I think it can be kept for a day after you have bought it, but beyond that it is not recommended. The taste of skate is predominantly a sweetish one and its texture is very unusual, the long grains being slightly reminiscent of spaghetti. Only the ribbed wings of this large, flat relative of the shark and dogfish are used. In France skate is extremely popular. It is a very strong tasting fish and the best accompaniments are either burnt butter, capers and vinegar (beurre noir) or mustard. This recipe is simple and quite delicious. Since it is originally a Normandy dish, cider could be served with it.

Raie à la Moutarde

Skate with Mustard Sauce

SERVES 4

15 ml (1 tbsp) unsalted butter
1 good wing of skate weighing about
    900 g (2 lb), cut in 4 pieces
15 ml (1 tbsp) Dijon mustard

1.1 litres (2 pints) double cream
salt and pepper
pinch of freshly grated nutmeg
60 ml (4 tbsp) finely chopped parsley

Liberally grease a shallow baking dish with the butter and lay the skate in it.

Mix the mustard in the cream, season with salt, pepper and the nutmeg and pour over the skate.

Cover with foil and cook at 180°C (350°F) mark 4, checking the fish frequently. It should take about 20 minutes.

Spoon the sauce all round the fish and baste to cover. Sprinkle with parsley and serve at once with a good light dry white such as a Sancerre or a Muscadet, or a chilled, light red wine such as Chinon.

Fishy mystique

I really think that a lot of nonsense is talked about fish. For some reason, when a chef is asked which type of food he likes to cook, if he answers fish, it is taken to mean that he is a great chef. Of course, many chefs love to cook fish. It is versatile and delicate, it requires careful handling and it needs delicate sauces. A rough hand has disastrous consequences. The range, type and variety of dishes which can be created from fish is wide indeed.

My favourite method of cooking fish is to steam it. However, certain kinds of fish taste much better cooked in certain ways. For example, sole tastes much better cooked *à la meunière*.

One method I do not have much enthusiasm for is poaching. If you immerse a piece of fish in liquid and poach it, it will invariably surrender some of its juices to the liquid in which it has been submerged. I therefore always steam fish and I find the ordinary straightforward *couscoussière* the most convenient piece of equipment for this.

My experience has also shown that it is pointless to add flavourings to the liquid in the steamer. I am always capable of registering the smallest aroma but I have never been able to notice on a fish any trace of aromatic liquid over which it has been steamed. The only thing I like to do before I steam a piece of white fish is to dip it in clarified butter and then place it in the steamer. This brings out its natural flavour and helps retain its moisture.

The great sea fish

The great, firm-fleshed delicately flavoured flat fish – turbot, brill, halibut and Dover sole (and to a lesser extent, lemon sole), delicately flavoured bass with its firm, lean, whitish pink flesh, John Dory and, of course, salmon (of which more later) are some of the primary fish used in the kitchens of good restaurants. It is very alarming to hear that the popularity of sea bass and its consequent over-fishing is causing serious difficulties with suppliers. It is an awful shame that this 'wolf of the sea', as the French call it, is under threat and has become extremely expensive.

This dish has been on my menu for the last six years. *Nouvelle cuisine* brought with it some strange paradoxes. From the sacred premise that ingredients should be left whole, not pulped, or smashed to pieces, to the banal practice of stuffing everything with a mousse, to me the turnaround, the contradiction, seemed bizarre.

Nothing can replace the texture and flavour of a perfectly executed mousseline of fish served up in the classical manner.

Mousseline de Sole et de Crabe
à la Sauce de Langoustines

A Mousse of Sole and Crab with a Dublin Bay Prawn Sauce

Illustrated on page 112

SERVES 10

800 g (1 lb 12 oz) lemon sole, skinned, filleted and perfectly trimmed

1 egg white

75 ml (3 fl oz) Sauce Crème de Ciboulette (page 235)

400 ml (14 fl oz) double cream

salt

clarified butter (page 241)

100 g (4 oz) fresh white crab meat

cayenne pepper

few drops of lemon juice

10 black truffle slices (optional)

350 ml (12 fl oz) Sauce Langoustine (page 242)

Dice the lemon sole into very small pieces and place it together with the egg white and the sauce crème de ciboulettes in the refrigerator to chill. Refrigerate the bowl of your food processor as well.

In the food processor, blend together thoroughly the fish, egg white and sauce until you have a homogeneous pulp. Add the cream in a steady stream and sprinkle in salt to taste. The salt will help stiffen the pulp and will give you a good idea as to how much more cream the mixture will absorb. It should be smooth and soft and not runny. Put the food processor bowl with the mousse back in the fridge. Prepare a bain-marie.

Lightly butter 10 timbale moulds.

Take the mousse out of the fridge and pack it into the moulds with a spatula, making a slight cavity in the centre of each one. Keep a little mousse back to top up the moulds at the next stage.

Combine a little clarified butter with the crab meat, sprinkle with salt, cayenne pepper and lemon juice and divide equally between the mousselines. Cover with more fish mousse and smooth over the tops. Tap the moulds well on a solid surface to fill in any air pockets.

Cover the surface of each one with tin foil. Place in the bain-marie and cook in the oven at 180°C (350°F) mark 4 for about 20 minutes. Touch the mousselines with your finger to determine whether they are done: they should feel slightly firm and only slightly wobbly.

If you are using truffles, gently warm the slices in clarified butter. Set aside.

Unmould the mousselines onto individual plates and pour over the langoustine sauce. If you are using truffles, drain the slices and decorate each mousseline with a truffle slice. Why not try serving a full-bodied white wine such as Clos du Val Chardonnay from California, or Champagne with this dish.

Monkfish, once called poor man's lobster (and now almost as expensive, I'm afraid), has become the cliché of *nouvelle cuisine* and we don't use it at all.

Enjoy brill. It lies in the shadow of its brother flat fish, the turbot. If you offer ten customers the choice between turbot or brill, eight of them will choose the former. For me, there is no contest. I far prefer brill's very delicate texture, and its finer flavour. I have a constant battle with my fishmongers to secure regular supplies of brill. Unfortunately, it is not always readily available, and it, too, is becoming a fashionable fish. Brill is smaller than turbot and its skin is lighter in colour. When buying whole turbot look out for fish that are not bruised and have no dark areas caused by accumulation of blood underneath the spine. The better fishermen make an incision at the very tip of the tail and bleed the fish, to remove all bruises and dark patches.

It is sad that nowadays trout plays such a minor role in good cooking and that trout generally have been rendered tasteless through farming. The most common way one encounters this fish is smoked. Freshly smoked trout is a great delicacy. But a fresh trout is even greater. In southern France, trout appears very frequently on the menus of the little inns and country restaurants.

Mediterranean fish soups

Since I first began to cook, classic, authentic Mediterranean fish soup has been an object for me to achieve and a recipe to master. Deeper and deeper research and deeper and deeper knowledge unearthed more and more varieties of fish, until in the end I could reproduce a true version, as close as possible to the real thing. True Mediterranean fish soup requires at least some of the following fish: red mullet, gurnard, rascasse, weaver fish, conger eel and crushed lobster or langoustine shells.

The best fish soup I ever made was in France where we were able to buy a mixture of little rock fish already put together in the market – all minuscule specimens of the real thing.

I think people are kicking hard and rebelling against the very strong emphasis on artful presentation which *nouvelle cuisine* has brought along in its wake. It is now coming to the point in restaurants where everything looks the same and everything is arranged in the same way. Monotony and repetition are the order of the day and it's exhausting to look at. The untidy dish which smells sublime and tastes even better is gradually creeping back. Our mothers and grand-mothers used to spoon food on plates with great ladles, and many a time, meat ragoûts and the great stews were presented in soup plates to trap the juices and the gravy. I think fish lends itself extremely well to this kind of presentation. After all, bouillabaisse is nothing but a ragoût of fish. You can use any selection of good-quality, firm-fleshed white fish for this recipe. You may or may not wish to serve this dish with aïoli, but if you do, and I think you should, don't forget some golden garlicky croûtons to go with it.

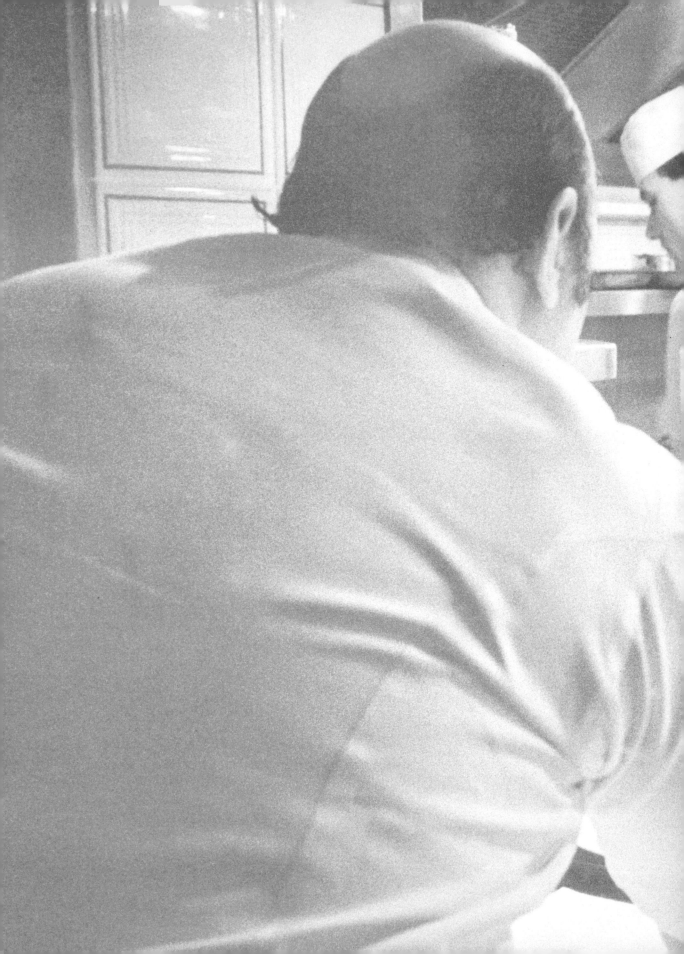

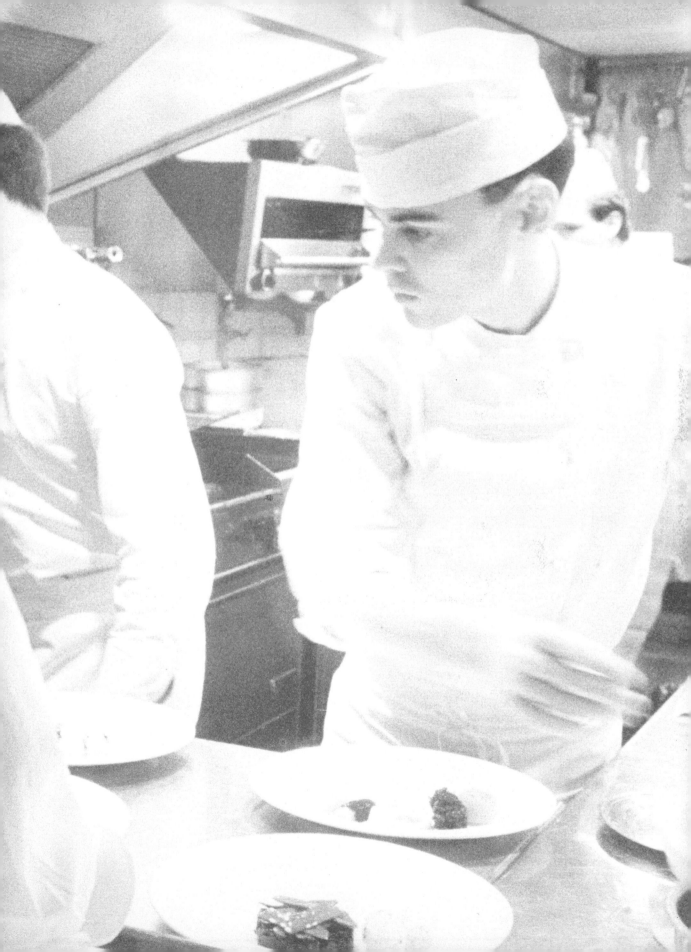

Ragoût de Poissons au Jus de Safran
Accompagné d'Aïoli

Ragoût of Various Fish with Saffron and Garlic Mayonnaise

SERVES 4

75 g (3 oz) butter
1 medium-sized 350 g (12 oz) red mullet
2 × 100 g (4 oz) fillets of sea bass, skin on
2 × 75 g (3 oz) fillets of sole
2 × 75 g (3 oz) fillets of brill, skinned
2 × 100 g (4 oz) fillets of bream, skin on
60 ml (4 tbsp) double cream
30 ml (2 tbsp) chopped shallots
300 ml (½ pint) dry white wine
150 ml (¼ pint) Fond de Poisson (page 230)

1 garlic clove, sliced
1 thyme sprig
1 bay leaf
60 ml (4 tbsp) finely chopped parsley
few black peppercorns
salt
pinch of saffron
Aïoli (page 238)
garlic croûtons fried in garlic-flavoured
    clarified butter (page 242)

Using 25 g (1 oz) of the butter, grease a large ovenproof dish and lay all the fish in one layer comfortably in it.

In a heavy stainless steel pan, mix together the cream, shallots, wine, fish stock, garlic, thyme, bay leaf, 5 ml (1 tsp) of parsley, peppercorns and the rest of the butter. Bring to the boil and then reduce by half over low heat. Strain. Pour the liquid over, cover with foil and bake at 190°C (375°F) mark 5 for 10 minutes, or until cooked.

Arrange the fish in equal quantities into 4 soup plates; add salt and the pinch of saffron to the remaining liquid. Spoon the liquid over the fish and place a blob of aïoli in the centre of each plate. Sprinkle with the remaining parsley and a few croûtons; serve with a robust white wine such as a Fixin.

Unfortunately, if you brand a fish as suitable only for coating with batter and frying in a sea of lard for the English national dish, fish 'n' chips, it is then very difficult to change its image. Though I find cod a wonderful fish, repeated attempts over the years to serve it in my restaurant to the public have failed.

I find the sweetly flavoured, firm, white-fleshed red mullet from Cornwall of exceptionally good quality and I like to serve these as a main course. They are a little less intense in flavour than their more brightly coloured Mediterranean counterparts which I keep for my fish soups – stronger in flavour and smaller in size, they can be liquidised more easily for this purpose.

Cornish red mullet are big, plump, magnificent firm-fleshed white fish. When you fillet them you have quite a lot of fish and for this recipe it is the Cornish red mullet which I recommend. Michel Guérard was once a guest at a luncheon where I cooked this dish, and afterwards he shook my hand and told me that he thought it stood out above all others.

Rouget au Beurre de Romarin

Fillet of Red Mullet with Rosemary-Flavoured Butter Sauce

SERVES 2

One 350–400 g (12–14 oz) red mullet,
cleaned and scaled
garlic-flavoured clarified butter
(page 242)

salt
cayenne pepper
200 ml (7 fl oz) Beurre Blanc au Romarin
(page 235)

Fillet the red mullet by running a knife from the base of the head to the tail along the back bone.

Trim the fillets, remove all the bones and make sure you do not tear or rupture the flesh. Trim off the tail end to allow two nice fillets. (You could wash the head and the back bone thoroughly, add the pieces from the tail and use them to make a stock for your next fish soup.)

Heat the garlic-flavoured clarified butter in a non-stick frying pan. Add the fillets, skin side down, and fry carefully, basting all the time for 1½ minutes. Turn the fillets over halfway. Season lightly with salt and cayenne.

Put the rosemary-flavoured beurre blanc on two warm plates and place the fillets in the centre. A dry white Meursault goes especially well with this dish.

Fresh and smoked salmon

I have deliberately left salmon until last because it deserves special mention. Wild salmon is the fish which spends part of its life in the sea, but is landed and caught from the rivers and the estuaries between February and August. Nowadays, farmed salmon is becoming increasingly more plentiful, but I personally have never liked farmed salmon as much as its wild brother, and I do not think it compares in any way. The flesh is flabby and the taste is milder. I am often surprised to see it on the menus of 'good' restaurants throughout the year. I have never liked its soft texture and I like its flavour even less.

The finest smoked salmon I have ever eaten was many years ago at the Château de Castel Novel when it still had two Michelin stars. I am extremely pleased that smoked salmon is no longer only eaten with a squeeze of lemon and a turn of the pepper mill. You now see it increasingly served in more versatile ways. In our kitchen, I have vastly expanded the range and treatment of smoked salmon. We now serve it with a chive cream sauce and warm crunchy cucumber. We also use it to encase a cold mousse of Dublin Bay prawns (see page 179). The international popularity of *gravad lax*, that superb Swedish recipe of preserved salmon with dill, has led to some new ideas and I plan to experiment with preserving salmon with fresh ginger.

Shellfish

And so to shellfish. My favourites are scallops, crab, Dublin Bay prawns (langoustines, which are like tiny lobsters), and mussels, which we use for one of our most delicious dishes, mussel soup with saffron. I much prefer the flavour of crab meat to lobster and the best size is between three and four pounds. I banish the so-called king of shellfish to a very inferior role in my kitchen. Lobster flesh is used as a garnish for fish dishes or in a salad with orange or truffle butter sauce. Lobster shells are used for lobster sauce. I treat langoustines in more or less the same way. As I have already said I make a cold mousseline from the flesh and dress it in a robe of smoked salmon and I use the crushed shells for my favourite soup (see page 62).

A freshwater favourite is the crayfish or *ecrévisse*. A soup or a sauce of *ecrévisse* is as good as a lobster soup or sauce and the tail meat is superior.

A recent dish on our menus is scallops individually wrapped in filo pastry and baked with some chives, a little garlic, salt and cayenne pepper.

Paper-thin filo is one of the most versatile and exciting pastries for the modern kitchen. For many years it was used solely for making crispy Greek baklava but, more recently, its use has spread and some of the top restaurants in France are beginning to use it to very good effect. My mind was preoccupied with using filo for many months before I settled on a number of recipes, one of which is this one for scallops. You can buy sheets of ready-made filo or strudel pastry in packets from delicatessens. You will need to have all your ingredients ready so that you can work fast when making these parcels, otherwise the filo will dry up and become flaky.

Bonbonnière de Coquilles St Jacques
au Beurre Blanc Pointillé de Poivrons Rouges
·
Scallops in Filo Pastry with Olive Oil, Chive
and Red Pepper-Flavoured Beurre Blanc
Illustrated on page 128

SERVES 2

clarified butter (page 241)

2 sheets of filo pastry 30.5 cm (12 inches) square

6 large fresh scallops

salt

100 g (4 oz) butter

25 g (1 oz) finely chopped spring onions

30 ml (2 tbsp) finely chopped chives

50 g (2 oz) garlic-flavoured clarified butter (page 242)

cayenne pepper

90 ml (6 tbsp) Beurre Blanc (page 234)

45 ml (3 tbsp) olive oil

5 ml (1 tsp) finely chopped red pepper

Brush some clarified butter on each of the sheets of filo pastry, and place one on top of the other.

With a sharp knife, cut 6 equal-sized squares of filo pastry. Lay each square across a tablespoon. Place a scallop in the middle of the pastry, sprinkle very lightly with salt, add a knob of butter, a pinch of chopped spring onion, 5 ml (1 tsp) chives and a little garlic butter. Push down the scallop into the recess of the spoon, season with cayenne and fold over the edges and sides of the filo pastry to make it look like a money pouch. Repeat this process 5 more times.

Brush the filo pouches with a little clarified butter. Arrange on a baking tray and bake in a 180°C (350°F) mark 4 oven for about 10 minutes. When the pastry is beginning to look golden and crisp, it is ready.

Mix together the beurre blanc, the olive oil, the remaining chives, and the red pepper and spoon in the centre of 2 plates. Place 3 scallop pouches on each plate, in the centre of the pool of sauce, and serve at once.

Serve with a good, crisp, dry white wine such as Puligny-Montrachet.

Salads

Vegetables to me mean three things. First I think of them in terms of salads, then as accompaniments to main courses in everyday cooking, and lastly I think of the new, exotic varieties being introduced from the tropics. The modern salad is a great feast of colour, texture and taste. In recent years, new and exotic salad leaves have been coming to us from across the Channel: *frisée, salade de mâche*, the curly green and red *batavia*, purple *radicchio* and the greenish and brown oak leaf lettuce *feuilles de chêne*. The *radicchio* has a slightly bitter taste. The curly endive (*frisée*) is slightly less bitter, oak leaf salad has a delicate sweetish taste and the lamb's lettuce or *mâche* is slightly more elusive. The various shades of green, the various shapes, the spindly leaves and the purple pleats of all these salads make up a lovely panorama when carefully arranged and served together. I dress them only with hazelnut oil, a little salt and a drop of lemon juice (never vinegar). Thankfully, more and more native growers are beginning to show some interest and I am quite certain that in ten, 15 or 20 years, we will be self-sufficient.

When it comes to oils, I use certain types for certain ingredients. I like Italian olive oil best – green virgin oil with a good flavour. I use olive oil for cooking salmon baked in salt, for fish soup and in globe artichoke salad or a salad of artichoke hearts, for example. I use hazelnut oil for dressing leaf salads and with avocados. A new invention of mine is to toss cooked vegetables such as carrots, courgettes or mange-tout in sesame oil just before serving.

This is an unusual way of eating smoked salmon, a veritable feast of colours in blacks, reds, different shades of green. The only thing to remember here is that you cannot allow the citrus fruit to marinate for longer than 2 hours in the lime syrup. It involves a lot of preparation and a lot of composition, but the end result is stunning and it is a very unusual salad.

You need to repeat again the same exercise as for the quail salad on page 106, and use the egg poaching rings in the centre of 2 plates to help arrange the ingredients. It goes without saying that you require the same salad ingredients and the same dressing. The only difference is that the plates should be cold and the salad should be placed on top of the salmon.

Salade de Saumon Fumé au Citrus Confit
Salad of Smoked Salmon with Citrus Fruit Segments

SERVES 2

6 smoked salmon slices	60 ml (4 tbsp) crème fraîche
Salad leaves as in Quail salad with Wild Mushroom Butter Sauce (page 106)	60 ml (4 tbsp) soured cream
60 ml (4 tbsp) granulated sugar	salt
4 limes	few drops of lemon juice
1 orange	15 ml (1 tbsp) chives
1 lemon	15 ml (1 tbsp) Tomates Concassées (page 186)
1 grapefruit	black lumpfish roe

Place an egg poaching ring in the centre of 2 cold plates. Fill each one with 3 slices of smoked salmon and top with salad leaves.

Melt the sugar in 200 ml (7 fl oz) of water and add the zest from 3 of the limes. Simmer for 20 minutes, leave to infuse and cool down. Strain and place in the refrigerator.

Segment the remaining lime, orange, lemon and grapefruit and steep in the lime syrup.

Whip the crème fraîche and fold in the soured cream. Whip to a stiffish consistency. Salt lightly, squeeze a few drops of lemon juice into the cream mixture and fold in the chives and tomato concassé very lightly. Make 6 individual quenelles, place on a plate and keep in the fridge.

Assemble as follows: drain the citrus fruit segments and place little bunches neatly together on 3 equidistant parts of each plate. Between the gaps, place the quenelles and dab some lumpfish roe on each quenelle. Remove the egg poaching rings and serve.

Serve with a pale dry white such as Mâcon-Viré.

If your idea of a salad is a mixture of simple salad leaves, this is probably something for you. Take a little bit more care than usual with the dressing and while keeping the dish simple, make sure you provide some variety in texture, colour and taste. Use large egg poaching rings to help keep the shape of the salad. You will probably find these in amongst your pastry equipment. On 2 warm plates, place 2 poaching rings about 10 cm (4 inches) in diameter. Your ingredients for a salad for two are as follows (use the same leaves as in the quail salad, page 106), but slightly more of them.

Salade aux Fines Herbes

·

Plain Mixed Salad with Fresh Herbs

SERVES 2
French bread for croûtons
melted goose fat
bacon for lardons
for the vinaigrette:
5 ml (1 tsp) white wine vinegar
30 ml (2 tbsp) hazelnut oil
5 ml (1 tsp) fresh lemon juice

1.25 ml (¼ tsp) Dijon mustard
salt and cayenne pepper
purple and green basil leaves
2.5 ml (½ tsp) fresh thyme leaves
15 ml (1 tbsp) chives cut to 2.5 cm (1 inch)
  lengths
15 ml (1 tbsp) of fresh tarragon leaves
mixed salad leaves

Make some croûtons from a French baguette, brush with melted goose fat and bake them in the oven until golden.

In a small roasting pan, cut some julienne of bacon and roast it until crisp to make lardons.

Mix together the vinaigrette ingredients and place them in a bowl. Tip over the herbs and salad and mix well, but lightly. In the centre of the 2 warm plates, place the warm sauce and arrange the rings on top. Fill them with the salad leaves and the herbs and place hot croûtons all round with hot lardons nestling on top. Remove the rings and serve.

Wild mushrooms

In September we await the bulk of the wild mushrooms, and as autumn advances, in come the fresh *girolles* and the *cèpes*, then in December and January, the black truffles start to appear. I use *cèpes* a lot in my cooking and I always invariably stock dried *cèpes*, too, so I can use them all year round. I also like dried *girolles* and use them to make light, very flavoursome butter sauces and to dress salads and other vegetables. I am very much in favour of dried wild mushrooms, because this way you can have their flavour without necessarily waiting for the season. I do not recommend buying them preserved in jars or tins – they are slimy and tasteless.

Fresh morels have an elusive flavour. Massive quantities of soil and grit accumulate in their many folds and when you try to wash them out you often

Bonbonnière de Coquilles St Jacques au Beurre Blanc Pointillé de Poivrons Rouges

Scallops in Filo Pastry with Olive Oil, Chive and Red Pepper-Flavoured Beurre Blanc

Paper-thin filo is one of the most versatile pastries for the modern kitchen and can be used in both sweet and savoury dishes. These little parcels of scallops are quick and easy to prepare and make a very attractive starter, but they do rely on good ingredients. You need nice, big, very fresh scallops, one for each portion. I like to bake the bonbonnières until the pastry is crisp and almost burnt on the top.

RECIPE ON PAGE 124

Escalope de Saumon
au Spaghetti de Concombre

·

Escalope of Salmon with Cucumber 'Spaghetti'

*This is a prime example of good ingredients
simply cooked. It looks pretty and tastes
sensational. For a little extra colour I have served
the steamed wild salmon with tomato-flavoured
beurre blanc sprinkled with chives and a
plain beurre blanc. The cucumber 'spaghetti'
make an interesting contrast of colour and texture
and offset the richness of the fish. This type of
presentation also goes well with brill or to
accompany meat you can make 'spaghetti' of
carrots or courgettes.*

RECIPE ON PAGE 182

end by smashing them up, they are so fragile, and this makes them impossible to cook. But dried ones are easily reconstituted in hot water (you can use the water as a flavouring for sauces) and remain firm and very edible. They also have a more concentrated flavour.

Morilles Farcies de Champignons
Stuffed Morel Mushrooms

SERVES 4

4 button mushrooms, finely diced
2.5 ml (½ tsp) chopped shallots
50 g (2 oz) butter

salt and pepper
2.5 ml (½ tsp) chopped parsley
4 large dried morel mushrooms, soaked in hot water for 30 minutes

Cook the button mushrooms, shallots and 25 g (1 oz) butter together until the mixture is dry, about 10 minutes. Add the salt, pepper and parsley.

When cutting the necks of the entrance to the cavity of the morels, tidy each one up. With a piping bag pipe the mushroom purée into the morel and fry in the remaining butter for 10 minutes until thoroughly cooked.

Champignons de Paris have a deeper flavour and a stronger taste than English button mushrooms, but I prefer to make my consommé with the native variety because they are more mellow. I am not keen on the texture or taste of the oyster mushroom and have not been as impressed as some others by the shiitake mushroom from Japan. I am generous with black truffles, which I enjoy, although I never use the white ones from Italy, which I find expensive and overrated.

Potatoes

The best potatoes in England come from abroad, from Jersey, Cyprus, Egypt and France. These countries all produce better potatoes than we do. A personal favourite when it comes to eating potatoes is the new season's Jerseys boiled with the skin on, with butter and chives, or rolled in breadcrumbs and deep fried with crispy, golden brown garlic and parsley.

Pomme Purée
Potato Purée

You might like to try making a purée of boiled potatoes with butter, milk and a little olive oil (or take a leaf out of Frédy Girardet's book and use only olive oil and milk). Season with salt, white pepper and a little nutmeg.

This is another very simple way of serving potatoes and it goes well with roasts, with chicken and with duck.

You'll need to allow a large potato for each person because there's quite a lot of wastage. Trim off the rounded sides so you only cut straight slices on the mandoline or in the food processor.

You'll also need a selection of little 4.5 cm (1¾–2 inch) 2.5 cm (1 inch) deep non-stick pans or tins.

Galettes de Pommes de Terre au Lard
Potato and Bacon Galettes

FOR EACH PERSON

1 large potato
1 rasher of lean bacon, finely chopped
goose fat or clarified butter (page 241)

salt and pepper
30 ml (2 tbsp) very finely grated Gruyère

Slice the potatoes very thinly. Wash and pat dry. Sauté the bacon and set aside. Liberally butter the tins with fat or clarified butter. Add 2 slices of potato. Season lightly with salt and pepper, sprinkle over a few pieces of bacon and add a little Gruyère. Repeat the layers 3 or 4 times more, seasoning each time. Cover each tin loosely with foil and bake in a 200°C (400°F) mark 6 oven for 20–30 minutes or until the potatoes are cooked and the tops are a mottled golden brown.

These simply cooked yet delicious potatoes go well with many dishes, especially roasts. They are almost the only deep-fried dishes we ever make.

Pommes à l'Ail
Garlic Potatoes

SERVES 2

6 new potatoes (½ the size of golf balls)
30 ml (2 tbsp) very fine, homemade
   breadcrumbs
2 eggs, well beaten
150 ml (¼ pint) groundnut oil for deep
   frying

50 g (2 oz) butter
2 garlic cloves, finely chopped
salt and pepper
2.5 ml (½ tsp) finely chopped parsley

Boil the potatoes then remove their skins. Roll them in breadcrumbs, then dip in the beaten egg, then roll again in the crumbs. Deep fry until golden. Drain well then keep warm on absorbent kitchen paper.

In a small frying pan melt the butter, mix in the garlic, cook until golden, season, add the parsley and pour over the potatoes.

Sweet Potatoes

Sweet potatoes reach us from Africa, the United States and Israel. Try making this purée of sweet potato. The taste is amazing.

Pomme Purée Douce

Sweet Potato Purée

The sweet potato is a vegetable I grew up with and which I knew very well in East Africa. Several varieties are available here including the orange-fleshed American potato, which tastes like a cross between a carrot and a pumpkin, and the grey-coloured African sweet potato. Simply boil the potatoes until tender then purée with butter, salt and pepper. This purée goes well with lamb and with duck.

Other vegetables

In Britain, a large proportion of a good restaurant's vegetable shopping basket now comes from France – artichokes, baby leeks, shallots, garlic, dark green crinkly leaf spinach, celeriac and aubergines, as well as baby turnips and many others. Courgettes and fine French beans come to us from Kenya and avocados from all over the world. We now have five colours of peppers: red, white, green, yellow and black.

I use asparagus in my kitchen as often as I can and I buy it throughout the year. I love the white asparagus from France when it is very tiny and I use green asparagus the rest of the year, because the season for white asparagus is very short.

The cabbage family, for generations considered to be a second-class collection of vegetables, is now winning greater praise. Modern chefs have reprieved them and the Savoy, red and white cabbages are now beginning to adorn the large plates in modern restaurants. Spinach cooked in lots of boiling salted water is the essential garnish for fish.

Going to market
– London versus Paris

I am often asked whether I go to the wholesale markets in the early hours of the morning to prod and to taste and to look and to order for my restaurants. I went to Smithfield market once to look at the meat and to the old Billingsgate market to look at the fish. I also visited the old Covent Garden on just one occasion. I shall never go again. The sheer ignorance about the produce they sell, the bad manners, the swearing, the rudeness I encountered from porters and traders was enough to deter me from the experience forever.

In direct contrast, I recently visited Rungis market in Paris. First of all, the sheer abundance, the variety and the quality of the produce left me totally dazed. Secondly, the good manners, the politeness and the genuine interest traders showed in our enquiries was very noticeable. It is difficult to begin to describe the variety of every size and shape of fish, shellfish, fruit, vegetables, herbs, cheeses, meats – the displays, the freshness, the colours – the sheer abundance. Perhaps if it was the same in England more chefs would climb out of their beds at five o'clock in the morning for an experience like this – I certainly would.

The kitchen garden

I am also asked repeatedly whether I grow my own herbs and vegetables. Unfortunately, the stories and the photographs of great chefs in cloth caps and heavy anoraks braving the cold weather of winter mornings is more a practice set up for the camera and for the cookery book than an everyday reality. I do not go to the markets in the early hours of the morning and I do not grow my own herbs and vegetables. If I did, I would have very little time to run my kitchen and my restaurant. I would rather leave the task to my greengrocer and to the various growers. Just as my greengrocer doesn't presume to break into my world of cooking, I do not intend to spend my time buying ingredients in the early hours and tilling the land to grow herbs.

Fruit

The subject of exotic fruits is one with which I am acquainted very intimately. Fruit, the arrangement of fruit and the making of fruit-based sorbets has been of great importance to my gastronomy. Fresh fruit goes so well with delicious dessert wines such as Sauternes, Barsac, Muscat de Frontignan and Muscat de Beaumes de Venise. Exotic fruits are not the only ones to be found in my kitchen. I like apples and I love oranges. I use melons, pawpaws, mangoes, kiwis, pineapples, passion fruit, figs and lychees as garnishes for fruit sorbets and for our famous tulip with vanilla ice cream and fruit. The best mango is the Alphonso from India, named after a Portuguese priest who first developed it in Goa. Mangoes now come from all over the world, but the best ones are from India, South America and drier parts of Africa. Kenya mangoes are not as good as those from Tanzania, and the small Alphonsos, alas, have a very short season in April and May.

There is one banana which I swear I would serve all on its own as a pudding, if it was available in this country. This is the red, giant banana of East

Africa. It has such an intense flavour and aroma that you could be eating it in one corner of a four-bedroom house and smell its perfume in every part of the building. My great sadness lies in the fact that many of these exotic fruits are flown into the country from around the world in an unripe state. A mango on a tree in a steamy African garden will ripen much better than in a warehouse in a wholesale vegetable market. Remember above all that apart from jam making and preserving, fruit is not for cooking.

In the pastry section of the kitchen, the nuts we use are walnuts, almonds, dark green pistachios and hazelnuts. We are unique in our restaurant in serving whole, roasted almonds coated with a hard layer of caramel as a petit four.

Herbs

I love dried herbs. I find very little sympathy with the single-minded pursuit of freshness for the sake of it, simply in order to say 'I only use fresh herbs'. Well I don't. I use chives always fresh, and I use thyme always fresh, but that's about it. I used to bring back dozens of sachets of mixed Provençal herbs and dried savory from our annual summer holiday in France. I use them often in many recipes and I find their intense flavour intoxicating. I use dried tarragon freely, but I avoid using dried thyme. When I make mussel soup, I use dry tarragon. When I make a delicate sauce, I use a sprig of fresh tarragon. In my Provençal fish soup I use dry, mixed Provençal herbs and dry savory. I always use fresh rosemary, because it is better fresh, but just as wild mushrooms and domestic mushrooms have their flavour concentrated when you dry them, the same applies to certain herbs. If you want to sum up the heady, unmistakable, concentrated scents of Provence, the single most important ingredient to use is dried Provençal mixed herbs. Remember, some of the pungency that assaults your nostrils as you stand under a pine tree on top of a hill in the Var comes from the herbs all around you which have been parched by the sun.

Spices

When it comes to spices, there is a short list which I always keep in the kitchen. These include allspice and juniper berries, star anise from Chinese super-markets, fennel seeds, whole nutmeg, and, of course, the saffron for my mussel and fish soups.

Green, pink, black and white peppercorns are much discussed. Green peppercorns are unripened berries from the pepper vine which is native to Asia. Madagascar is the name most prominently associated with the growing of pepper. The sun-dried green peppercorns become the black peppercorns of such good aroma. The dried core of the ripened fruit of the pepper vine is the white peppercorn. I prefer the taste of the green peppercorns in brine to the freeze-dried variety ones which I think are overpowering. And I find the taste of pink peppercorns bizarre. The best taste comes from the freshly ground black peppercorn. White pepper has too much power and intensity.

As you see, the produce, the ingredients which you use, are the heart of a good dish. Do not be misled by fashion. Remember: dried herbs; crab is less expensive than lobster; duck foie gras can be marvellous. The heretofore accepted fallacies relative to the selection of raw ingredients – the early morning market visits, only use fresh herbs and others already discussed – are for the glossy magazines or TV series rather than real life. The main principle is to be fussy: not to take second best. You must select your prime ingredient, learn to identify it, to understand and to work it with respect and restraint. These are the secrets of good cooking.

'*My favourite methods
of cooking are primitive. I cannot easily
forget the taste of a partridge baked
in clay or the smell of the
green pigeons of Africa
grilling over an
open fire.*'

CHAPTER FIVE

Methods of cooking

I first became acquainted with one particular way of cooking food when I was a boy. I went to a primary school amongst the coffee and banana plantations in the foothills of Mount Kilimanjaro. The area around the school was so fertile that the school relied extensively on the vegetables and fruit which grew in its own gardens and on the little allotments and peasant farms surrounding it, which also supported chickens and pigs. It was those chickens and the partridges which fed with them that provided us children with our first excursions into cookery. As with many boys of that age, the catapult was an essential part of our armoury and since the mountain slopes abounded with bird life, we had ample scope to develop our skills with this highly effective weapon.

I soon learned how to dig a hole in the side of a steep bank and thus create my first clay oven. Instinct and common sense flourish in the young. I immediately set about 'seasoning' the earth around the oven by lighting fires and letting the red embers burn deep into the earth to provide a good insulation. The crack shots among us were responsible for the supply of chickens, partridges and green pigeons. We used to disembowel the birds, salt them inside and coat them with layers of mud, feathers and all. Thus sealed, the birds were put into the oven to cook slowly for hours. Those first primitive cooking smells were unforgettable. The baked clay coating was chipped away, removing the feathers with it. The aroma was incredible. When I taste partridge now, I simply cannot find the excitement or the intensity of flavour to compare with those early years. Inadvertently, I suppose, I was taking my first steps in cooking.

Another primitive method of cooking which was also an essential part of my youth was roasting on a spit over an open fire. Fresh lemons were always at hand. The fire would be lit under a lemon tree and we could reach out for a lemon and squeeze it over the roasting bird. Thyme was also abundant and the smells from those early simple attempts at cooking were sensational. Lemon, thyme and melted butter – what a heavenly combination! At our house in the south of France we used to love eating this sort of simple food. We just reached out and picked fresh lemons from the tree and grilled cutlets of lamb and whole chickens flavoured with local thyme.

As the years rolled on and I found myself standing behind a stove wearing whites, I became attracted more and more towards the two methods of cooking which reminded me of my youth: grilling and roasting became my own personal favourites. To this day I associate food cooked this way with good, fresh, strong flavours. I was very surprised when I first set foot in England to see the boiled maize. In Africa the norm was always to roast maize over an open fire and to hear the crackling sound of the bursting grain. That was the way the Africans ate their maize and the only way I knew.

The simplest, most generally accepted definition of cooking is 'the application of heat to a raw material'. The way in which this heat is applied to various raw materials, be they meat, fish, or vegetables, is really what constitutes the various methods of cooking. Nowadays the processes and methods of cooking have become entangled with two new elements: the march of science and technology and the dictates of modern living.

Grilling

What is grilling? The term causes a great deal of confusion. Is cooking under a restaurant salamander or a domestic overhead grill, grilling? When you place a piece of meat on a modern lava rock charcoal-simulated grill, do you in fact grill? If you are using a Hibachi with real charcoal at the bottom of your garden, is that grilling? When you are turning a chicken, or when modern science turns it for you constantly and subjects it to heat from the top and from the side, is that, in fact, grilling? When you have an open fire in a fireplace, or in the open air and you have a suckling pig which you are constantly turning, is that grilling? If you have a fire made of pine wood, vines and olive and you place the meat directly on it, is that grilling? So many different ways of grilling, or spit roasting are now common that the true method and concept of grilling has been lost. To my mind, when as children we used to spreadeagle green pigeons and partridges, run a skewer right through the carcase (the spatchcock method), place them three or four inches above a wood fire and baste them with lemony, herby butter using the leaf of a pawpaw plant, *that* was grilling. But some people might say that was spit roasting! It is a fine point. Grilling, for me, is the method that produces the most delicious aromas in cooking. In grilling it is quite tricky to cook food to the required degree and also ensure that you have preserved all the juices. It is more difficult, for example, to cook a piece of chicken on the grill than it is to cook a piece of lamb. My general rule, as far as possible, is to avoid cooking white meats such as veal and chicken this way, because they are both fairly lean and both must be cooked right through, not pink or red, while still remaining moist. Veal and chicken contain the kind of bacteria which must be eliminated by cooking before the meat is fit for human consumption. Lamb and beef lend themselves better to grilling because they contain a higher proportion of fat. They are safe to eat rare. The meat is more juicy when it is reddish pink and is less likely to dry out.

Roasting

When we cook food inside an oven, we subject the food to an enclosed heat. Modern technology is constantly giving us new ovens and new ideas in the development of ovens. The earliest ovens were difficult to control and were heated from underneath by coal and wood and there is much to be said for the authenticity and the honesty of baking or roasting food in such an oven. The idea has stayed with us over the years and still exists today in the shape of a traditional solid fuel stove such as the famous Aga. I have never cooked on an Aga, but it seems that everyone who owns one refuses to cook on anything else. In practical terms, though, for both the professional and domestic kitchen, it is best to talk about the speed and controllability of the modern oven (I do not include a microwave oven here as it is not really capable of browning or crisping – two essential parts of roasting).

The smaller the raw ingredient (e.g. a piece of steak, or a portion-size of fillet of turbot) the less suitable it is for this type of cooking. Ideal subjects for roasting are full-size birds such as chickens, ducks, pigeons, partridges, grouse, pheasants, quails, or legs or shoulders of lamb, whole fillets or ribs of beef, and so on. A recent development is the convection oven and even more recently the steam-assisted convection oven. This type of oven circulates the hot air and introduces the heat more frequently to the object you are roasting, more repeatedly and more evenly than an ordinary oven. Another great application of convection for professionals is the pastry oven. When making pastry you need the even distribution of heat, you need speed and you need controllability. At our restaurant in Shinfield, for a year I used exclusively three powerful convection ovens. I find the speed and the effectiveness of a convection oven invaluable. The slight disadvantage I find with a fast convection oven is that because of the speed with which a joint or a chicken cooks, the crispness which normally occurs with longer, slower roasting might be slightly lacking, although this is unlikely to occur with a less powerful domestic oven. This obviously applies particularly to smaller birds and joints which by their nature require less cooking.

What to do with duck legs is always a problem for a restaurant. These days we use the breasts only for so many dishes and then find we have legs galore left over. One very useful and pleasant solution to the problem is this recipe. If you use pork fat, render the fat yourself in your kitchen, by dicing finely 900 g (2 lb) of belly of pork and cooking it on a very, very low heat. Remember to use a heavy cast iron, enamelled pan to cook the ducks in. Because a lot of extra fat will be released from the skin of the duck legs, it is important to use a large enough pan to accommodate the extra fat which will be released.

Confit de canard has such a truly French ring to it, almost like the signature of General de Gaulle. Everything is catered for in this recipe – economy, long life, wonderful taste. It's all there.

Confit de Cuisses de Canard
Preserved Duck Legs

SERVES 6

for the confit:

600 ml (1 pint) goose or pork fat	12 Jamaica allspice berries
1 onion	6 crushed juniper berries
2 medium-sized carrots, scraped and quartered	salt
2 shallots	12 duck legs
6 cloves garlic	*for the sauce:*
2 bay leaves	600 ml (1 pint) Demi-Glace (page 228)
1 sprig of thyme	300 ml ($\frac{1}{2}$ pint) red wine
1 sprig tarragon	5 ml (1 tsp) Confiture d'Echalotes au
small piece of orange rind	Cassis et au Vin Rouge (page 151)
36 black peppercorns	24 crushed peppercorns
	100 g (4 oz) butter
	salt

To make your confit, in a large, heavy, cast iron enamelled saucepan with a tight-fitting lid, melt the fat and add all the vegetables, the herbs and the aromatics. Add the duck legs (arrange them carefully), cover with a lid and cook for 2–3 hours in a 150°C (300°F) mark 2 oven, checking periodically to ensure that the fat is not bubbling violently. If it does, the meat will fall off the bones. Remove the pan from the oven and leave everything to cool overnight. Next day, place in the refrigerator and leave there for 2 more days. The duck will keep extremely well for a week or up to 10 days under the solid fat.

To serve the confit, remove the duck legs from the fat. Place, skin-side down, in a heavy roasting pan and cook in a medium 180°C (350°F) mark 4 oven until the skin becomes very crisp, about 15–20 minutes. If you are worried that the heat might dry the skin unduly, cover with aluminium foil.

Meanwhile, make your sauce. Cook all the ingredients together and reduce to a syrupy consistency. Strain into a clean pan and, stirring constantly, thicken with the butter.

Pat dry the duck legs on absorbent kitchen paper and arrange crosswise, allowing 2 legs per person, in the centre of warm serving plates. Pour over the sauce and serve at once. Serve with rich red wine, a burgundy such as a Pommard or a Provençal such as Château Vignelaure.

A further extension of the convection oven and the most modern step in this direction has been the professional cook-and-hold convection oven. This enables the chef to cook a joint and to hold at the degree of doneness and at the temperature required until it is ready to be served. My own prediction is that this type of oven is going to become more widely available and more commonly used – it is the ideal instrument for serving hundreds of meals at banquets and other large scale functions.

I have, incidentally, become very excited by a method of cooking vegetables in the oven. I call this confit of vegetables. It is an easy way of preparing and cooking vegetables and the flavours are concentrated well (though it does also concentrate the acidity). With boiled vegetables the acidity is lost, but some of the flavour is, too. The sugar which is added to the confit helps to balance the acidity.

The container referred to in this recipe is the sort the Chinese use for take-aways. Cooked in this way, vegetables retain all their flavour and go exceedingly well with roast lamb. As Harold McGee points out in his book, when you do not boil vegetables you allow too much acidity to concentrate in the fibres. This is a method of cooking vegetables which I stumbled across by chance and which has excited me. I pass on the secret to anyone who wants to try it. If you wish to eliminate excess acidity in the vegetables, all you have to do is blanch them well, in which case you have to make allowance for the cooking time in the oven.

If you don't have one of these metal containers, use a gratin dish lined with 3 layers of kitchen foil. Put the vegetables, in separate foil parcels, in the dish and cover tightly with 3 more layers of foil. They may take slightly longer to cook than in a metal container.

The 'turned' vegetables in the ingredients list here refers to the technique of shaping carrots, potatoes and the like into small, uniform, torpedo-shaped pieces. You do this by literally turning them in the hand and paring them into shape with a sharp knife. Large vegetables may have to be quartered lengthways first.

Confit de Legumes
Roast Vegetables

SERVES 4

1 medium-sized fennel bulb, well trimmed, green stalks removed, quartered

4 potatoes, 'turned' into 7.5 cm (3 inch) pieces

4 carrots, 'turned' into 7.5 cm (3 inch) pieces

4 stalks of celery, well trimmed, and cut into 8 × 5 cm (2 inch) lengths

2 courgettes, 'turned' into 7.5 cm (3 inch) pieces

4 × 7.5 cm (3 inch) long asparagus spears

4 garlic cloves, well trimmed

4 medium-sized shallots, well trimmed

4 button onions, well trimmed

4 large dried morel mushrooms, well trimmed and soaked in hot water for 30 minutes

60 ml (4 tbsp) clarified butter (page 241)

4 tarragon sprigs

4 thyme sprigs

20 black peppercorns

5 ml (1 tsp) sugar

salt

Separate all the ingredients into 4 portions. Place in an aluminium container and slide the lid into place.

Cook at 180°C (350°F) mark 4 for about 15 minutes or until all the vegetables are tender and cooked through.

This dish goes well with roasted and grilled meat. It is very easy to make – you literally screw up the vegetables in foil and throw the foil parcel in the oven. The aroma which comes from the oven while they are cooking is sensational. The vegetables will be soft and will remain whole.

Confit d'Echalotes, d'Ail et de Petits Oignons
Whole Shallots, Garlic and Button Onions Roasted in the Oven

SERVES 2

2 medium-sized shallots, very well trimmed

2 large garlic cloves, well trimmed

2 button onions, well trimmed

15 ml (1 tbsp) clarified butter (page 241)

thyme sprig

tarragon sprig

3 or 4 peppercorns

salt

Place all the ingredients in the centre of a 15 cm (6 inch) square piece of kitchen foil, gather up the edges and screw together into a loose, sealed ball.

Cook in the oven at 180°C (350°F) mark 4 for 40 minutes until all the vegetables are thoroughly cooked and are soft and mellow in flavour.

To roast food successfully, you have to know when to season and where to season. By trial and error you have to learn which ingredients help brown or crisp the skin of poultry or game. You must understand why you baste food. And when it is cooked, you must always allow whatever you have roasted to rest in a hot, sealed place such as a hot cupboard or an oven. Why? In an oven, a piece of meat subjected to very high heat will contract and have a tendency to shrivel, the fibres shrink as they become fiercely agitated by the heat. This has to do with being relaxed or tense (an animal killed under stress will yield tougher meat). After roasting, the fibres, the connecting tissues and the fats between the tissues must be allowed to relax. The more they relax, the more tender the food will be – chicken, for example, will be wonderfully tender and moist if allowed to rest for three quarters of an hour. I find roast chicken at its absolute peak while it is still warm, at that point when the jelly is just beginning to form round it but before it gets cold.

Certain ingredients help crisp the skin or surface of what is being roasted: for beef or lamb, brushing with butter and a very light powdery application of flour will help it brown and crisp; brush the skin of birds with honey to create a brown, crisp surface; if you apply coarse salt to the skin of a duck, you will get a drier crisper result. If you rub with lemon, you get a good flavour and a crisper result, too. Chicken or duck can be painted with honey and melted butter, sprinkled with dried Provençal herbs, coarse salt and freshly crushed black peppercorns to obtain a crisp brown skin, and after cooling down this produces a most delicious and aromatic jelly. If you want to serve the chicken cold with dollops of this jelly, it stops being a meal, it becomes an experience!

The method of cooking the chicken recipe overleaf is the same as for Canette de Challans au Miel (page 109). If you like to eat chicken skin, you should remember that it has a very high fat content and that there is a high concentration of germs. You must therefore be very careful to cook the skin of chicken to a very crispy, crackling consistency. There is no better recipe to achieve this than the one which follows. Honey and coarse salt dry out the flesh very thoroughly and also give a heavenly flavour. Honey also makes a wonderful jelly and if you eat this chicken dish cold, which you could very easily do, with a green salad with fresh herbs, warm rice and the sweetish jelly, you will soon forget the meaning of sauce.

Carré d'Agneau Rose en Croûte de Fines Herbes

Best End of Lamb with a Brioche and Herb Crust

The natural affinity of lamb with herbs and garlic is exploited in this robustly flavoured dish. The Provençal herb-flavoured crust is complemented by a light garlic purée which has been flavoured with green peppercorns. I think lamb should be served rare. Once cooked, the trick is to allow it to rest for a while to develop a nice pinkness. Simply cooked vegetables, well presented, include carrots and asparagus or a bed of spinach topped by gratin dauphinois. A filo pastry parcel containing mushrooms adds a contrast of texture and flavour.

RECIPE ON PAGE 101

Assiette Savoreuse

*Hot Foie Gras with Caramelised Oranges
on Toasted Brioche*

*This is one of the most popular, and most
attractive, of our starters. It is a rich concoction
in which slices of foie gras are quickly cooked
and served on toasted brioche. Caramelised
oranges go particularly well with foie gras and
balance the richness of the liver. The light
veal reduction flavoured with cognac and fruit, and
the salad leaves which have been dressed in
hazelnut oil, also help offset the richness of the
main ingredients.*

RECIPE ON PAGE 174

Poulet Rôti au Miel

Roast Chicken with Honey, Peppercorns and Coarse Salt

SERVES 2

1 × 1.6 kg (3½ lb) plump, maize-fed free range chicken
25 g (1 oz) very soft butter
30 ml (2 tbsp) honey

15 ml (1 tbsp) crushed peppercorns
15 ml (1 tbsp) coarse salt
2 cloves garlic, finely sliced
1 sprig tarragon

Smear the chicken with the soft butter and paint the skin thoroughly with the honey. Season with pepper and salt and place the sliced garlic and the tarragon in the cavity.

Roast in a 180°C (350°F) mark 4 oven for 45 minutes. Switch off the oven and leave the chicken inside for a further 45 minutes. At this point, either carve it and serve it with the juices, or eat it cold with spoonfuls of wobbly jelly, warm Basmati rice and a green salad made with cos lettuce and herbs.

Serve with a light, fruity red wine such as a Cru Beaujolais.

Incidentally, in my opinion, the only way to cook a whole salmon is also in the oven. You simply lay the fish on well-buttered aluminium foil, stuff the cavity with spring onions, thyme, tarragon, peppercorns and salt, pour over generous drops of good white wine, place 4 or 5 bay leaves along its back, fold the foil over, roll it tight to seal and place it in the oven on a baking tray, or in a shallow roasting tin. Cook it for 25 minutes in a preheated medium-hot 180°C (350°F) mark 4 oven, switch off the oven, and leave it there to cool. In about one and a quarter hours you should have the most perfectly cooked salmon. This is the best and easiest way to cook fish. This cooking time is approximate for a 2–3 kilo (4½–6½ lb) fish.

An important aid to roasting in modern professional kitchens is the blow torch. It is fashionable and nutritious to leave meat pink and underdone and in many good restaurants the blow torch is now used to brown the skin. A few seconds of its intense heat will soon char the thin skin of a quail or a pigeon and improve the flavour. On the subject of skin, two vital characteristics should be pointed out. It is wise to remember that skin should be cooked thoroughly until it is crisp for it contains an overwhelming preponderance of germs and microbes and also has a high concentration of fat.

The salamander

Going back a little again to the general subject of grilling, I always have a very powerful salamander in my restaurant kitchens. This is rather like a domestic overhead grill but the sides are enclosed and the heat is more powerful. Professionals do not particularly associate this piece of equipment with grilling, but there is one exception. Over the course of many years I have very successfully grilled cubes of calves' liver, interspersed with bacon and bay leaves in a cast iron pan under the salamander. I baste the meat with clarified butter, lemon, red wine and port, then deglaze the pan with this mixture, reduce the juices and then roll the brochette around in the sauce until the liver is well covered. I find that the salamander is very effective for flashing (browning) crumbs of bread or brioche and finishing cream and egg sauces in gratin dishes.

I have repeatedly tried to 'grill' steaks in my salamander but I have never found the taste satisfactory. I have now come across a piece of equipment which is quite superb. It is a simple, electric grill with bars and a tray underneath which should be filled with water. The steam created by the water keeps the meat moist and the clarified butter and lemon and herbs with which I baste the meat drips into the hot water; the fumes created thus envelop the meat and impart to it a delicious aroma. This little grill has been a great revelation to me. It produces a stronger, truer charcoal flavour than any actual charcoal grill I have ever come across.

With the planning of my Battersea kitchen, and the restrictions which space placed on its design, I decided to invest a large sum of money in a cooker that had attached to it one of the most useful pieces of equipment I have encountered. The heavy, stainless steel griddle plaque which was located on one side of my Garland cooker was a revelation. I used it as a grill and as a source of heat for my very fast copper pans. I regularly use the griddle for fillet steaks, noisettes of lamb and beautiful côtelettes d'agneau. A little secret I have indulged myself in is to use truffles to decorate meat. I cut the truffles into thin slices, coat them with clarified butter and place the truffles on it for a few seconds on either side. The aroma from the truffle is incredible. Char broiling, or griddling, call it what you like, it was a great revelation. In his book *On Food and Cooking*, Harold McGee devotes considerable attention to this method of cooking and I was delighted to find no hint of disapproval in its use. There is no better, faster way of crisping the fat or skin covering a breast of duck than on the griddle. Because the surface of the griddle is so intensely hot, I only allow the flesh side of the duck breast to come briefly into contact with it, and only for just long enough to brown it. The rest of the cooking then takes place with the surface of the skin in contact with the surface of the griddle. The incredible concentration of heat that a griddle gives you, which a professional chef knows anyway from his solid-top cooker, provides a good way of cooking, searing and crisping all kinds of meats.

I never grill fish. I think probably the only time this sort of thing is a great success is when one is sitting in a taverna on a Greek island or in a slightly more fashionable seaside restaurant in St Maxime or St Tropez. The Greeks would probably offer you whole firm-fleshed fish such as trout or red mullet, grilled over charcoal with herbs and a squeeze of lemon and some olive oil. In France, correspondingly, you might be offered a small sea bass grilled whole over charcoal nestling in amongst fennel, finished off with Pernod and served with a beurre blanc. But grilling fish such as turbot or salmon over an open fire or on electric bars is not all that sensible. Fish contains less fat than red meat, and the precious little amount of juice and fat it does have is something to be preserved. It is more likely to be lost in grilling and the result would be a chewy and tasteless product. Very oily fish like sardines, basted extremely well, do taste sensational off the grill, but are very rarely encountered on restaurant menus.

Three particular ingredients lend themselves superbly to charcoal grilling. A beautifully marbled piece of Scotch beef is to me probably the most ideal ingredient for grilling because it is naturally so well lubricated that it will not dry out or lose its flavour. Lamb cutlets (and brochettes) and spatchcocked quails are also ideal candidates for grilling.

Avoiding totally the argument about whether you should salt before or after you grill, it might be as well to concentrate on basting a piece of meat thoroughly well with some pure groundnut oil and a little bit of butter, sprinkling it with dry Provençal herbs and grilling all sides of the meat, including the outer edges. Charcoal grilling and grilling generally, although ostensibly the easiest of cooking methods must be done properly. I do not like to marinate meat for too long. I simply smear it in oil and let it rest in a mixture of dried Provençal herbs for about 10 to 15 minutes. Whatever you are cooking, remember always to take it out of the refrigerator about an hour before you plan to cook it. Avoid turning the meat over too many times. Once you have placed a well oiled piece of beef on a very hot grill, have heard the first sizzle and seen the first puff of smoke as it hits the bars, you must leave it there. To mark it well with clear diamonds, lift the meat carefully with a pair of tongs and turn at an angle of 45 degrees; do the same on the other side and do not forget to cook the side of the meat as well. Always baste continuously with the herbs and oil. For the simplest and most delicious meal, squeeze some lemon juice on a plate, add 25 g (1 oz) of butter and 30 ml (2 tbsp) of demi-glace sauce (page 228). Chop some parsley and mix everything together on the plate. Put the plate in a hot oven, let everything melt together and when you have finished cooking your steak, let it rest on this plate. Add salt and pepper and pour over the cooking juices. Baste the steak with this liquid as it rests, for the next 10 or 15 minutes, then serve with some sauce béarnaise (page 236). I love to cook quails and lamb cutlets the same way.

I read with an incredible amount of pleasure, Harold McGee's explosion of the theory of 'The sealing of meat' (ie by browning the meat on all sides the essential juices are retained) in his book *On Food and Cooking*. I never, in fact, did give much credence to this theory. It was always much more important for me that the meat looked properly browned. If this so-called browning also served as a coat to preserve the juices, so much the better, but the primary reason why I did it was to brown the surface. I browned the meat more than sealed in the juices. Poor Escoffier! One of his theories has been scientifically and conclusively demolished.

I am not a great fan of the casserole or the stew, the *ragoût* or the *daube*. Occasionally in France I have enjoyed a *civet* made with wild boar and local wine or perhaps a really well-made *boeuf bourguignon*. I would never, however, cook this way whether at home or in the restaurant. These days at least the most popular form of stew is a curry and I leave that to the experts!

Frying

Frying is probably the most indispensable and the most widely used of all methods in French cuisine. I would like to mention in passing a particular method of dry frying salmon which I personally like very much. I sear one side of a flattened-out escalope of salmon in a very heavy pan and leave the other side entirely uncooked. The fish is then allowed to finish cooking in the pan for about 5 minutes, off the heat.

I do not care very much for deep frying, and have hardly ever used this method. In my early days in Dulwich, I did make some rather rustic, delicious, deep-fried garlic potatoes though to the best of my memory that was the only time I ever made use of the process. I do not entirely discount its use in the future.

Close relatives of frying are sautéing and braising or pot roasting. The cooking utensils to achieve these methods, and the temperature required to get the best results from each one, are all different. You must use a deep sided pot with a lid to pot roast a pheasant and it takes a long time at a low temperature.

This is a truly rustic dish for an informal occasion. I just cannot remember how I came across this dish. I cannot find a basis for it in any cookery book, so it must have come straight out of my head. While it is not the lightest of dishes, it is none the less quite delicious. The chances are that you will want to eat more than you ought to — beware, it is very rich. Aïoli is a mayonnaise heavily scented with garlic and although it may do your cholesterol count a lot of good, you may find it somewhat difficult to digest. These vegetables are at their best two days after they're made. Beyond the fifth or sixth day, they may begin to go sour. To stretch their life as much as possible, remove them to a clean, dry container each day.

To make this dish you will need a large, enamelled cast iron pan.

Les Legumes à l'Aïoli

Pickled Vegetables with Garlic Mayonnaise

SERVES 10

600 ml (1 pint) groundnut oil
300 ml ($\frac{1}{2}$ pint) dry white wine
150 ml ($\frac{1}{4}$ pint) white wine vinegar
sprig of fresh rosemary
2 bay leaves
sprig of fresh thyme
sprig of tarragon
15 ml (1 tbsp) sugar
15 ml (1 tbsp) black peppercorns
6 carrots, well scraped and cut into 4 cm ($1\frac{1}{2}$ inch) long × 0.5 cm ($\frac{1}{4}$ inch) square batons
1 small white cauliflower, divided up into little fleurettes

2 heads of broccoli, broken up into little fleurettes
6 very dark green courgettes, seeds removed, cut into batons the same size as the carrots
1 cucumber, seeds removed, the rest cut into batons the same size as the carrots and courgettes
1 each red, yellow and green pepper, seeded, quartered and cut into 1 cm ($\frac{1}{2}$ inch) strips
salt
Aïoli (page 238)

Over medium heat, in a large enamelled cast iron pan, simmer the oil, wine, vinegar, all the herbs, the sugar and the black peppercorns. Cook gently for 10 minutes and then skim.

Now cook the vegetables. First immerse the carrots and cook for 30 seconds. Then add, one at a time, the cauliflower, broccoli, courgettes, cucumber and lastly the peppers. Stir carefully to avoid breaking or smashing up the vegetables. Cook all the vegetables together for 1 minute. Season to taste with salt.

Remove from the heat, and with a slotted spoon, remove all the vegetables from the liquid. Place in a large glass bowl and pour the liquid over. Allow to cool. Cover and refrigerate for two days.

Serve on a large platter and pass the aïoli separately.

Serve with a robust red wine such as a burgundy or Rhône wine, or a fruity white such as Gewürztraminer.

This preparation of shallots is not really a garnish, nor is it a recipe. It is, however, a very vital ingredient in the making of my favourite brown sauces including the sauce in tournedos aux échalotes confites (page 98). Easy and relatively quick to make, it will keep well for a few days in a sealed plastic container in the refrigerator. This sauce also goes well with steamed sea bass.

Confiture d'Echalotes au Cassis et au Vin Rouge
Caramelised Diced Shallots in Cassis and Red Wine

MAKES ABOUT 150 ml ($\frac{1}{4}$ pint) 450 ml ($\frac{3}{4}$ pint) red wine
90 ml (6 tbsp) very finely chopped shallots 150 ml ($\frac{1}{4}$ pint) crème de cassis

Over medium heat in a small, uncovered saucepan, cook the shallots in the red wine and cassis very slowly until all the liquid has evaporated.

Making sauces

In French cuisine, you must have a *sauteuse* or a *sautoir* in which to fry quail, woodcook, chicken, a duck breast, a fillet of beef or a lamb cutlet. A heavy iron pan can be a substitute for the copper *sauteuse*.

Traditionally, the meat or bird is cooked and browned and then rested in a warm place while the sauce is finished in the pan in which it was cooked. The fat (usually clarified butter or groundnut oil) is discarded, the pan wiped and then deglazed with alcohol, a few spoonfuls of the relevant stock are added and reduced, thickened and then poured over the meat.

But I never favoured this method because it relied on the fact that you always had a bird of the same age, size, weight and fat content, that its temperature was always the same when you put it in the pan, that the temperature of the pan was always the same, that the clarified butter was always of the same clarity and that you deglazed the pan with cognac at the right temperature. In short, if you could manage always to do everything exactly the same from A–Z the results would be spectacular and I would be in favour of this method.

The ideal versus reality

But what happens in reality? The birds vary, each one is smaller or scrawnier or fatter than the last; or maybe you are not feeling particularly well that day, maybe it's now the end of the bottle of cognac rather than the beginning and by mistake you have put in a little extra butter to thicken the sauce – a million things can be done differently. Yet you use the correct method of cooking with different results every time! For this reason I have always concentrated on making a sauce separately, before the service, and bringing it to the point where I could finish it off under the most difficult circumstances, without any variations. In this way, I always achieve better results and total consistency. The sauces are clearer, shinier and have more flavour. It is this method that is the foundation of my reputation as a saucier. Recipes for some of my sauces, sweet and savoury, are to be found in chapter nine.

Steaming

Nowhere is the marriage of a good sauce to a good ingredient more clearly evident than with fish, and fish to me means steaming. Steaming allows you both to preserve the look and the colour of a fish and to concentrate the flavour. This is particularly important for the professional chef. If you poach, some of the flavour will inevitably be lost and some of the juices will flow into the poaching liquid. Apart from this loss of taste, there is also a loss of sparkle and shine. If you use the bouillon or *nage* to make the sauce, you might achieve a beautiful sauce, but it can never be consistent. But if I steam the fish (or cut it into thin fillets and cook it under the salamander or grill) and have a separate sauce ready, it is far easier to control its final taste and appearance. I steam escalopes of salmon with the skin on and remove it after it is cooked. This gives the salmon a very bright, fresh appearance, like a freshly skinned fish.

I prefer to use lemon sole for this dish. This is another fish which is often relegated to second class status, the main objection being its very soft flesh. It cooks very quickly and you must be careful not to overcook it. Dover sole is unquestionably a superior kind of fish, but in my opinion, the best ways to eat Dover sole are either meunière on the bone, meunière filleted, or baked in the oven with mushrooms and vermouth (page 72). I am quite certain that both types of sole taste a lot better on the bone, than off it. Perhaps this is the reason why after filleting, various stuffings are traditionally used in order to enhance the taste. This recipe calls for a lemon sole double filleted into 2 wide double fillets joined together. Sauce Langoustine (page 242) makes a good alternative to Beurre Blanc, and you can, if you wish, omit the pastry case garnish.

Paupiettes de Sole au Crabe

Paupiettes of Sole stuffed with Crab

Illustrated on page 65

FOR EACH SERVING
30 ml (2 tbsp) very fresh white crab meat
5 ml (1 tsp) very fine julienne of fresh
  ginger blanched in 150 ml ($\frac{1}{4}$ pint) water
  sweetened with 5 ml (1 tsp) sugar
90–120 ml (6–8 tbsp) clarified butter
  (page 241)
cayenne pepper
juice of $\frac{1}{2}$ lemon

one 350 g (12 oz) lemon sole, skinned and
  double filleted
1 garlic clove, finely chopped
$\frac{1}{2}$ shallot, finely diced
3 mushrooms, very finely diced
salt and pepper
7.5 cm (3 inch) puff pastry case (page 248)
90 ml (6 tbsp) Beurre Blanc (page 234)
chopped fresh chives

First prepare the crab meat: in a small stainless steel pan, lightly fry the ginger and the crab in a little clarified butter.

Sprinkle with cayenne pepper, a little lemon juice and set aside to cool.

Trim the sole fillets well and place a spoonful of the crab mixture in the centre of each one. Bring over both ends to meet in the middle and overlap slightly. Skin side should be on the outside.

In another pan fry the garlic and shallot in clarified butter until well cooked, then add the mushrooms, salt and pepper and a little lemon juice. Stir-fry quickly for a few seconds only.

Fill the little puff pastry case with this mixture and heat through well in the oven at 180°C (350°F) mark 4. This will take 3–4 minutes.

Pour some clarified butter over the sole fillets and place joint side down in a steamer (I use a couscoussière). Drizzle some clarified butter over, a little salt and a squeeze of lemon. Steam very carefully for 2–3 minutes, then rest the fish on absorbent kitchen paper until required, keeping them warm.

Place the hot puff pastry case in the middle of a warm plate. Arrange the 2 fillets of sole stuffed with crab on either side of the pastry case. Make sure there is no excess moisture on the fillets. Spoon the Beurre Blanc over the fillets and a little more on the plate. Sprinkle with freshly chopped chives and serve at once.

Serve with a full flavoured white such as a burgundy.

I have attempted without success to steam vegetables. I am afraid I do not like this method. The primary reason is that it requires a very short burst of an exceedingly high heat and steam to cook the vegetable through, without the loss of its colour.

If you overcook them, very dark green vegetables like beans and broccoli lose their character and their colour. The addition of soda or copper coins to preserve the colour is self-defeating. You may preserve the colour, but you smash up the vegetables, and copper contains poisons.

Boiling

Although I have experimented with new and exciting methods of cooking vegetables, I still find that for some, the best results come by cooking them using salted boiling water. When cooking green vegetables such as courgettes, French beans, mange-tout or broccoli, the first point to remember is that you must cook them in enormous quantities of water. There is really only one rule to remember when boiling vegetables

Large Amounts of Boiling Water Will Suffer a

Relatively Small Temperature Drop when the Vegetables are Added

If anybody wants to understand the principle of boiling vegetables they should read and re-read this sentence until it is firmly and clearly understood in their mind.

The more you trim your artichoke before boiling it, the less time it will take to cook, but if you start cutting and trimming too much in the beginning, unless you take precautions, the cut edges will turn black. Have some cold water acidulated with lemon juice ready to prevent any blackness developing. The cooking time will also vary depending on the size of the artichoke and how well you have trimmed it. Either way, you'll find it difficult to cook an artichoke in under 20 minutes, and a sure way of checking if it is done or not is by pulling off the leaves on the side as you go along. If they come off very easily, the artichoke is cooked. For this recipe, you cook it whole first, then remove the leaves and the choke from the centre and trim it round the sides. This recipe is a good way of using up any leftover Hollandaise.

Coeur d'Artichaut à la Duxelles de Champignons Sauce Hollandaise

Artichoke Heart with a Purée of Mushrooms and Hollandaise Sauce

SERVES 1

1 medium-sized artichoke
½ lemon
2.5 ml (½ tsp) salt
15 ml (1 tbsp) Sauce Hollandaise
for the duxelles
2.5 ml (½ tsp) very finely chopped shallots

4 button mushrooms, very finely chopped
25 g (1 oz) butter
pepper
2.5 ml (½ tsp) very finely chopped parsley

Cook the artichoke in a large pan full of boiling water to which you have added the ½ lemon and salt.

Meanwhile, make the mushroom *duxelles*. Fry the shallots and the finely chopped mushroom in butter until the vegetables are soft and their liquid has evaporated. Season with salt and pepper and add the parsley.

Drain the artichoke and allow to cool. Remove the leaves and the choke and trim the edges.

Fill the artichoke heart with the *duxelles*, cover with Hollandaise and glaze under a hot grill or salamander. Serve at once.

The practice of serving green vegetables very crisp and crunchy to conform with the so-called rules of *nouvelle cuisine* is a misconception. You really have to decide whether you are going to serve them raw or cooked. I like to boil beans, for example, well, leaving only a tiny amount of crunchiness. When I can turn a bean into the shape of an 's' without it springing back into a straight line, then I know it is correctly cooked.

The only beans which I like to serve in my restaurant are the very fine, extra thin green haricots verts from Kenya. Unfortunately, these days it is now common practice in many restaurants to serve plainly boiled hot beans as a vegetable. I personally prefer to serve them as a little garnish dressed with hazelnut oil and sprinkled with lemon and salt and very fine quantities of minutely chopped blanched shallots.

In recent years the influence of the East has been considerable and modern French cuisine has absorbed ideas from China, Japan and Thailand, in particular. An analysis of three basic processes are central to Chinese cooking: steaming (in many-layered Chinese steaming baskets), stir-frying (in a wok) and lastly boiling. When a Chinese chef boils a duck, he boils it for hours and hours and hours. Of all these methods, one of the most interesting is stir-frying. The thin metal wok is placed directly over the flame so that food in it cooks very fast, and instead of having the fried taste left in your mouth, stir-fried food reminds me, or brings to my palate a slight hint of smokiness, almost a char-grilled taste.

But the techniques of steaming and stir-frying vegetables brings with them the disadvantage that acids within the vegetables are retained rather than diluted. When you boil vegetables these acids are dispersed. With stir-frying the cooking process is very rapid, because the surface temperature of the wok is higher than the boiling temperature of the water and because the foods being stir-fried are always cut into small portions. I cook spinach by blanching it quickly in boiling salted water, draining it thoroughly and tossing it in garlic flavoured clarified butter spiked with lemon juice and seasoned with salt and pepper.

Cooking eggs

Soufflés are considered to be the ultimate egg dish. People are frightened of soufflés and ask what the trick is. There is no trick. It is simply the technique. Modern ovens give you the evenness of temperature which is essential. Simply make sure that the paper is fully around the mixture, that you have not overbeaten the eggs and finally run the knife between the mixture and sides of the ramekin. This will ensure that it will rise evenly.

For many years I was terrified of soufflés. So much drivel and nonsense about technique, the wrist, etc etc . . . has been talked about them. I also think that although a soufflé looks very attractive if it has risen evenly and looks very neat and trim, we should not be brainwashed into believing that this is necessarily how they must always look. If a soufflé is moist and well risen, and if it truly tastes of what it purports to be, then it doesn't matter one little bit if it looks like an untidy chef's toque.

Soufflé au Café et au Rhum

Coffee and Rum Soufflé

SERVES 2

10 ml (2 tsp) granulated coffee

60 ml (4 tbsp) rum

15 ml (1 tbsp) Crème Pâtissière (page 246)

3 egg whites

knob of butter, melted

15 ml (1 tbsp) caster sugar

15 ml (1 tbsp) icing sugar

Dissolve the coffee in 10 ml (2 tsp) of rum. Blend this well into the crème pâtissière.

Whip the egg whites by hand to a slightly loose consistency and fold into the crème pâtissière. Brush two medium ramekins with the butter and sprinkle with caster sugar.

Pour the soufflé mixture into the ramekins and run a clean spatula across the top to form an even surface. Run the point of a knife all along the edge, between the lip of the ramekin and the mixture. This helps the soufflé to rise and avoids sticking.

Cook for 15 minutes at 220°C (425°F) mark 7. Once out of the oven, sprinkle with the remaining rum and icing sugar.

Serve with a good dessert muscat such as Muscat de Beaumes de Venise.

This is probably one of the most famous soufflés of all time, deservedly so, in my opinion. The only other soufflés I like are coffee and rum and coconut.

Soufflé au Grand Marnier

Grand Marnier Soufflé

SERVES 2

15 ml (1 tbsp) Crème Pâtissière (page 246)

45 ml (3 tbsp) Grand Marnier

7.5 ml (½ tbsp) pure natural orange essence

3 egg whites

25 g (1 oz) butter, melted

15 ml (1 tbsp) caster sugar

15 ml (1 tbsp) icing sugar

Mix the crème pâtissière with the Grand Marnier and orange essence.

Whip the egg whites and gently fold into the Grand Marnier mixture.

Proceed as in the previous recipe, buttering and sugaring the ramekins, running the point of a knife round the edge and cooking in the oven at 220°C (425°F) mark 7 for 15 minutes. Sprinkle with icing sugar and a few drops of Grand Marnier.

Serve with a good dessert wine such as Sauternes.

Scrambled eggs

An enjoyable egg dish and a versatile one is scrambled egg. I use neither cream nor milk, simply season them and beat the eggs, perhaps with the addition of some pieces of asparagus or mushrooms. Scrambled eggs with truffles is a luxurious dish where the eggs will benefit from the addition of a little single cream.

New technology

The last 15 years have seen the arrival, acceptance and wide use of certain key items of machinery. The impact of these products on modern cooking has been very important. In the very early Seventies the Robot Coupe arrived. This professional version of the domestic Magimix merely made the blender a little more practical and easier to use, as well as expanding the use and application it could be put to. The great advantage of the Robot Coupe is that it made mousselines easy. Its introduction coincided with *nouvelle cuisine* and the proliferation of the *coulis* and hot and cold mousses.

Sorbetières

Another brilliant modern tool, though a very expensive one, is the *sorbetière*. This enables the professional chef to create a range of ice creams and fruit sorbets very easily and very quickly. The consistency which some of the modern equipment can achieve is truly spectacular. All my ice creams and sorbets are made in *sorbetières*. These are now also available in domestic sizes and are certainly worth the investment if you eat lots of ice creams. No other method achieves quite the same perfect result. I often serve them with a mixture of fresh fruits (*panaché de fruits frais*).

It is never easy to give exact times when it comes to beating and churning. So much depends on the individual machine, on the quality of the fruit, the temperature at which the liquids are set to freeze. And it also depends on personal preference when it comes to the ideal consistency. Some people like sorbets slightly runny, some like them firm. It is not possible, therefore, to say that you *must* leave a wild strawberry sorbet for 11 minutes in the machine, or that you *should* allow 15 minutes for a vanilla ice cream. Basically all ice creams and sorbets take between 10 and 20 minutes.

Here are a few guidelines for dealing with fruits of any description when making ice creams and sorbets:

o   Never use carbon knives to cut fruit. The acid in the fruit reacts with the metal and produces a nasty metallic taste which will taint the fruit. Use only stainless steel knives or silver spoons.

o   For the same reason do not use tin sieves.

o   The acid varies between fruits – some, such as grapefruit, have a high acid content while others, such as strawberries, less so. The acidity of the fruit will affect the quantity of sugar syrup and therefore freezing times and consistency. As a general rule, the higher the acid content, the more sugar you need.

o   Your sorbet will only be as good as the fruit that has gone into it.

o   A squeeze of lemon always accentuates the flavour of the fruit.

o   Three things retard the rapid freezing of sorbets: alcohol, high sugar content and very high acidity.

o   Never use egg whites. You can achieve very fluffy sorbets without them. I find they neutralise the taste of the fruit.

Here is the basic recipe for making sugar syrup, which is used in all my sorbets.

Sirop

·

Sugar Syrup

MAKES 600 ml (1 pint)   600 ml (1 pint) water
225 g (8 oz) granulated sugar

Dissolve the sugar in 300 ml ($\frac{1}{2}$ pint) of water. Bring to the boil for 1 minute. Remove from the heat, then add another 300 ml ($\frac{1}{2}$ pint) of water. Allow to cool.

Sorbets

The beauty of a sorbet is in its taste and texture, and I find that very sweet dessert wines go well with these. Here are recipes for seven of my favourites to illustrate the point. In the following chapter, when we deal with the subject of presentation, I shall include some more. We love to serve them in a *tulipe* (page 165), often with assorted fresh fruits and dressed with lime syrup (see photograph on page 209).

As with all sorbets, the secret here is in the quality of the fruit. The pineapple should be just ripe, not overripe or beginning to turn black. For me, a sorbet is a wonderful way of eating pineapple, while at the same time preserving the spirit of one of the great marriages – pineapple and kirsch.

Sorbet à l'Ananas et au Kirsch

·

Pineapple and Kirsch Sorbet

Illustrated on page 209

SERVES 8   600 ml (1 pint) cold sugar syrup (above)
1 large pineapple   150 ml ($\frac{1}{4}$ pint) kirsch

With a sharp knife, cut off the skin of the pineapple, taking care to cut it all off. Slice the pineapple lengthwise into 4 and cut out the hard central core. Slice the pineapple into thin pieces and put in the blender with the sugar syrup.

Blend thoroughly and pass through a *chinois* or stainless steel sieve into a bowl.

Place the liquidised pulp in the sorbetière and freeze for about 10 minutes. Halfway through, add the kirsch and continue to freeze until the sorbet is soft and glossy. Do not allow it to become over-beaten or grainy.

The aroma of wild strawberries is so pungent, yet so delicate at the same time, it is as if someone sprayed them with an aromatiser just before they were picked. Nature, however, has balanced matters by making wild strawberries so fragile it is difficult to keep them for any length of time. This is why sorbets were invented! When your wild strawberries are suddenly beginning to lose their freshness, don't panic, because you can convert them into a most delicious sorbet.

Sorbet aux Fraises des Bois
Wild Strawberry Sorbet

SERVES 8

700 g (1½ lb) wild strawberries
600 ml (1 pint) cold sugar syrup (opposite
    page)
juice of 1 lemon

Mash the strawberries in a blender and strain through a *chinois* or conical stainless steel sieve. Make sure you leave behind all the tiny pips. You may have to strain this through a tammy-cloth.

Mix in the syrup and put the mixture in the sorbetière. Freeze for 10–15 minutes. Halfway through, add the lemon juice and taste.

On the one occasion when I was lucky enough to find the most perfectly sweet and perfumed fresh lychees, I made the single best sorbet I have ever tasted in all of my life. Since that day, I have never again found the good enough quality fruit necessary to achieve the same result. There is, however, one reliable way of coming as close as possible to a very good lychee sorbet every time and that is to use tinned fruit.

Sorbet aux Lichees
Lychee Sorbet

SERVES 2–4

450 g (1 lb) tinned lychees (stoned), with
    their syrup
juice of ½ a lemon, strained.

Put the tinned lychees and their syrup into the bowl of a blender and purée well.

Strain through a *chinois* or conical stainless steel sieve and add the strained lemon juice. Place in the sorbetière and freeze for 10–12 minutes.

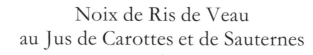

Noix de Ris de Veau
au Jus de Carottes et de Sauternes

Veal Sweetbreads on a Bed of Carrots and Sauternes Sauce

Following the premise that one of the greatest marriages in French cuisine is carrots and sweetbreads, I decided to make a special carrot sauce to go with simply cooked sweetbreads. The flavour and aroma of the sweet wine are brought out by the carrots, and wedges of lemon balance any sweetness. The sweetbreads are presented here on a bed of spinach and accompanied by vegetables of complementary colours: simply cooked carrots and asparagus in a tartelette with Hollandaise sauce and a little portion of gratin dauphinois.

RECIPE ON PAGE 171

Caille Rôtie au Madère
et Sa Galette de Pommes de Terre

Roast Quail with Madeira Sauce
and Shredded Crisp Potato Cake

This is a relatively new invention of mine, a variation on the quail salad with mushroom butter sauce recipe. It is a supremely pretty dish, the colour of the diced red pepper garnish contrasting sharply with the slices of jet-black truffles. The richness of the wild mushroom sauce is balanced by the bed of sweet and sour red cabbage and the potato galette.

RECIPES ON PAGES 108 AND 186

Unfortunately this sorbet has become a cliché of *nouvelle cuisine*. Passion fruit sorbets are everywhere and yet when you choose one, it rarely comes up to your expectations. Look out for passion fruits from Kenya. They should be a deep purple and beginning to shrivel and wither.

Sorbet aux Fruits de la Passion

Passion Fruit Sorbet

Illustrated on page 209

SERVES 8
30 passion fruits

600 ml (1 pint) cold sugar syrup (page 158)
juice of ½ lemon

Cut your passion fruits in half on a plastic tray or over a bowl so you catch all the juices.

With a stainless steel or silver spoon, scoop out not only the pips and the yellow membrane round the pip, but also the little purple bits inside the fruit. This is very important for colour. Make sure you catch all the juices and tip the juices, pips, yellow membrane and the small purple bits into the blender.

Pour over the sugar syrup and blend thoroughly to reduce the pips to pulp. Strain through a *chinois* or conical stainless steel sieve, pressing hard to squeeze out all the liquid. Turn into sorbetière, add a squeeze of lemon, and freeze for 10–15 minutes.

We came across this extraordinary sorbet for the first time at Vergé's Moulin de Mougins near Cannes. We liked it so much that I determined to make it and to serve it, either between courses in an elaborate gastronomic menu, or indeed as the finale to a rather rich meal.

Sorbet aux Pamplemousses Roses

Pink Grapefruit Sorbet

SERVES 8
4 pink grapefruits
600 ml (1 pint) sugar syrup (page 158)
juice of ½ lemon

50 ml (2 fl oz) or one liqueurglass of ice-cold Noilly Prat or very dry French Vermouth
fresh mint

Cut the grapefruits in half with a stainless steel knife and squeeze out every ounce of juice over a stainless steel strainer. Make sure you extract all the juice.

Add the juice to the sugar syrup. Mix in the lemon juice and pass all the liquid through a tammy-cloth or fine sieve.

Pour the mixture into the sorbetière and freeze for about 10–15 minutes.

Serve in large individual wine glasses with the ice-cold vermouth poured over the top and decorate with fresh mint.

Melon must be the most cantankerous fruit available to man. Too much melon is a bad thing for the digestive system – in ancient Greece this fruit had the dubious reputation of being believed to be poisonous. Although melon is one of my favourite fruits, it can also be one of the most disappointing. No amount of sniffing, pressing or weighing will cause it to surrender its secret; you never know whether you are buying a round cucumber, or a fragrant, delicious fruit. The biggest culprits are melons from France, from the Charentes and Cavaillon. When good, they are sensational. Even the Ogen is very much a hit-or-miss proposition. In my experience I have found the Galia melon from Israel the most consistently reliable. Having said all this, the best melon sorbets I have ever made were with Ogens.

Sorbet au Melon
·
Melon Sorbet

SERVES 8
1 large, fleshy, heavy, aromatic Ogen
   melon, halved and deseeded

600 ml (1 pint) cold sugar syrup
   (page 158)
juice of 1 lemon

With a silver or stainless steel spoon, scoop out the flesh from the melon into a bowl. Get as close to the skin as possible to reach the darker green flesh which is located underneath the skin.

Place contents in the bowl of a blender, pour over the syrup and blend.

Pass through a *chinois* or conical stainless steel sieve and add the juice of ½ a lemon. Taste the mixture, and add more lemon juice if you think it needs it.

Freeze in a sorbetière for 10–15 minutes.

I have never found it necessary to use fresh blackcurrants for this classic and very delicious sorbet. Instead, I use frozen berries, which are readily available throughout the year. Apart from anything else, the colour of blackcurrants is very intense. If you want to make this a very special dish you could pour a little champagne over the sorbet just before serving – like a frozen kir royale!

Sorbet au Cassis
·
Blackcurrant Sorbet
Illustrated on page 209

SERVES 8
1 kilo (2.2 lb) fresh or frozen
   blackcurrants

600 ml (1 pint) cold sugar syrup (page 158)
150 ml (¼ pint) crème de cassis
juice of ½ lemon

Place the blackcurrants in a blender. Pour over the sugar syrup, blend thoroughly and strain through a *chinois* or conical stainless steel sieve.

Stir well and add the crème de cassis and the lemon juice.

Turn into a sorbetière and freeze for 10–15 minutes.

This has been an old faithful dessert on our menus for many years. When I got fed up with making it, there was an enormous outcry and customer after customer asked for its reinstatement. There is no doubt that the iced armagnac taste with a vanilla-flavoured chestnut purée is another of those marriages ordained by nature.

Parfait a l'Armagnac aux Marrons Glacés
Armagnac-flavoured Ice Cream with Chestnut Purée

SERVES 10

9 egg yolks

hot sugar syrup made from 200 g (7 oz) sugar and 300 ml (½ pint) water flavoured with a split vanilla pod, reduced to a thickish syrup

75 ml (3 fl oz) armagnac

450 ml (¾ pint) double cream

1 × 200 g (7 oz) can of vanilla-flavoured chestnut purée

10 whole marrons glacés in vanilla syrup

Put the egg yolks in the bowl of a mixer or blender. Mix at ¾ speed and dribble the very hot syrup over the eggs as they are beating. The contents should swell and reach the top of the mixing bowl. Allow to cool.

Stir the armagnac into the double cream and whip it until it is almost as thick as crème Chantilly. Set aside.

When the egg and syrup mixture has cooled, fold the whipped cream into it and mix well.

Have ten 200 ml (7 fl oz) plastic cups to hand. Spoon the parfait mixture into the cups, tap a little, fill to the top and place in the freezer.

The next day, unmould the parfaits and put a tablespoonful of chestnut purée on each individual parfait. Place a glistening, syrupy, whole marron glacé on the top of each one. If you have any purée left over, form little quenelles of purée and serve with 2 spoons.

The colour and flavour of this ice cream can be rather elusive. You have to, therefore, make certain that you obtain very dark green pistachios, and that you use enough of them to produce the real flavour. A good pistachio ice cream is a perfect partner to a chocolate marquise.

Glace aux Pistaches
Pistachio Ice Cream

SERVES 8

1 recipe Glace à la Vanille (page 57)

800 g (1¾ lb) pistachios, shelled, skinned and chopped

Blend the ice cream with the chopped pistachios. Mix them together well and freeze again for a few minutes in the sorbetière.

I often like to present my ice creams or a selection of sorbets (*panaché de sorbets*) or fresh fruits (*fruits frais assortis*) in *tulipes* – little home-made biscuit baskets, often accompanied by Lime Syrup (page 244).

Almost the same mixture, shaped in a different way, is used to make *tuiles*, below, curled biscuits which also go well with fresh fruits, ice creams or sorbets and are irresistible! You must work *very quickly* when they come out of the oven hot because unless you shape them immediately they will quickly harden and become unmanageable. So, get all your remekins or wooden spoons ready in advance.

Tulipes
Plain Biscuit Baskets

MAKES ABOUT 25

100 g (4 oz) butter, softened
225 g (8 oz) plain flour

225 g (8 oz) sugar
7 egg whites

Cream the butter, then add the flour, sugar and egg whites and beat together thoroughly until smooth.

Spread out in teaspoonsful on a greased baking sheet and bake in a 190°C (375°F) mark 5 oven until golden brown – 5–6 minutes. Have ready a good number of ramekins which stack into each other.

When the biscuits are ready, quickly remove each one with a palette knife and put it in a ramekin dish, gently pressing it into shape. Place another ramekin on top and set aside. Repeat with the remaining biscuits. When cool, remove them from the ramekins.

Tuiles aux Amandes
Almond Tiles

MAKES ABOUT 25

50 g (2 oz) butter
50 g (2 oz) plain flour
350 g (12 oz) sugar

7 egg whites
350 g (12 oz) almonds, skinned and finely sliced

Cream the butter, then add the flour, sugar and egg whites and beat together thoroughly until smooth. Then add the chopped almonds and mix well.

Spread out in teaspoonsful on a greased baking sheet and bake in the oven at 190°C (375°F) mark 5 until golden brown – 5–6 minutes. Have ready some wooden spoons with medium-thick handles.

When the biscuits are ready, quickly remove each one, shape them by winding them around the handle and allow to cool.

This praline ice cream is an outright sensation. It is not very difficult to make, yet it is very rare to find one which has the true taste of burnt sugar and crispy almonds. The process of making a caramel is very tricky and sometimes dangerous. Exercise extreme care to avoid burning yourself. Once beyond a certain temperature when sugar begins to caramelise, it retains heat and keeps on cooking. It is important, therefore, to make your caramel in a copper sugar pan, because this way the temperature is more controllable.

Glace Pralinée
Praline Ice Cream

SERVES 8

1 recipe Glace à la Vanille (page 57)
200 g (7 oz) sugar

450 g (1 lb) flaked almonds, toasted until just golden

Put the vanilla ice cream in the refrigerator.

In a very heavy, cast iron pan, or better still, a copper sugar pan, melt the sugar with 60 ml (4 tbsp) of water and proceed to caramelise over a high heat.

Prepare a large piece of double thickness foil (about 30.5 cm (12 inches) wide and 45.5 cm (18 inches) long); spread it out.

Mix the almonds into the caramel just before you take it off the heat.

Pour the almond caramel mixture onto the foil and spread. Allow to cool.

When it has set completely, break it into large chunks in a pestle and mortar and reduce these to tiny cubes.

Spoon the vanilla ice cream into the sorbetière and freeze for about 12–13 minutes. Add the crushed praline and freeze for a further minute. If you prefer a less crunchy texture, put the crushed praline into the sorbetière before you start freezing.

This ice cream must rank as one of the most sensuous tastes I have encountered. I did not invent it. I owe its existence to Frédy Giradet and am dying to taste it one day at his restaurant at Crissier near Lausanne. My own customers who eat it never do so without comment. The colour is a deep, dark beige and sprinkled with freshly roasted crisp almonds, it is sublime.

Glace au Caramel
Caramel Ice Cream

SERVES 8

250 g (9 oz) sugar
1 vanilla pod, split in half

200 ml (7 fl oz) double cream
12 egg yolks
300 ml (½ pint) milk

In a heavy, cast iron pan or a copper sugar pan, placed over low heat, make a liquid caramel from the sugar and the vanilla pod. Take great care when the sugar begins to colour and stir continuously over a consistent heat.

The colour should be a deep golden brown. Remove the pan from the heat and stir in the double cream. Be careful of the explosions of fierce bubbles. Keep stirring until the cream and the caramel are thoroughly blended. You may have to return the pan to the heat.

Beat the egg yolks. Bring the milk to the boil and pour it over the yolks, stirring well without cooking the eggs.

Pour the milk and eggs into the caramel. Return to the heat and bring to just below boiling point; do not allow to boil or the mixture will curdle. Remove from the heat and discard the vanilla pod. Leave to cool and then place in the sorbetière. Freeze for about 15 minutes.

Sous-vide

As I have said earlier, new technology is influencing both style and content of food. Over the last two or three years, because the Roux brothers have been in the midst of it, the method of *sous-vide* has become very prominent. From an initial concept as a means of vacuum packing and as a means of preserving the life of a fillet steak, or a fillet of fish, it has developed to a fully fledged cooking process where a completely cooked dish with its sauce and its vegetables is vacuum packed as a portion, and is reheated to be served on a plate in a restaurant some time later. However persuasive the arguments in its favour, I personally do not approve of the use of *sous-vide* in restaurants, or in special restaurants set up to provide only this kind of food.

I prefer to stick to classic principles. This way, you will enjoy a perfect piece of steamed fish, the aroma of roasting meat, the flavour of a perfectly grilled game bird, well cooked vegetables tasting of themselves. New inventions should be complementary rather than short cuts to the true methods of cooking.

'*I cannot easily be led
away from a deeply felt conviction that cooking
is a science. Once you have fought skirmishes
with the liquids and the solids, battles with
the temperatures and the textures,
once you have won the war, there remains
the armistice and a short journey
into the realms of fine art.
First you conquer the science
of cooking then you present
the food in an art form.
Art begins where science ends.*'

CHAPTER SIX

Presentation

he look of food is of paramount importance and the constant task of any great chef is to avoid fussy presentation, to achieve simplicity, with restraint, to create a controlled composition that is uncluttered, sharp, clear and defined in appearance as well as taste. I have always been aware that the first sight people have of the plate and the food on it goes a long way towards influencing them and their appreciation of the food. To me it has been obvious all along that the chef must arrange the food on the plate as he wishes to see it presented to the customer. It was not always so: the waiter's involvement in the presentation of food has a long and undistinguished history.

In 1984, Egon Ronay awarded us his 'gold plate' award as Restaurant of the Year. For the announcement of the award he had devised a celebratory meal and invited four chefs and their teams to cook a four-course meal. Each chef and his team had to cook for 30 people, making a total audience of 120. One of the dishes the Chez Nico team planned to prepare was a boned duck breast, its skin made crisp by the application of honey, coarse salt and crushed black peppercorns. It was a simple dish and there was not much danger in its presentation. All the chefs, however, were extremely nervous about the way their sauced food would be carried from the kitchens of the hotel to the banqueting room. An army of waiters was specially commandeered each year to attend to this ritual. At one point an ageing continental waiter picked up one of my plates of duck and held it carelessly at an angle of 45 degrees. The sauce went all over the rim of the plate and nearly tumbled over the side. I saw red and gave the waiter a piece of my mind. His reply was typical: 'Young man, I have been in this business for 40 years and you cannot teach me a thing.'

The demise of the waiter

Inherent in this episode and its ramifications is the crucial difference made by the modern revolution, which occurred in both the kitchen and the service of food with the arrival of *nouvelle cuisine*. A stupid waiter like that is now no longer permitted to spoil the work of a chef. In the past, according to classical convention, the main courses were served to the customer by the waiter in silver dishes. This meant that the chef finished his work when the food was dished out in the kitchen on to the silver tray or copper pan. The sauce was poured on top and the garnish arranged on the side. The waiter then took it all the way into the dining room, placed it by the side of the table, took a warm plate, cleaned it and deposited it on the side. Lifting a fork and spoon, he would thus begin to destroy the careful way in which the chef arranged his work. Waiters usually transferred the contents in a haphazard way, messed up the side of the plate, wiped it off with a napkin and left long, lingering, greasy marks to tell the tale.

The emancipation of the chef

Imagine what severe rethinking had to take place to stop this vandalism. Apart from anything else, restaurant managers, head waiters, senior waiters all looked towards the chef with the same disdain as the public. *Nouvelle cuisine*, if it didn't do very much else, did at least emancipate the chef, and it raised him to an elevated position above that of waiters and head waiters. The chef became a star. And what does a star do? He performs. The chef began to perform. The public was his audience. His character and his signature were there on the plate. The chef now began to arrange and present the food directly on the plate in the kitchen. The waiter merely carried the plate to the customers. This was the first major change which many people associated with the coming of *nouvelle cuisine*. The chef had become an artist.

When I first began to cook, I had not had to endure the old careless methods of serving food, the sloppy wiping of the side of the plate. Instinctively, the colour of the plate which appealed to me was pure, pristine white. It was a sparkling canvas against which shiny sauces, deep colours and beautiful arrangements could best be shown off. From a very early stage, therefore, I became a devotee of the white plate. I had grasped the principles, but sought to improve my presentation further.

The plate, now seen as an artist's canvas, became important, and the constant search for ever more stunning, bigger better plates that held their temperature longer were in demand. Colour, arrangement, garnishes and saucing, slicing and fanning all became of prime importance and it was in the presentation of food that some of the staggering new talent began to manifest itself. Food as art had arrived.

This dish is a combination of classical with modern, imaginative cuisine. The constant search for new tastes, new flavours and vivid colours has brought us carrot sauce. I have found that when you combine carrots with Sauternes, you get a lovely perfume. Carrots have traditionally been natural partners with sweetbreads and one of the best ever sweetbread dishes I have eaten was thin escalopes of sweetbread on a bed of caramelised carrots. A quick variation on that theme would be to caramelise some carrot strips and serve the sweetbreads on the top. You will need to begin this two days before you plan to serve it.

Noix de Ris de Veau
au jus de Carottes et de Sauternes

Veal Sweetbreads on a Bed of Carrot and Sauternes Sauce

Illustrated on page 160

SERVES 2

2 perfectly rounded, very white
   sweetbreads from the pancreas
900 ml (1½ pints) aromatic bouillon,
   flavoured with carrots, onions, shallots,
   bay leaf, thyme, peppercorns, 1 lemon
   slice, 45 ml (3 tbsp) vinegar
120 ml (8 tbsp) clarified butter (page 241)

salt and pepper
150 ml (¼ pint) Demi-Glace (page 228)
45 ml (3 tbsp) Madeira
10 ml (2 tsp) truffle juice
300 ml (½ pint) Jus de Carottes (page 241)
30 ml (2 tbsp) pine kernels, fried in butter
   and lightly salted

Soak the sweetbreads overnight in salted water. Next day, drain well and poach in the aromatic bouillon for 35 minutes. Remove, press down with a heavy weight and leave overnight again in the refrigerator.

Trim off any bits of fat, sinews, membrane and veins from around the sweetbreads.

In a heavy cast iron pan, heat the clarified butter until it sizzles, add the sweetbreads and fry for about 10 minutes until crisp on all sides. Season and set aside.

In a small pan, reduce the demi-glace with the Madeira to a syrupy consistency and add the truffle juice. Coat the sweetbreads with this mixture.

Dress 2 warm plates with the carrot sauce and place the sweetbreads in the centre. Sprinkle with salted, buttered pine kernels and serve at once.

Serve with a rich red wine such as a Côte Rôtie from the Rhône.

The way in which I perceived traditional classical French cuisine was that the chef cooked his piece of fish or meat, placed it in the serving dish, made his sauce, poured it over and added two or three important garnishes. He then either sent a main vegetable to accompany it, or arranged them all around the dish, or just piled them in a corner. In later years, restaurants started to send vegetables on side plates to accompany the main dish. Rather than engage in the cooking, the presentation and arrangement of the garnishes and the vegetables separately, I thought it would be a wonderful idea if I could combine the three and send one whole dish complete in its entirety.

There has always been an interminable debate in my mind which I have extended to the members of my kitchen. How do you present quails? Do you bone and then stuff them? Do you roast them plain? Do you just cook the breasts? Or do you present them whole, on the bone and stuffed with a lovely farce? If you ever wish to resolve this argument, the smell alone will give you the answer. If just one person is eating these quails and they are tucked away in a corner of the restaurant, the whole dining room is enveloped in the heavenly, elusive aroma. This is a recipe which, along with half a dozen others, is one of the most evocative dishes I have ever placed before my customers. When I once took it off the menu, the demand for its reinstatement was so loud, I had to put it back.

Les Cailles Farcies au Fumet de Truffes

Stuffed Quails with a Brown Truffle Sauce

Illustrated on page 96

SERVES 2

4 plump quails, gutted and cleaned
30 ml (2 tbsp) clarified butter (page 241)
for the stuffing:
1 slice ordinary white bread, edges
  trimmed
90 ml (6 tbsp) milk
150 g (5 oz) cleaned chicken livers,
  sinews, membranes and bile removed
2 whole eggs
15 ml (1 tbsp) chopped parsley
1 crushed clove garlic
5 ml (1 tsp) green peppercorns
2.5 ml (½ tsp) ground allspice
4 crushed juniper berries
90 ml (6 tbsp) cognac

salt and pepper
1 rasher bacon, very, very finely chopped
90 ml (6 tbsp) double cream
15 ml (1 tbsp) pine kernels, roasted
for the sauce:
150 ml (¼ pint) Demi-Glace (page 228)
25 ml (1½ tbsp) cognac
15 ml (1 tbsp) diced truffle peelings
30 ml (2 tbsp) truffle juice
squeeze of lemon
25 g (1 oz) butter
salt and pepper
4 thick round croûtons of brioche cut out
  from the centre with a pastry cutter,
  toasted

172

Prepare your stuffing. Soak the slice of bread in the milk and squeeze dry. Blend the bread and all the remaining ingredients for the stuffing to make a smooth, soft mixture.

Season the cavities of the quails. Stuff the birds with the mousse. Paint the quails with the clarified butter and roast at 180°C (350°F) mark 4 for 20 minutes. At this point, to finish them off, a good restaurant kitchen would have a blow torch. Brown them all over with the blow torch, set aside and keep warm. In a domestic kitchen, the alternative would be to flash them under a very hot grill.

Make the sauce. In a heavy, stainless steel pan over medium heat, reduce the demi-glace and the cognac to a syrupy consistency.

Add the diced truffles, cook a little more, sprinkle in the truffle juice and a few drops of lemon juice, then thicken with a knob of butter.

Season well with salt and pepper.

Place 2 croûtons on each plate and settle the quails on top. Pour the sauce carefully over the quails and serve with a rich red claret such as Ch. Les Ormes de Pez.

Foie gras

At the age of 37 I neither knew what goose liver was nor had any inkling of how geese and ducks are fattened. My financial investment in learning about foie gras must have added up to a few thousand pounds. At first, I used to buy the livers and not know what to do with them. I ruined an awful lot of goose and duck livers and spent many sleepless nights pondering over the buttery mass wondering where I had gone wrong.

Gradually, however, the Prince of Ingredients surrendered its secrets as I read and read and reread all the information I could gather. It was some years before I plucked up enough courage to put goose liver on my menu. Nowadays, more often than not, we use duck livers in our dishes. Remember to keep any buttery juices left over in the pan when you've cooked foie gras. They add a wonderful flavour to pâtés and terrines.

There is absolutely no question that foie gras and truffles are my favourite luxury ingredients.

This is the most popular, and one of the most attractive, of all our starters. The secret of this recipe is to use the right frying pan at the right temperature when you cook the foie gras. The aim is to char and brown the surface of the goose liver all over and to leave the inside nice and pink and soft. Have all the ingredients assembled and ready before you begin, because the frying part takes only a few seconds. This is a mouth-watering dish and one which has attracted a considerable amount of attention over the years. It is nearly impossible to make successfully at home.

Assiette Savoreuse

Hot Foie Gras with Caramelised Oranges on Toasted Brioche

Illustrated on page 145

SERVES 2

30 ml (2 tbsp) brown sugar

60 ml (4 tbsp) clarified butter (page 241)

6 orange segments, pith removed

200 ml (7 fl oz) Fond de Veau (page 227)

30 ml (2 tbsp) cognac

25 g (1 oz) good butter

15 ml (1 tbsp) hazelnut oil

salt

4 small lamb's lettuce leaves

2 oak leaf lettuce leaves

2 slices of brioche

2 slices of fresh foie gras each 1 cm ($\frac{1}{2}$ inch) thick and weighing about 100–150 g (4–5 oz) each

Preheat the grill so that it is very hot. Melt the brown sugar in the clarified butter and brush the orange segments. Caramelise under the grill for 20 seconds and keep warm. Do not cook them through or they will fall to pieces. Set aside.

Over a high heat, rapidly reduce the veal stock until you have a tablespoon left. Add the cognac and a knob of butter and simmer until the sauce is thick. Remove from the heat and keep warm.

Pour the hazelnut oil and the salt in an empty bowl and brush the bowl with the lamb's lettuce leaves. Do the same with the oak leaf lettuce leaves. Arrange the lightly oiled leaves decoratively on one side of each of 2 serving plates.

Toast the slices of brioche and place one slice on each plate, on the opposite side to the salad leaves.

Heat a cast iron frying pan to a very high temperature – the pan must be very hot. Put the slices of foie gras in the pan, without any fat. Turn over with a palette knife after 15 seconds. Leave to cook for another 15 seconds and season lightly with salt.

Place the foie gras on top of the brioche and arrange the caramelised oranges on top. Pour over the sauce. Serve with a Sauternes or other good-quality white dessert wine.

There is one vital thing to remember about foie gras. Because the liver is full of fat, if left in the fridge, it solidifies and becomes hard. If left in an ambient temperature in the kitchen, it will be too soft and floppy to handle. Remove, therefore, the liver from the refrigerator and leave it in room temperature for no more than $\frac{1}{2}$ to 1 hour before you intend to begin preparing this dish.

By the time you finish your process of deveining the liver, scraping off the membrane and removing the dark green bile located at the tip between the two lobes, your liver should be soft and supple. If it begins to get too soft, put it back in the refrigerator to firm up.

To make this dish you will need a 1.4 litre ($2\frac{1}{2}$ pint) enamelled cast iron terrine with a lid, and plenty of time. Ideally, the finished dish should be left to mature for 2–3 days in the refrigerator before eating.

Terrine de Foie Gras avec sa Gelée au Sauternes

Terrine of Duck or Goose Liver with Sauternes Jelly

SERVES 15

90 ml (6 tbsp) white port
90 ml (6 tbsp) fine cognac
30 ml (2 tbsp) Madeira
120 ml (8 tbsp) dessert wine such as
  Sauternes or Barsac
very fine sea salt
caster sugar

15 ml (1 tbsp) finely ground white pepper
1.25 ml ($\frac{1}{4}$ tsp) quatre épices (cinnamon,
  clove, Jamaica allspice, pepper)
2 fresh duck livers, weighing about 350 g
  (12 oz) each
clarified butter (page 241)
500 ml (16 fl oz) Gelée au Sauternes
  (page 230)

Mix together the port, cognac, Madeira and wine and stir in 30 ml (2 tbsp) salt, 15 ml (1 tbsp) sugar, the pepper and the quatre épices. Stir well together, and try to dissolve as much of the ingredients as possible. Leave in the refrigerator for 2 hours.

Line a sieve with 3 or 4 layers of wet muslin and strain the liquid through. This way you eliminate the black specks of the pepper and the quatre épices, while still retaining the flavours.

Prepare the liver. Force open the 2 lobes which make up the liver. With a small, very sharp knife, scrape off the fine membrane which covers the entire liver. Next follow the bloody veins and sinews down the centre of the lobe and the various forks off it. Remove all these veins. This is a laborious process, but very necessary. In order to get to all the veins, you will probably require to slice open the thicker of the 2 lobes.

When you have cleaned the liver, arrange the slices and lobes on a big tray side by side. Sprinkle over the strained liquid and keep on basting and turning over from time to time. Leave in the refrigerator for 30 minutes.

Meanwhile have a bain-marie (water bath) ready which is large enough to take your terrine containing 5 cm (2 inches) of water. Brush the inside of the terrine all over with clarified butter. Begin to arrange your pieces of liver and press down with your fingers and the back of a spoon to flatten out slightly. Sprinkle small quantities of the marinade between the layers and add a pinch of salt and a pinch of sugar as you go along. Pack to the top, sprinkle a little more liquid and a pinch of salt and sugar and cover with kitchen foil. Settle the terrine into the bain-marie, cover with the lid and cook in a 200°C (400°F) mark 6 oven for 15 minutes.

Remove from the oven, lift out of the bain-marie. Place it on a heatproof tray, take off the lid and let it cool for 40 minutes. A thin film of beautiful golden yellow fat will have formed on the top of the terrine.

Loosely cover the terrine with cling film and place a flat piece of wood on the top which evenly covers the surface. Add a heavy weight, press down well and leave in the refrigerator to cool. Quite a lot of fat will be released during the pressing-down

Marquise au Chocolat

Rich Chocolate Dessert

*This is very rich, a chocolate lover's
dream dessert. Over the years I have served it in a
number of ways, always with bright green
pistachios. Here they have been blanched, peeled
and rolled in sugar syrup. Sometimes I omit
the nuts as a decoration and serve a pistachio sauce
instead. Other times I surround the chocolate
with genoese sponge soaked in rum to cut the
richness of the dish. Here it is served simply, with
orange-flavoured crème anglaise.*

RECIPES ON PAGES 195 AND 245

Timbale de Saumon Fumé
à la Mousse de Langoustines

*Round Pillow of Smoked Salmon filled
with a Mousseline of Dublin Bay Prawns*

*This pretty starter is designed to appeal to
people who like something simple. Smoked salmon
makes an attractive and versatile wrapping
for a seafood mousse, and the richness of the main
ingredients is balanced by the olive oil vinaigrette
decorated with chives and peppers. The
timbale is garnished with lumpfish roe, which I
think is underrated, and a quail's egg dipped
in paprika. As an alternative to shellfish we also
make this dish with a mousse of smoked trout
or with a filling of cream cheese with chives.*

RECIPE ON PAGE 179

process, so by placing the terrine on a tray you can avoid a mess (do scrape up the fat, it is wonderful for use in recipes such as mousse de foie de volailles).

Remove the wooden plank and the weight and pour a little melted fat over the terrine to make a 1 cm ($\frac{1}{2}$ inch) layer of rich foie gras butter.

After 2 or 3 days in the refrigerator, place the terrine in warm water for a few seconds and unwrap the cling film. Wrap the terrine neatly in kitchen foil. Refrigerate until ready to serve.

To serve, slice neatly through the foil with a very sharp knife and remove the foil band all around. Cut the gelée au Sauternes into small neat dice and serve with the slices of terrine.

A good dessert muscat such as Muscat de Frontignan goes well with this dish.

Food as an art form

The new style of presentation of food and the inevitable art form it had become appealed to the public. The bandwagon of pretty pictures in glossy magazines and illustrated cookery books began to roll. Food became the 'in' thing internationally, and the best chefs became stars, almost overnight. Eating out became increasingly popular, and I personally began more and more to apply my mind to the total eating out experience, to presenting food well to my customers. It was no longer sufficient just to provide good food. The first impact had to be a visual one, an assault on the eye, and only when the eye was fulfilled, amazed, satisfied, would happy expectations be triggered off in the palate and the nose. Food had to be a feast for the eye as well as the palate. The way ingredients were cut and laid out on the plate was now of paramount importance for food critics and customers alike.

Smoked salmon not only looks very attractive but also makes an excellent wrapping for delicately flavoured fillings such as cream cheese or a shellfish mousse. This can make a beautiful starter if you stretch it to serve four people, but can be very rich. The way to handle it, therefore, is to make sure that the quantity of smoked salmon and the richness of the mousse of Dublin Bay prawns will not be so overwhelming as to spoil the rest of your meal.

However you choose to serve this dish, exercise great care with your portions and serve it with a vinaigrette or with a sauce which will cut the richness slightly. A sauce made of lemon juice and olive oil with peppers and chives (as here) or one made from soured cream spiked with lemon juice are two types of sauces that go with this dish. You may omit using the gelatine if you plan to allow the timbales to set in the refrigerator overnight.

Dublin Bay prawns (also called langoustines or scampi) look like tiny lobsters and have a similar, delicate flavour.

Timbales de Saumon Fumé à la Mousse de Langoustines

*Round Pillows of Smoked Salmon filled
with a Mousseline of Dublin Bay Prawns*

Illustrated on page 177

SERVES 2

4 thin slices of smoked salmon
6 uncooked peeled Dublin Bay prawns
bouillon:
   120 ml (8 tbsp) white wine
   1 bay leaf
   1 sprig of thyme
   1 garlic clove, sliced
   6 black peppercorns
   pinch of salt
   300 ml (½ pint) water
50 g (2 oz) butter
1 gelatine leaf (optional)

60 ml (4 tbsp) cognac (optional)
75 ml (5 tbsp) double cream, chilled
salt
cayenne pepper
30 ml (2 tbsp) olive oil
juice of ½ lemon
5 ml (1 tsp) finely chopped chives
5 ml (1 tsp) finely diced skinned red
   peppers
2 Iceberg lettuce leaves
5 ml (1 tsp) Danish lumpfish caviar
2 lime segments

Line 2 small individual ramekins with the smoked salmon, allowing the edges to flop over the sides.

Make a mousse with the Dublin Bay prawns: poach the prawns in the bouillon. Do not cook them for more than 1 minute in the boiling liquid. Remove the prawns, cool and refrigerate. Boil the bouillon down to a tablespoon of syrupy liquid. Strain, allow to cool down and refrigerate.

Place the prawns in the bowl of a blender, add the reduced bouillon and butter and blend until very smooth.

Melt the gelatine leaf in a little cold cognac and leave aside to cool. (Remember, you may omit this stage if you are going to allow the timbales to set in the refrigerator overnight.)

Lightly whip the double cream and fold into the prawn purée (make sure both the cream and prawn purée are at the same cold temperature).

Add the gelatine and cognac, if used. Adjust the seasoning with salt and cayenne pepper and pack the mousse into the lined ramekins. Fold over the bits of overlapping smoked salmon. Mix the olive oil and the lemon juice, add the chopped chives and the chopped peppers and set aside.

Chop the Iceberg lettuce very finely. Make a ring of chopped lettuce in the middle of 2 plates to form a base. Invert the timbales of smoked salmon on to the lettuce. Spoon the pepper-chive vinaigrette round them.

Place a blob of caviar on the top of each timbale and press down gently. Decorate with lime segments to give a contrast of colours and freshness of taste.

You could serve a good quality, light dry white such as Pouilly Fumé or a fruity white such as Gewürztraminer with this dish, although I think iced vodka is really the only drink which goes well with smoked salmon.

Presentation is very important to me – almost the most pleasurable part of cooking. There is a natural flow in the colours, in the arrangement of food on the plate. The pleasure I get from presenting food well has always been in direct contrast to the painful processes of cooking fish or meat, or preparing a salad. These cooking processes always arouse in me great waves of anger and frustration, but presentation of the final result on the plate pacifies my raw nerves and gives me an immense amount of pleasure.

The cooking revolution produced a situation whereby lightly cooked ingredients, especially vegetables, gave good colour while at the same time producing more intense flavours. You could *see* and *taste* the quality of the food. Just as green vegetables were vibrantly colourful, meat was moist and pink and steamed fish glistened white or pink on the plate. The process was circular. The search for colour in food had caused desirable side effects such as lighter cooking and new ways of cutting food.

Presenting fish

This terrine should only be made with fresh salmon. It is an ideal way of using the tail end of a whole salmon which is left over after you have cut chunky escalopes from the middle of the fish for other recipes. Visually it is very attractive, for it combines the lovely dark spinach green with the soft, bright, pinky orange of the salmon. It is also a good excuse for serving a homemade mayonnaise full of green herbs.

For this dish you will need a 900 ml ($1\frac{1}{2}$ pint) porcelain terrine with a lid.

La Terrine de Saumon aux Epinards

Terrine of Fresh Salmon
with Spinach and Shallots

SERVES 10

900 g (2 lb) tail end piece of fresh salmon, skinned and boned
15 ml (1 tbsp) clarified butter (page 241)
150 g (5 oz) butter
30 ml (2 tbsp) chopped shallots
350 g (12 oz) young, dark green spinach, just cooked, thoroughly squeezed and drained
7.5 ml ($1\frac{1}{2}$ tsp) chopped fresh tarragon
7.5 ml ($1\frac{1}{2}$ tsp) fresh thyme leaves, thoroughly washed

15 ml (1 tbsp) fresh chopped chives
few fresh mint leaves
15 ml (1 tbsp) chervil
salt
pepper
pinch of nutmeg
75 ml (5 tbsp) Noilly Prat or very dry French vermouth
2 bay leaves
Mayonnaise aux Fines Herbes (page 238)

Slice the tail pieces of salmon horizontally into 1 cm ($\frac{1}{2}$ inch) thick slices. Lay on a plate and cover tightly with cling film to prevent drying out.

Brush the bottom and sides of the porcelain terrine with clarified butter.

In a large frying pan melt the butter and fry the shallots very, very lightly. Add the spinach and herbs (except the bay leaves), plus salt, pepper and nutmeg. Let the spinach soak up the butter. Heat through thoroughly and set aside, allowing the spinach to become completely cold. Prepare a bain-marie.

Begin to layer the terrine. First line the bottom of the terrine with the salmon to cover the entire area. Spread some of the cold spinach mixture over it, continuing with the salmon and the spinach until you end up with the salmon on the top. Pour over the Noilly Prat, place 2 bay leaves on top. Place 2 layers of kitchen foil over the surface and close with the lid.

Place in the bain-marie in the oven and cook at 180°C (350°F) mark 4 for 20 minutes. Remove from the oven, take the terrine out of the bain-marie and leave to cool down.

When completely cold, weigh down with a plank of wood and a heavy weight. Place in the refrigerator for 24–48 hours. Remove from the terrine, place it in the middle of a large square piece of kitchen foil, chill again for a couple of hours and slice to serve, cutting through the kitchen foil. Gently remove the foil and arrange on serving plates.

Pass the mayonnaise round separately. Serve with an intensely flavoured white wine such as Chignin Bergeron from Savoie.

Brill is my favourite fish. If you were to ask ten fishmongers if they prefer brill to turbot, it's a safe bet that seven out of ten of them would agree with me. Of these two great, flat fish, for some inexplicable reason, turbot in this country is considered a far superior creature, whereas in France, brill is much liked and thoroughly respected for texture and flavour. I suspect people are suspicious of the name 'brill' – turbot sounds much more grand. For whatever reason, this wonderful fish should, I believe, be elevated to a position among the princes of the sea.

Brill is usually a smaller fish than turbot and its flesh is a little thinner, its grain and texture slightly finer. It does not keep as well as turbot.

Barbue en Rouge et Blanc

Fillet of Brill in Two Sauces

FOR EACH SERVING

60 ml (4 tbsp) clarified butter (page 241)
one 175 g (6 oz) fillet of brill
juice of $\frac{1}{2}$ lemon
salt
cayenne pepper

45 ml (3 tbsp) hot Sauce Crème de
    Ciboulette (page 235)
45 ml (3 tbsp) hot Coulis de Tomates
    (page 237)
15 ml (1 tbsp) chopped fresh chives

Preheat the grill and grease the grill pan with 15 ml (1 tbsp) of butter. Pour the remaining clarified butter over the fish and place in the grill pan. Grill for about 2 minutes or until cooked.

Remove from the grill. Pour over the lemon juice, sprinkle with salt and cayenne pepper and keep warm.

On a warm plate, spoon over the sauces, one on each side of the plate. Sprinkle the fresh chives over the Sauce Crème de Ciboulette. Place the brill in the centre and serve at once. Serve with a good, full-flavoured white burgundy such as a Mercurey blanc, or with a Chardonnay from Australia or California.

Salmon is steamed *with its skin on* so that, when the skin is removed after cooking, the flesh underneath is a spanking fresh pink. It has not come into contact with water, or fat, or with the bottom of a pan or with any other surface. You thus achieve freshness, intensity of flavour and good colour. Another advantage, in my view, is that steamed fish has a beauty and a flavour which fish poached in the traditional way lacks, having surrendered so much of its flavour to the bouillon in which it was cooked.

This dish looks stunning. You have the light pink of the salmon, the pale green of the cucumber and the sparkling golden green of good virgin olive oil. Serve with a little beurre blanc and a sprinkling of diced tomatoes.

Escalope de Saumon
au Spaghetti de Concombre

Escalope of Salmon with Cucumber 'Spaghetti'

Illustrated on page 129

FOR EACH SERVING
15 ml (1 tbsp) clarified butter (page 241)
1 escalope of salmon weighing about
   150 g (5 oz)
coarse rock salt

½ cucumber
1 large ripe tomato
good quality virgin olive oil
15 ml (1 tbsp) chopped fresh dill
60 ml (4 tbsp) Beurre Blanc (page 234)

Pour the clarified butter over the salmon and sprinkle with a pinch of the salt. Steam for 10 minutes or until cooked through, but still moist and pink inside.

Meanwhile, peel the cucumber and cut 20 cm (8 inch) long, thin ribbons on a mandoline. Trim off and discard the seeds and the skin to leave only ribbons of cucumber flesh in between. Slice finely into long spaghetti-like lengths. Sprinkle with more salt and set aside to drain in a colander.

Cut the tomato in 4 pieces. Remove the seeds and run a sharp, pointed knife between the flesh and the skin. Dice finely and immerse in 30 ml (2 tbsp) olive oil. Warm slightly and set aside.

Wash the cucumber and plunge it in boiling water for 3 seconds. Toss in 15 ml (1 tbsp) hot olive oil and chopped fresh dill.

Spoon the beurre blanc onto a warm plate. Arrange the cucumber spaghetti on the sauce and add the salmon. Pour over the tomato and olive oil and serve.

Serve with a great white burgundy such as the intensely flavoured Puligny or Chassagne-Montrachet.

Turbot with shellfish sauce made from lobster, crayfish, crawfish, langoustines or prawns is one of the classic combinations of French *haute cuisine*. My own preference is for langoustine because it has a unique taste, sweet and pungent and the flavour is more pronounced. Puff pastry is something that goes well with the dish and with the flavours. Rather than present it empty, I like to fill the puff pastry case with a creamy purée of leek.

Feuilleté de Turbot
au Coulis de Langoustines
·
Fillet of Turbot served in a Puff Pastry Case, Creamed Leeks and a Dublin Bay Prawn Sauce

FOR EACH SERVING

3 × 7.5 cm (3 inch) spears of green
  asparagus
50 g (2 oz) butter
30 ml (2 tbsp) Fond de Poisson (page 230)
30 ml (2 tbsp) chopped leek (white part
  only)
30 ml (2 tbsp) double cream
salt

cayenne pepper
10 cm × 5 cm (4 × 2 inch) puff pastry case
  (page 248)
150 g (5 oz) piece of perfectly trimmed
  fillet of turbot, sliced horizontally into
  2 thin escalopes
15 ml (1 tbsp) langoustine butter (see
  Sauce Langoustine page 242)

Poach the asparagus in lightly salted boiling water until just cooked. Top with a knob of butter and keep warm.

Melt 25 g (1 oz) of butter in a non-stick pan, pour in the fish stock, add the chopped leek and double cream. Cook together slowly for about 5–6 minutes.

Reduce to a soft purée in a blender, then sprinkle with salt and a little cayenne pepper. Fill the pastry case with this purée and keep warm. Prepare a steamer.

Put a knob of butter on each of the pieces of turbot, sprinkle lightly with salt and steam for 6–7 minutes or until just cooked.

Have a warm serving plate ready, bring the langoustine butter just to the boil and pour in the centre of the plate.

Arrange the food so that the puff pastry case is slightly away from the centre. Place the pieces of turbot, overlapping, in the centre of the plate. Add the asparagus pieces on the other side and serve at once.

Serve with a similar great white wine to the one suggested above.

Serving meat

When it comes to serving beef you might suddenly tire of seeing a great hunk of crusty fillet in the middle of the plate, its sauce cascading from it like a shining drape. You may suddenly wish to see if you can improve this. At various times I have either decided to cut the fillet horizontally into two big pieces (making two beautifully red, fantastically juicy medallions) or to slice it vertically, arranging the slices in a fan. Served with a light translucent, brownish red Madeira sauce, the effect is stunning. Offal, especially liver, can cause presentation problems. But if you serve it in pastry cases on a bed of strongly coloured, well-flavoured sauce, it's sensational.

This is one of my all-time favourites. Blackcurrant liqueur (*crème de cassis*) is a truly lovely drink in its own right and when you add a little to a brown sauce it makes it sparkle and shine and it gives it a vivid dark mauve colour. Apart from anything else its taste is sensational with a slightly smoky after effect — in combination with calves' liver, it is delicious. This dish is liver and bacon fit for a king or queen.

Feuilleté de Foie de Veau au Cassis
Calves' Liver with Puff Pastry and a Blackcurrant Sauce

SERVES 2

85 g (3½ oz) butter
15 ml (1 tbsp) olive oil
½ a medium onion, very finely diced
2 rectangular puff pastry cases, measuring
    7.5 × 5 cm (3 × 2 inches) (page 248)
150 ml (¼ pint) Demi-Glace (page 228)

20 ml (4 tsp) crème de cassis
6 thin 1 cm (½ inch) thick escalopes of
    calves' liver, about 6.5 cm (2½ inches) in
    diameter
salt and pepper
few drops of blackcurrant or raspberry
    vinegar

Melt 50 g (2 oz) of the butter in a heavy cast iron pan, add the olive oil and fry the onion until it is brown and slightly caramelised. Set aside and keep warm.

Heat through the puff pastry cases in the oven and fill them up with the onion mixture. Set aside and keep warm.

In a small, stainless steel pan, reduce the demi-glace and the cassis to a syrupy consistency. Add 15 g (½ oz) of butter and set aside.

In a large heavy griddle pan, melt the remaining butter and when it begins to smoke, add the escalopes of liver. Cook for 15 seconds on either side. Sprinkle with salt, pepper and a few drops of vinegar. Set aside.

Pour the sauce over 2 warm plates in equal quantities. Place the puff pastry cases with the onions in the middle and arrange 3 escalopes on each puff pastry case, allowing the slices to cascade down over the sides. Serve with a rich, fat red wine such as the seldom seen red Meursault from Burgundy.

The search for new ingredients

The search for new shapes and colours has also meant a search for new ingredients of all kinds, especially fruit and vegetables. Salads began to develop in variety and a mixed plateful of radicchio, oak leaf salad, red batavia and the curly endive looks stunning. Different shades of green, different shades of maroons and reds reveal a kaleidoscope of colour when cleverly arranged together and shown off and are a far cry from the salad days when a 'tossed salad' meant the massacre of what might have been perfectly good ingredients in gallons of acid vinaigrette in the bottom of a big bowl.

Garnishes and vegetables

To a professional chef, garnishes and vegetables both decorate and provide the final touch to a dish. If hats were compulsory for all human beings, then garnishes and vegetables would be an equivalent, unconditional law for finishing off a main course perfectly. It is the garnishes and the way they are cooked and presented which indicate a chef's calibre, his talent and attitude of mind. They provide the colour and variety and are the means by which he can fill in the most important areas of his canvas.

The garnishes and vegetables which I have included in this chapter are very much a hotch potch from which to pick and choose. Select those which appeal to you and which best accompany the main ingredients and the sauce of a chosen dish. Remember certain rules: sweet things with lamb and duck, crisp potato with fillet of beef, *duxelles* of mushroom, spinach and asparagus with fish, *gratin dauphinois* with lamb, with beef fillet, with duck and with offal.

A classic dish, simply cooked, gratin dauphinois can be used to accompany many types of meat and poultry dishes. Its ideal partner is a roast saddle of lamb encrusted with brioche crumbs, herbs, garlic, parsley and dried Provençal herbs. These days, I serve tiny, individual-sized portions of this dish as one of my garnishes.

Gratin Dauphinois
Sliced Potatoes Baked with Cream and Garlic
Illustrated on page 80

SERVES 6
4 medium-sized potatoes
75 ml (3 fl oz) milk
75 ml (3 fl oz) double cream

salt
pinch of nutmeg
1 garlic clove
15 ml (1 tbsp) clarified butter (page 241)

Peel the potatoes and slice very finely on a mandoline. Soak in cold water to remove the starch.

Boil together the milk and the cream, season with salt and add the nutmeg.

Rub a 15 × 30.5 cm (6 × 12 inch) rectangular roasting pan with garlic. Brush it with clarified butter.

Drain the potatoes and dry thoroughly on absorbent kitchen paper. Spread the potatoes in thin, closely packed layers, adding a little creamy liquid between each layer. The mixture should not be more than 2 cm ($\frac{3}{4}$ inch) thick. Pour the rest of the liquid on top and bake in the oven at 180°C (350°F) mark 4 for about 30–45 minutes or until nicely browned on top.

I make this little potato dish in small 7.5 cm (3 inch) flat non-stick ovenproof galette pans. If you like *rösti*, this is very similar. These galettes go particularly well with quail or beef. Remember too, that the richness of offal will cry out for something simple to balance it and on certain occasions, rice or a light purée of potatoes flavoured with olive oil are the most appropriate accompaniments.

Galettes de Pommes de Terre

Shredded Crisp Potato Cakes

Illustrated on page 96

SERVES 1 or 2
1 medium-sized potato

45 ml (3 tbsp) groundnut oil or goose fat
salt and pepper

Peel the potato and cut in 0.25 cm ($\frac{1}{8}$ inch) thick slices. Trim the edges into square slices. With a knife cut into *julienne* and mix in the groundnut oil or melted goose fat. Season with salt and pepper.

Heat up 2 small galette dishes and divide the potato mixture between them.

Place these dishes on a hot plate or under a hot grill and cook for 45 seconds until the top is crisp and golden. Turn the galette over and cook for a further 45 seconds. Serve at once.

Tomates concassées

I use tomatoes in several ways as garnish. *Tomates concassées* is a method familiar to everyone in my kitchen. When a *concassé* has been prepared properly from firm, bright red tomatoes, it provides a vivid red colour for garnishing hot and cold starters, main courses and fish. To prevent the tomato from becoming soggy we no longer blanch it in hot water to remove the skin. We merely quarter it, slice off the seeds, then run the point of a very sharp, small knife between the skin and the flesh. When you do that you are left with 4 petals. With a very sharp knife and a light hand, and taking care not to crush the tomato, you slice it into little cubes, perfect *tomates concassées*. We lay them on absorbent kitchen paper and then put them away in the fridge. To use them, we turn a teaspoon of *tomates concassées* in olive oil and tarragon and use it as a garnish.

Tomato butter is another popular way of using these vegetables. We purée the liquid from whole tomatoes which have been pushed through a sieve, then simply thicken it with butter and sprinkle with chopped chives. While we make tomato petals as a decoration, we *never* make tomato roses.

Several years ago, therefore, I began to develop another style. I searched for lots of vegetables with different colours and played around with combinations according to which vegetable accompanied which fish or meat best of all. I developed a selection of small tartelettes filled with different purées and different vegetables covered by different sauces, each designed to complement different dishes.

A little tartelette filled with a purée of apple and topped with a glazed lemon segment goes very well with duck; a tiny tartelette of leeks with bacon looks and tastes good with kidneys in mustard sauce; another tartelette with a purée of mushrooms and glazed with sauce hollandaise complements both fillet of sole and fillet of beef; a little round potato galette with a piece of foie gras in the middle enhances a fillet steak.

For the tartelettes, you make the puff pastry case first by baking it blind for a short time in the oven – the pastry is prevented from rising uncontrollably by the empty flan tin placed on top of it while it is cooking in the oven. Endless different fillings can be used for these versatile little tartelettes. I find them a useful receptacle for ratatouille and for prawns. Simply mash the prawns down with eggs and cream and bake them in the oven. Lobster, crab and other shellfish are delicious done this way.

Petites Quiches
·
Puff Pastry Tartelette Cases

MAKES 4 TARTELETTE CASES
Puff Pastry (page 247)

Roll out the puff pastry until it is no more than 0.25 cm ($\frac{1}{8}$ inch) thick and use it to line 4 small 6.5 cm ($2\frac{1}{2}$ inch) individual flan cases.

Have ready 4 more small flan cases the same size as the others. Place an empty flan case inside each of the pastry-lined ones and press them lightly. Bake in the oven at 180°C (350°F) mark 4 for about 10 minutes or until just cooked. Remove the top flan case and set aside.

Petites Quiches aux Poireaux
·
Tartelettes of Leek and Bacon

SERVES 4

60 ml (4 tbsp) finely chopped leeks (white
    part only), blanched and well drained
60 ml (4 tbsp) double cream
4 egg yolks

20 ml (4 tsp) very finely sliced bacon,
    blanched
salt and pepper
4 tartelette cases (page 187)

Mix together the leek, cream, eggs, bacon, salt and pepper. Allow any excess liquid to drain.

Divide the mixture among the flan cases. Bake in the oven at 180°C (350°F) mark 4 for 6–8 minutes or until the mixture sets. Remove the tartelettes carefully from the flan cases and serve warm.

Petits Flans à la Purée de Champignons Sauce Hollandaise
·
Tartelettes with a Mushroom Purée and Hollandaise Sauce

SERVES 4

10 ml (2 tsp) finely chopped shallots
16 button mushrooms, very finely diced
100 g (4 oz) butter
salt and pepper

15 ml (1 tbsp) very finely chopped parsley
4 tartelette cases (page 187)
60 ml (4 tbsp) Sauce Hollandaise
    (page 237)

In a stainless steel pan fry the finely chopped shallots and mushrooms in the butter and cook together until the purée is dry. Add salt, pepper and parsley and with a palette knife, spread the mixture inside each of the flan cases. Even out well and cover the tops with hollandaise. Glaze under a hot grill or salamander for a few seconds only and serve at once.

Petits Flans de Champignons Sauce Béarnaise
·
Tartelettes of Diced Mushrooms with Béarnaise Sauce

SERVES 4

24 button mushrooms, quartered
100 g (4 oz) butter
15 ml (1 tbsp) Madeira

salt and pepper
2.5 ml (½ tsp) finely chopped parsley
60 ml (4 tbsp) Sauce Béarnaise (page 236)
4 tartelette cases (page 187)

Fry the quartered mushrooms in very hot butter, add the Madeira and stir over high heat until the liquid has almost evaporated. Season with salt and black pepper and sprinkle with parsley.

Place some Béarnaise sauce in each flan case, spoon the mushrooms on top and serve.

Tartelettes au Fromage de Chèvre

Tartelettes of Feta Cheese, Provençal Herbs and Courgette

SERVES 4

60 ml (4 tbsp) paper-thin round slices of courgette	4 egg yolks
50 g (2 oz) feta cheese	salt and pepper
20 ml (4 tsp) double cream	dry Provençal herbs
	4 tartelette cases (page 187)

Blanch the courgettes quickly and drain well on absorbent kitchen paper. Mix together all the rest of the ingredients with the courgettes and fill the flan cases with the mixture.

Bake in the oven at 180°C (350°F) mark 4 for 8–10 minutes or until set. Carefully remove the tartelettes from the flan tins and serve at once.

My mind constantly revolves round the idea that each main course with its distinctive sauce should be accompanied by two distinctive garnishes which are special to it as well as being served with other vegetables which are common to all dishes. For example, the ideal accompaniment to fish is fluffy, buttery, shiny green spinach.

Asparagus, mange-tout and spinach

I always think of these three vegetables as a trio in concert. I suppose it is because I love them so much and because they go well with most fish dishes. The thing to remember about spinach is that it should be cooked in vast quantities of salted water and it has to be squeezed dry. Cooked spinach can absorb a lot of butter (I often use clarified garlic butter) and served this way it is at its finest. I prefer a squeeze of lemon juice to a pinch of nutmeg as a final dressing for cooked spinach.

Asparagus also goes well with fish. I like to dice it diagonally in 2.5 cm (1 inch) batons and arrange it on plates in little heaps all round the edges. In the kitchen, as far as possible, we never send asparagus, mange-tout, carrots, or any other vegetables out without first tossing them in clarified butter.

Mange-tout peas, or snow peas as they are called in America and Australia, are now available very nearly all year round. The tiny fine, green ones are the very best. They need virtually only a few seconds in boiling salted water and a knob of good, fresh butter.

Always cook vegetables in stainless steel pans or in enamel-lined cookware. Their natural acidity or the use of salt or lemon in cooking can cause a reaction with aluminium utensils.

Broccoli

I usually cut up a head of broccoli into *fleurettes* and stalks. The stalks are quite delicious, with a very strong flavour: they should not be discarded. Trim well, then turn into olive shapes (double the size of an actual olive) and serve together with other turned vegetables.

Cook broccoli in enormous quantities of water, slightly salted, to preserve its green colour. If you wish to serve the *fleurettes* later, plunge them straight into ice cold water after cooking.

I think the combination of hollandaise with broccoli is a sensational marriage. For stunning effect, you can make a cluster of cauliflower and broccoli *fleurettes* and arrange them on a plate on a bed of hollandaise, or in a small tartelette case, alternating green with white.

Courgettes, tomatoes and feta

Courgettes are ideal vegetables for stuffing with rice, breadcrumbs, Provençal herbs and Parmesan cheese, or with a little ratatouille, or simply with tomatoes *concassé* flavoured with herbs, garlic and parsley. In any of these ways, they are sensational accompaniments for lamb.

A new type of courgette is beginning to appear more regularly in our markets. This is the round courgette from Provence. I suspect its season may not extend much beyond the longish Provençal summer.

Remember to blanch courgettes well first, then stuff them, reheat them and dribble with heavily scented clarified butter just before serving.

A skinned, scooped-out tomato filled with a *concassé* of tomato, olive oil and basil goes well with salmon flavoured with coarse salt and topped with hot olive oil, giving a colourful result redolent of Provence. A tartelette of feta cheese, Provençal herbs and paper-thin courgette slices goes well with lamb.

Confits

I have recently begun to serve special *confits* of vegetables, an amalgam of five or six different types of vegetables cooked together in a sealed container or aluminium foil with clarified garlic butter, a little sugar and some thyme (page 142). In recent months, this has been my greatest discovery and the idea is firmly planted in my mind that I will hardly ever want to boil another vegetable again.

Carrots and mushrooms

You do not have to 'turn' carrots in order to serve them this way, though in the restaurant we do always turn them (that is, pare them with a knife, turning as we cut, until they form olive shapes), then glaze them in chicken stock and honey and serve them as a garnish. You can serve them either as small batons, or slice them very finely on a mandoline.

Carottes Glacées au Miel

Carrots Glazed with Honey

SERVES 4

300 ml (½ pint) Fond de Volaille, reduced
    to 15 ml (1 tbsp) (page 229)
50 g (2 oz) butter

5 ml (1 tsp) honey
2 medium carrots cut in 2, 'turned'
salt and pepper

Put the chicken stock, butter and honey into a small saucepan.

Over medium heat, cook the carrots, uncovered, for 6–7 minutes in the syrupy liquid. They should be slightly crunchy. Season lightly with salt and pepper.

This dish goes well with beef and chicken and with game birds. Glazed tiny vegetables are a favourite of mine and they look very good presented in a little tartelette. Tiny onions can be treated in the same way (they should be boiled first in salted water and then glazed). Don't overcook them or they will break up and disintegrate.

Petits Champignons Glacés au Vin Rouge

Glazed Button Mushrooms in Red Wine

SERVES 2

600 ml (1 pint) red wine
15 ml (1 tbsp) sugar
12 black peppercorns

pinch of salt
300 ml (½ pint) Fond de Volaille (page 229)
12 button mushrooms, cleaned and well
    trimmed

Mix all the ingredients together except the mushrooms and boil down fast, uncovered, for about 15–20 minutes in a small stainless steel casserole until the liquid becomes syrupy.

Grill the mushrooms lightly for a few minutes and then add them to the syrupy liquid. Turn them over to coat and warm through.

Chefs are now looking all the time for new ways of cutting vegetables. One of the more successful innovations is 'spaghetti', long strips of spaghetti-shaped cucumber, courgette, carrot or kohlrabi cut on a mandoline. One of the most successful dishes we have recently made is a spaghetti of cucumber which,

Tulipe à la Vanille Aux Fruits Frais Assortis au Coulis de Framboises

*Vanilla Ice Cream served in a Tulip Case
with Fresh Fruit and Raspberry Sauce*

*This is a very personal dish, entirely of
my own making. It takes time and patience to
prepare. First you must slice all the fruits — here
we have used grapes, oranges, kiwi fruits,
blood oranges, nectarines, mangoes, plums — choice
of fruits will depend on what is in season.
Then you place the vanilla ice cream in the tulip
case, arrange the fruits on top, dribble over a little
more lime syrup and serve in a pool of fresh
raspberry sauce.*

RECIPES ON PAGES 165, 57 AND 244

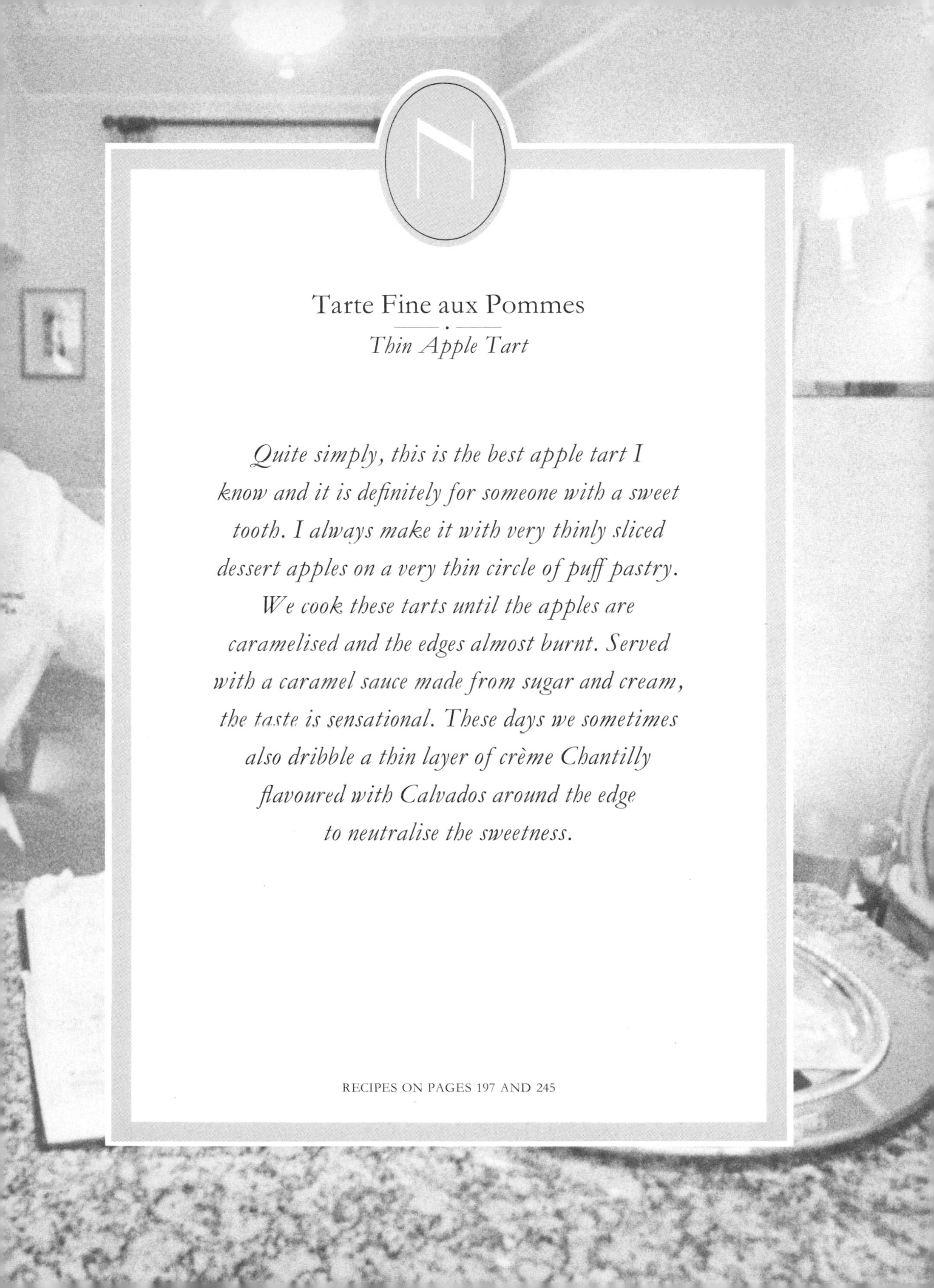

Tarte Fine aux Pommes

Thin Apple Tart

Quite simply, this is the best apple tart I know and it is definitely for someone with a sweet tooth. I always make it with very thinly sliced dessert apples on a very thin circle of puff pastry. We cook these tarts until the apples are caramelised and the edges almost burnt. Served with a caramel sauce made from sugar and cream, the taste is sensational. These days we sometimes also dribble a thin layer of crème Chantilly flavoured with Calvados around the edge to neutralise the sweetness.

RECIPES ON PAGES 197 AND 245

when tossed with dill and olive oil, produces a stunning visual effect and tastes delicious too. I do not know whether it is safe to argue that the skill with the knife in modern kitchens is now more widely applied. We seem to have mountains of vegetable work all the time. Vegetables are very finely diced (brunoise), they are 'turned' into olive shaped pieces or cut into 'spaghetti', sweet peppers and tomatoes are skinned, lettuce and sorrel are finely shredded: all require skill with a knife.

Tasteless art

The new emphasis on presentation did have one drawback. Many chefs became artists at the cost of all else: they decorated the plate to such a point that the purpose and true nature of the dish was lost totally. Plates became cluttered with fruit and even flowers. A garnish must be edible, and furthermore it must enhance the main ingredient of the dish. For many second-rate chefs, a large plate and a pound or two of sliced fruit covered a multitude of sins. Yet lack of quality or freshness of an ingredient is not easy to disguise with this type of cooking. Food magazines were also to blame. A clever photographer and a carefully oiled brush to sharpen the image created an equality on the page between the good and the indifferent. People who admired the 'art' in magazines in many cases were fortunate not to have to eat the real thing. But readers of the magazines or buyers of the illustrated cookery books in many cases did not fare so well – the insipid vegetable terrine is one example which springs readily to mind. How many people over recent years have been seduced into the (lengthy) process of preparing this dish only to be bitterly disappointed. Its very attractiveness often belied an insipid end result.

With so much emphasis on the art side, food is beginning to look as if it was made to be photographed or looked at, not to be eaten. The 'food designer' is the latest phenomenon in the world where food is presented for photography. Out come the little brushes to paint shiny surfaces on scallops, brown liquid out of little bottles emulates an authentic brown sauce and yellow liquid masquerades as a saffron sauce. It is quite incredible to think that if the spotlight had to fall on one man as being responsible for the movement towards colour photographs of food and its presentation, it would be Michel Guérard. The other books from the great chefs of France which followed his formative work, *Cuisine Gourmande*, were nothing but very much of the same. Now food pictures are everywhere, not all of them are honest representations of the recipes from which they came and by no means all of them taste as good as they look.

Good presentation also requires good cooking skills, experimentation and thought. I hold very sincerely an impression of what is perfect, what is good and what constitutes an advance within my own parameters, not whether I can serve a fillet of salmon or a fillet of beef in 20 different ways. For me, improvement, perfection and good cuisine means the developing – and improving – of a particular dish. For example, if you pass a brown sauce or a veal stock several times through a muslin cloth it becomes clearer and clearer as a consequence and the end result is a shinier, more translucent sauce. You can achieve a depth of colour to a sauce by browning your veal bones more or can get a richer glow if you add more tomato; the addition of a tiny amount of a liqueur of *cassis* could brighten up the sauce and make it look like a jewel.

I do not proclaim that I cook food better than other people. One thing I should be allowed to do, however, is to proclaim unequivocally that I have no peers in my presentation of sorbets and ice creams and of fruit. My usual way of presenting fruit is on a white plate with a very light green background. That green background is my lime syrup. Having spent my youth in Tanzania and Kenya, in an exotic, tropical garden, I have come to know the colours, the tastes, the textures of my native Africa so terribly well. We arrange fruits and sorbets in the most devastating way. Have a look at the illustrations on pages 192 and 209.

This chocolate marquise looks sensational if you make sure you use really fresh, strong green pistachios. The quantities of ingredients for this chocolate cake are standard in my kitchen. It usually makes about 24–30 slices. The container I use for this Marquise au Chocolat is a long 45.5 cm (18 inch) terrine made of very light aluminium. If you wish to halve this recipe, then my advice is to use an ordinary 1.1 litre (2 pint) terrine.

The type of chocolate you use is also very important. Meunier chocolate, which is the most common cooking chocolate, will give you very good results, but we use a French-made 'Barry' in the restaurant. You can, if you like, serve this with Orange-flavoured Crème Anglaise (page 245).

Marquise au Chocolat
Rich Chocolate Dessert
Illustrated on page 176

SERVES 24–30

145 g (4¾ oz) dark chocolate, melted
12 egg yolks
250 g (9 oz) caster sugar
45 ml (3 tbsp) granulated coffee, dissolved
    in 60–70 ml (4–5 tbsp) of water

100 g (4 oz) clear honey
275 g (10 oz) best quality unsalted butter
165 g (5½ oz) cocoa powder
450 ml (¾ pint) double cream
clarified butter (page 241)

Mix the melted chocolate, egg yolks, sugar, coffee and honey together.

Cream the butter and mix it with the cocoa powder, then stir this into the chocolate honey mixture.

Whip the double cream into soft peaks and fold into the mixture.

Brush the bottom and sides of the terrine all over with melted butter and line with cling film. Pour the chocolate mixture into this and place in the refrigerator to set. It is best to make it the day before you use it.

Unmould the terrine by dipping it into hot water for 10 seconds and then inverting it very carefully.

Remove the cling film and run a palette knife evenly over the top and sides to smooth it out.

If you really want to drink with this, try a glass of champagne or a delicious dessert muscat.

This chocolate mousse is a lighter version of our Marquise au Chocolat.

I think one of the best ways of serving a chocolate mousse is scooped into round balls with a giant ice cream scoop and served nestling in very light tulip pastry cases.

It is important to use the best quality ingredients you can lay your hands on for this very rich dessert – the finest black chocolate.

Mousse au Chocolat

Chocolate Mousse

Illustrated on page 208

SERVES 12

130 g (4½ oz) cocoa powder
300 g (11 oz) dark chocolate, melted
45 ml (3 tbsp) clear honey
45 ml (3 tbsp) granulated coffee

90 ml (6 tbsp) rum, Grand Marnier, cognac or armagnac
7 whole eggs
7 egg yolks
300 ml (½ pint) double cream

Mix the cocoa and melted chocolate together, then stir in the honey. Dissolve the coffee in the liqueur of your choice.

Whisk the whole eggs and yolks together, then whip the cream to the point where it just forms peaks.

Fold together ⅓ of the cream, ⅓ of the egg mixture and all the chocolate. Fold the next ⅓ of the cream and ⅓ of the eggs and amalgamate well. Remember to fold rather than mix. Finally, fold in the remaining cream and eggs carefully. Pour into a large glass bowl and allow to set in the fridge.

As with the chocolate marquise, above, you could drink champagne with this or a glass of dessert muscat.

This is easily the best apple tart I have tasted. The secret is in the quality of the apples, the thinness of the slices, how well you caramelise them and the caramel sauce itself which makes a simple tart look superb.

Tartes Fines aux Pommes
Thin Apple Tarts
Illustrated on page 193

SERVES 2

4 Golden Delicious dessert apples, peeled, halved and cored

2 thin rounds of puff pastry (page 247), 15 cm (6 inches) in diameter, pricked with a fork all over to prevent rising

10 ml (2 tsp) caster sugar

knob of butter

Syrop (page 158)

Sauce Caramel (page 245)

Cut the apples into very, very thin slices and arrange around the pastry bases in a circle, starting at the edge and working towards the centre as in the classic manner.

Sprinkle the apples with sugar, then divide the butter in 2 and dot over the surface of the apple slices.

Bake the tarts at 170°C (325°F) mark 3 for about 10–15 minutes or until the pastry base is cooked and light brown in colour. If the apples have not caramelised well, either cover the edges of the pastry with tin foil and glaze under a salamander or fierce grill, or caramelise with a blow torch. Glaze with sugar syrup and serve with caramel sauce and a good dessert wine.

Petits fours

I determined early on to avoid serving petits fours which you see everywhere else. This is a petit four which the famous restaurant Hiely in Avignon has served with great distinction for many years.

Meringues
Meringues

SERVES 12

100 ml (7 tbsp) egg white

200 g (7 oz) sugar

100 g (4 oz) almonds, roasted and chopped

Put the egg white and the sugar into a round-bottomed copper bowl, and heat to 70°C (158°F), whisking continuously.

Warm the bowl of a mixer. Tip the meringue mixture into the bowl and whisk at top speed until cold. Fold in the chopped almonds.

Put into a piping bag and pipe 2.5 cm (1 inch) blobs onto a non-stick baking sheet. Cook at 180°C (350°F) mark 4 for 20 minutes until firm.

My favourite petit four. I have not seen it anywhere else and I have not eaten it anywhere else. This is an idea that came straight out of my head. Once you start eating these, you just cannot stop. Allow two per person with coffee.

Amandes Caramelisées
Caramelised Almonds

SERVES 12
24 whole almonds

225 g ($\frac{1}{2}$ lb) sugar
2.5 ml ($\frac{1}{2}$ tsp) glucose syrup

Blanch the almonds in boiling water, skin them, dry them and roast in the oven till golden.

Boil the sugar with 120 ml (8 tbsp) of water and the glucose until the sugar begins to colour. Aim for a deep, rich, light brown caramel colour.

With a tiny, 2-pronged fork, dip the almonds individually into the caramel and place onto a marble surface to cool. Store in an airtight container to prevent the caramel coating from becoming soft. It is best to eat them the same day.

This is another simple petit four which I find irresistible. Oranges are one of my passions in life and this is a wonderful way of using the peel.

Orangettes
Caramelised Orange Peel

SERVES 12
3 large, very deep orange-coloured
  oranges

550 g (1$\frac{1}{4}$ lb) caster sugar

Cut the base and top off the oranges. Cut each one diagonally into 4 quarters. Peel the flesh from each quarter and cut the zest into sticks, 0.5 cm ($\frac{1}{4}$ inch) thick and the whole length of the orange quarter. Although you do not need all the pith, some of it should adhere to the skin.

Cover the orange zest with cold water and bring slowly to the boil. Simmer gently for 5 minutes. Strain, and repeat this operation another 3 or 4 times.

Return the pan and the orange sticks to the heat and add 300 g (11 oz) of the sugar. Over a very, very low flame cook for over 1 hour, stirring continuously with a wooden spoon.

Spread the orange sticks onto a grill pan to drain off any excess syrup. Then, when dry, roll the sticks in the remaining sugar.

This is another one of our little petits fours which are different. We try to make these little strawberry tartelettes so small that you can eat them in one mouthful. The pastry we use is the crumbliest of all and the word *sable* (sand) perfectly describes its fine texture. You can experiment with the flavour by adding vanilla essence, rosewater, Pernod, kümmel or orange or lemon essence instead of Grand Marnier.

Tartelettes aux Fraises
Tiny Strawberry Tarts

SERVES 12

Make 12 × 2.5 cm (1 inch) diameter tartlet cases from pâte sablée (page 248)
crème pâtissière to fill the pastry cases (page 246)

12 tiny strawberries, hulled
30 ml (2 tbsp) thick sugar syrup (page 158), flavoured with 15 ml (1 tbsp) Grand Marnier

Fill the tartlets with crème pâtissière, roll each strawberry in the syrup mixture and place on top.

The principles of presentation

At home, you may not have the time or the equipment to create the elaborate presentations you see on the plate in good restaurants. But principles remain the same: do not overgarnish, where possible serve the food on one plate, although the family-style of serving vegetables in the middle of the table gives added enjoyment. With the food, remember that you can, with practice and hard work, continually improve the look and flavour of a dish. Do not be afraid to use white china for a stunning effect. Remember, too, that the table is the background to the presentation of your food. Glasses and cutlery must gleam, linen napkins and tablecloths should be crisp and free of creases and folds. Note the difference between linen and paper ones. Use fresh flowers liberally to create the perfect setting for the meal.

At home, or in a restaurant, the presentation of a dish should enhance its character. The extreme practices of the 'artists' and charlatans has caused the inevitable backlash. And now a second restaurant revolution is at hand, *la cuisine de grande-mère* or 'granny food', which has come to us from France. Under this influence, presentation is almost studiously casual and garnishes may be a purée of potatoes or a portion of lentils rather than exquisitely sculpted carrots. Hearty, honest, traditional dishes such as pot au feu are once again in vogue.

Here at last is a new challenge for the real chef who cooks real food and does not merely make pictures.

'These days front of house is just
as important as the kitchen. Very few people who are just
brilliant chefs make a success in the restaurant world.
Décor, comfort, lighting, rapport with and interest in
the customers all come into the equation. I'm always dying to
know who my customers are, what makes them tick, where
they live and what they do.
We remember their names, their likes and dislikes. In the
end it is all to their advantage. The livelihood of a
good restaurant may well in the end depend on
good, caring service. The best restaurant is
the one where you're recognised.'

CHAPTER SEVEN

The restaurant world today

 ho knows what makes a successful restaurant? Price, location, décor, comfort, service, and lastly, food. Whoever attempts to answer this question never gets anywhere. There are so many variables to do with personalities, atmosphere, image and honesty, the mood of the moment, fashion and *luck* (if you're busy when you start, the chances are you'll continue to be busy). It is no bad thing that food has become fashionable. It is no longer expected that in fashionable restaurants the food must be bad. The modern revolution in food began in the early Seventies in France with Bocuse and Guérard and the coining of the phrase *nouvelle cuisine* by Gault et Millau. The new lighter cooking used fresh ingredients and a slightly oriental look.

Granny food

Having extracted most of the goodness and virtues of 'la nouvelle cuisine' the great chefs are now turning their backs on it. Plates are still large, vegetables are still crisp and fresh ingredients are still to the fore. However, it is now *la cuisine de grand-mère* or Granny Food which is being rediscovered by the French public. Mashed potatoes, lentils, humble root vegetables, like swede or turnips, and cheaper cuts of meat simmered for a long time feature on stylish menus in France. Some years ago these chefs competed with each other for elaborate displays of presentation and recherché ingredients. Now, they will serve you a pot-au-feu, combining a recipe from their mother with some of the new cooking methods to produce this new style of food. This trend will surely speed around the world as quickly as did the vegetable terrine and the sliced breast of duck. But even this is false modesty. There is also some concern in France at the undermining of the sound base of French cooking by the intrusion throughout Europe of the American fast food conglomerates with their limitless budgets and sophisticated marketing techniques. Some of the great chefs have even spent their own money to form a committee to fight the invasion of the hamburger and the spare rib. They see the danger that the French tradition of being raised on honest food and devoting oneself early to the pleasures of the table will be lost in a sea of tomato ketchup and synthetic bread. It is ironic that at a time when we are more health conscious than we have ever been, when pages and pages are being written on diets, additives, etc, that there should be an unprecedented boom in the sale of so-called junk food; that it has invaded France, the cradle of cuisine, and been received so warmly by so many people is a matter of grave concern.

The influence of France

France is undoubtedly the centre of European gastronomy and it must be hoped that the chefs will win their fight. France's influence is still enormous on the cuisines of other countries I have visited. In Germany, 'la nouvelle cuisine' lives on. Native chefs serving French food are making great advances towards 2 and even 3 star status but it must be said that the food is becoming almost too precise and too stylised and possibly lacks the heart of the truly great food of France. Similarly in Holland, a country which has always steadfastly resisted advances in gastronomy, chefs are being encouraged and good restaurants are appearing. Unusually, Belgium is not, as many people think, full of people drinking beer and eating chips with mayonnaise. Apart from its superb chocolates, Belgium has a tradition, particularly in Brussels, of great restaurants. Because of its geographical location it is also the first beneficiary of major advances in French cuisine. In Scandinavia, the improvement in restaurants is notable in those which serve a form of French food, although there is a resurgence of interest in national dishes. The food in Italy has always been seen at its best in the home or in the humble restaurant using the best local ingredients. *Michelin*, however, are now discovering significant and important Italian restaurants and the outlook for food there is highly encouraging. Hats off to the Italians, whose pasta-based repertoire has provided the fiercest resistance to American-style fast food. Unfortunately, though, the only 3-star restaurant in Italy is French, not Italian.

And so in Europe the good efforts of the French are having to counter the force of the Yankee dollar. In America itself *nouvelle cuisine* has been firmly Americanised. Presentation in significant restaurants is of paramount importance. Yet the large variety of vegetables is grown with the emphasis on looks and colour which totally ignores any flavour. I find, too, the legendary American beef tasteless and inferior to Scotch and French. To me, many American restaurants prefer to sell the look rather than the taste and in many cases they are selling a theme to cover the absence of any genuine inspiration or talent. Despite the paranoia in America about health foods, salt-free diets and additives, it seems to me that popular eating is dominated by restaurants with their evil smell of bottled sauces and their sweets and chocolates of poor quality. It must be hoped that the movement towards native American ingredients will produce a genuinely good national cuisine, but 'Californian cuisine' should stay in California. For how can any cuisine, supposedly from a specific country or region, bear such widely differing hallmarks as Parisian-style bentwood chairs, very fine vermicelli with scallops (renamed rather fancifully scallops with angel's hair), fruits in savoury sauces, pawpaw and mango in salads or grilled guinea fowl on a bed of salad leaves? Yet all these disparate elements are part of what is called Californian food, so I suppose it is a specific cuisine. But does it deserve to be?

It is, of course, England that I know best. England has a clear insight of ideas from France, America, India and Hong Kong as a result of the Empire, and lately from almost every other country that can claim to have a national cuisine. The rise of the ethnic restaurant has been a great phenomenon over the last 10 years. Korean, Thai, Mexican, Brazilian, African, Burmese, even Irish, restaurants have sprung up and are flourishing. What is it that makes Indian and Chinese cooking, in particular, so irresistible to the English? Why do the untutored taste buds of the average Briton respond so favourably to this food? I love Indian and Chinese but I am surprised how the garlic served there is warmly received, though when it comes from a French kitchen it is less popular.

Big business versus small businessmen

Because of this popularity and because of the presence of funds from abroad, particularly the Chinese who are fleeing from Hong Kong, ethnic restaurants are no longer the humble corner site in a rundown suburb. In London they are competing in the centre for prime sites; they are driving the independent chef/patron into the suburbs, or into the country. There are so many obstacles conspiring against the high quality restaurateur when he begins: rents, rates,

planning applications, licensing laws etc. The picture is bleak for the small man, the inspired amateur or the gifted young chef trying to begin. In London many public houses are being transformed into American-style cocktail bars and are owned by large conglomerates. They have premium sites and an alcohol licence, which enables them to serve drinks and food and also to oppose anyone else who threatens their monopoly. The group executive from one of these companies clumsily directs operations as the big money from England or America develops these faceless chains.

Egon Ronay has said that to establish a 3-star restaurant in London requires an investment of £1–1.5 million. If this is so, you first have to obtain the money, service the loan: someone at the end of the day has to pick up the bill. Therefore, in London these large sites become big, buzzing theme restaurants. Out goes the talent in the kitchen, in comes the simple cooking process for high volume, and the conveyor belt of American-style service.

Starting with the premise that you want to provide good food on a comparatively small scale is wrong. The economic conditions in England currently conspire against the good restaurant. There is a property owning democracy created by easy money from the building societies. On the other side of the coin, however, as domestic property prices rise and mortgages increase, the available disposable income for a good diner out is cut. Property is sucking in money out of people's pockets on a large scale and the boom in property in fact contributes to a decline in living standards. It is certainly true in England that a suburb with its tidy gardens and lawns, clean, quiet and civilised – in every way a conservative area – will not support a good restaurant. People's disposable income is consumed by their houses, their children's education and so on – there is little left over for the 'luxuries' such as eating out or good clothes. Go instead to an area dominated by doctors, solicitors, barristers and intellectuals who stand politically on the left and you are likely to succeed.

Sky-high property prices

A selfish restaurateur might say that what England needs is a bout of inflation to bring incomes in line with property values and put disposable money back on the streets. Incidentally, in London the troubled theatre trade may say the same, too. The property developer in England is supreme and from his coat tails hang all the little men – restaurants and others – who try to make a living. Property prices throughout France are virtually static. Even in Paris or the Riviera towns, property prices have never risen as they have here. Restaurants pass from generation to generation. There is a tradition of family and communal help. These are some of the reasons why food in France has always been so much cheaper.

In England the Business Expansion Scheme (BES) is an attempt by the government to help the small businessman. The BES has been taken up by the restaurant world because it is beyond the scope of the friendly bank manager to help set up a restaurant and the sums are too insignificant for merchant banks or the Stock Exchange – we're talking about between $£\frac{1}{4}-\frac{1}{2}$ m. But with this scheme the small businessman is required by law to adopt all the trappings of big business. This means not only an ever-increasing amount of paperwork but the hiring of expensive lawyers and accountants. For a small man this, as well as high rates and wages causes a vicious spiralling circle of rising costs which the eventual customer does not wish to know about or pay for. The BES scheme is being manipulated by the big catering empires to get bigger.

At our first restaurant in 1973 we charged seven pounds for two, in 1987 we charge ninety pounds for two, but our profit margins were higher all those years ago. The lawyer, the estate agent, the butcher, they all put their prices up as they like but when customers visit your restaurant they will be heavily critical if you do the same. It cannot be said often enough that the restaurateur is providing you not just with food but also service, linen, flowers, tables, chairs and so on. The maintenance of standards does not achieve business. In London, at least, there are some forces against the domination of the great chains. Although it is not unique, I think it wrong that so large a portion of middle range restaurants – the famous Wheelers, Mario & Francos and Maxims group – should all be owned by one company: Kennedy Brookes plc. One of the principals, Roy Ackerman, is a personal friend but I cannot see the justification for so much power in the hands of a few people when it comes to eating out, especially when their standards are so abysmally low.

The success stories

Yet there are still some individuals in London who have achieved success, despite everything. Praise is due to Albert and Michel Roux, whose restaurants were the first to be awarded three Michelin stars in England. I hope, however, that they will be remembered more for their excellence than for their attempt to take a shortcut to millions by the strange method of preparing convenience food – *sous-vide*, in which food is pre-prepared, portioned out, sealed in a bag and reheated for sale in proper restaurant premises. Their French counterparts Michel Guérard, Roger Vergé, Paul Bocuse augment their income by publicising their businesses through self promotion – books, lecture tours, special appearances, consultancy work and the promotion of own-label wines,

Mousse au Chocolat

Chocolate Mousse

This is another very pretty dessert. I always serve chocolate mousse in a tulip case and here we have exploited the classic mint, chocolate, nuts combination. The mousse itself has a real chocolate flavour — there's very little cream in it. I always flavour my crème anglaise with orange and here the flavour of the sauce is echoed by using a segment of orange as a garnish.

RECIPES ON PAGES 196 AND 165

Panaché de Sorbets et de Fruits Frais au Sirop de Citron Vert

Sorbets with Lime Syrup

Blackcurrant, passion fruit and pineapple with Kirsch — I always serve these three sorbets together. The fruits are selected to contrast with the sorbets in both colour and taste. It takes time to arrange a dish like this. First we slice all the fruits which are then dressed with lime syrup. Contrary to the practice in most French restaurants, I like to serve sorbets, like ice cream, in balls. The finishing touch is an almond tuile, lightly dusted with icing sugar.

RECIPES ON PAGES 158, 162 AND 163

foods and champagnes. Praise also is due to Langan's Brasserie in London – a restaurant that feeds 600 people a day to a decent standard through the hard work of Richard Shepherd and, some may say despite the publicity, the talent of co-owner Peter Langan.

Pierre Martin has brought to London real French seafood and despite themselves, the English now enjoy it. There is more sheer honesty in his restaurants – in terms of food, price and décor than in any other truly French restaurant except Alain L'Hermitte's Mon Plaisir. For sheer dedication and staying power, as well as someone to look up to, Pierre Koffmann is probably the giant of the London scene. For sheer brilliance, energy and ambition Raymond Blanc is ahead of all the others. The great educators, teachers and mentors are Anton Mosimann at the Dorchester, Michel Bourdin at the Connaught and the Roux brothers in their two respective temples of gastronomy, Le Gavroche and the Waterside Inn. Their protégés are scattered all over the country and sometimes themselves have created new restaurants fostering the teaching of good food.

The trend towards the adulation of the chef will, I hope, play itself out. The good work done by teaching the young to cook and inspiring them to open their own restaurants is of more value than the self-adulation which is revelled in by the profession at the moment. When you group yourself within a profession, you are saying 'I am the greatest'. As an amateur, I shall not join any of these self-congratulatory groups. I have always said that it is not a college training, it is not the ability to belong to associations, that makes great chefs. Forces for change, for development and for advancement will inevitably be resisted by associations, professional bodies and societies. I believe that the young man or woman wanting to be a chef should begin by working in an important kitchen. The process of going through the catering college is outdated. It reflects the knowledge and principles of yesteryear that can no longer be of use – though if colleges worked closer with chefs and recognised the leaders in their profession, I might change my mind. If a professional body of chefs could advise and revise the syllabus, I might understand. Colleges in England making stocks from powder, preserving old recipes, old methods and old ideas are in the way. Let the colleges buy Harold McGee's book and then they will see whether the teaching is in tune with modern thinking. If it is, I will eat my hat.

It is thought the young chefs, through whatever means, must be encouraged to stand up for good food and sound methods. The individual opening a restaurant benefits from the advance in modern communication and the advances in modern travel. Japanese methods of presentation can be complimented in Los Angeles as easily as in London. Young chefs will find cookery books competently translated and readily available. They will discover suppliers who will help to find the most difficult ingredients to enable them to create the dish they have read about or seen. In return for this, they may have to pay the price. There is still a need to overcome the large corporations, the rising prices and the marketing techniques which convince potential customers that a restaurant without a theme is no restaurant at all and to go out simply to eat good food is boring. I will believe that the trend all over the world is towards good food when I see a McDonalds close down and be replaced by a restaurant run by a young chef in search of three Michelin stars.

'A gin and tonic
says a lot about you as a person.
It is more than just a drink, it is an
attitude of mind. It goes with
a prawn cocktail,
a grilled Dover sole,
Melba toast and
Black Forest gâteau.'

CHAPTER EIGHT

The customer is not always right

*I*f anyone were to ask me how I would like to be remembered, I should like to reply 'as the man who could never understand why so many people believe in the maxim "the customer is always right"'. I'm afraid that I am totally evangelical in my belief that this is just not true. I feel very secure in the knowledge that the great Fernand Point was certainly not dominated or guided by this rule. If there is one request I could make to enable me a flashback of his golden era at the Pyramide in Vienne, it would be to see him presiding over those great kitchens and deporting himself in front of his customers. I have not yet had the courage to present a bill to the customer who lights a cigarette after his hors d'oeuvre, though, there are very many times when I have wished I could have done so. Nor have I served a *gâteau marjolaine* at the start of a meal to a customer drinking LaTour Blanche.

I think some clever Frenchman somewhere in the past said that we get the politicians we deserve. It was the great Brillat-Savarin, the nineteenth-century French author of *La Physiologie du Goût*, who declared that the destiny of nations depended on the manner in which they eat. He would probably have gone on to say that by and large we get the restaurants we deserve and in a geographical context the more sociologically dead an area is, the less likely it is able to support good restaurants. In England, a supreme example of a sociologically dead area, according to Christopher Driver, ex-editor of *The Good Food Guide*, is Reading and its environs, and by God how true that is!

213

The comparatively low sales of major restaurant guides, particularly of the prestigious and mysterious *Guide Michelin*, show the lack of general interest in good food. More significant for the restaurateur is the sinister fact that these low sales reflect the lack of authority and the lack of trust which these guides command. A Frenchman who enters a restaurant listed by *Michelin* knows more or less what to expect. He will be aware of the standard of food to expect and the level of service he will receive because he will have been informed of them by the guide's rating system. In England, around 40,000 copies of each edition of the *Guide Michelin* are sold, while in France, the figure is closer to one million. A Frenchman dining out in France will be surprised if something goes wrong in a restaurant. A customer in England is, on the other hand, suspicious from the start. He will ask on the telephone 'What sort of restaurant is it?' 'What are the prices?' 'Can you describe to me some of the dishes you offer?' 'Can I bring my own wine?' Depending on my mood, I have on several occasions given the following answers: 'We do a little bit of everything, Chinese, a little bit of Indian, a little bit of Uruguayan, a little bit of Spanish, some Italian and some French cooking'. As for prices I might say: 'Oh very expensive, about £100 a head!' Or on one occasion when I felt very jumpy, I told the man on the line, 'If you ask the price – you can't afford it!' On another occasion, I told someone who wanted to bring his own wine that he could bring his own food and his own waiters too! The other day, a lady tried to ask if we were a good restaurant – I happened to be in a very calm and particularly mischievous frame of mind, so I lowered my voice and mustering all the seriousness I could, I said to her 'As a matter of fact this is not a very good restaurant and I don't advise you to come and eat here' to which, slightly taken aback, she thanked me profusely for being so honest and bid me a good day in a very charming manner. . . .

The concept of a good restaurant

Only a very small percentage of the population understands the concept of a good restaurant and the trust that is required on both sides in order to achieve the highest standards. A performer needs an audience, an appreciative audience. A Frenchman knows that a Michelin rosette against the name of a restaurant, especially one where the chef is the owner, reflects the skill, the training, the dedication, the professionalism and the extensive thought that has gone into the selection of good ingredients, the creation of good recipes, the compilation of well-balanced menus and the way in which very fresh ingredients have been put together, cooked and presented. If escalope of salmon is on the menu of a good restaurant, it means that wild salmon is in season, that it is fresh salmon, that it is beautifully trimmed, steamed or poached, or that it has been cooked to just the right point. The sauce which accompanies the salmon will have been created specifically to complement it. It is hardly an afterthought. So if someone says 'I think I will have no sauce at all', it would be like asking a greater shoemaker to make you a pair of shoes without soles – I suppose you could still wear the shoes, but it's not the same.

The concept of a good restaurant takes it for granted that it is a spotlessly clean establishment, that table settings are sparkling, the kitchens are impeccable, and that management will spare no expense (hygiene is a very expensive business) to avoid poisoning its customers. The customer has to have taste and appreciation; he must understand what is involved and place his trust in the restaurateur. To get the best out of a good restaurant, you have to place your faith on the line and understand the effort, the toil and the heartache and the tears that go into it. It is not only disappointing but infuriating when having gone to considerable lengths to create a dish, a customer will ask for, say, a grilled Dover sole and a bottle of tomato sauce. I remember a Texan millionaire who came to dinner at our restaurant in Battersea. He said that since he and his companion were on a diet, could we therefore give them very simply steamed fillets of sole? When the fish arrived he produced a bottle of Texas chili sauce, asked for a silver sauce boat and proceeded to spread it all over his fish. This sort of thing happens even in top restaurants.

Advising customers

In our restaurants it has always been one of our most important rules that customers should be guided, assisted and, if necessary, cajoled into a well balanced meal. My wife is positively meticulous in the pursuit of this golden rule, many times to the dissatisfaction and displeasure of the customer. It really means that if he or she asks for a mousseline of sole with a langoustine cream sauce, then there is no point whatsoever in following this with a course of chicken with a cream sauce flavoured with foie gras. One cream sauce followed by another cream sauce is asking for trouble and, invariably, the restaurant will be to blame, yet nearly 99 per cent of the time our desire to please and to help people enjoy their meals by careful planning is misconstrued as an attempt to dictate. From the moment the order is accepted for a mousseline of sole with a *beurre blanc*, followed by a fillet of turbot in a Champagne sauce, the damage is done. Allow people to eat two such unbalanced dishes and they will not enjoy their meal. Advise them against it and they may not come back.

If only customers would realise that a visit to a good restaurant is not the beginning of a battle. They have come to relax, to be amused, for their senses to be titillated, for their palates to be teased, and their appetites satisfied. Eating out is not a war and the encounter with the head waiter should not be a battle of

words. Ordering food should never be taken as an opportunity for sly remarks or jokes at the waiter's expense or at the expense of the restaurant. Top flight restaurateurs put every ounce of their thought, their energy and their thinking behind everything that they do. Good waiters are not there to pit their wits against the enemy, or to bolster their own egos.

It is not much fun being a waiter in England. Customers look down on the profession, generally, and the English themselves look upon this profession as beneath their dignity. Service is mistaken for servility. To be a waiter is to be servile and that won't do for a great, proud race. But the French, too, are a proud race and the Americans, even prouder. In France the profession is recognised officially, it is respected, it is honourable and is exercised with skill, with pride and with professionalism. In America, a waiter is almost as important as the head of the corporation, and is treated with similar respect.

Until a few years ago, chefs, likewise, had no status. They were part of the service and the service meant a lower scale of dignity. The image of the chef was of a simple, humble person, someone with little ambition, a plodding, shuffling body who did the dirty work. But today, things are changing. The chrysalis has burst and the butterflies are beginning to emerge. The clothes we wear in the kitchen are smart, they are sparkling clean, they are brilliant white, they are well-tailored. The great chef is now a star. Modern life, modern stress, the pursuit of health, the pursuit of enjoyment, the search for new horizons have opened up the horizon of the chef and his frontiers are constantly being pushed forward on to new grounds, new tasks, a new search for a new style and a new method.

Restaurateurs in general, and this one in particular, love to give service, to give good food, to show manners, to show great generosity, to laugh, to smile, to greet their customers politely. But restaurateurs in general, and this restaurateur in particular, do not react favourably to frivolity or rudeness or pomposity, the desire to show off and the desire to proclaim to all and sundry, both staff and other diners, that they are very important people. This kind of attitude gets very short shrift with us. Hence the polarisation, over the years, into two groups of people – they either love us or they hate us.

Booking the table

'A table for four, at eight, name of Smith.' Surely this kind of person would not even address members of his family quite so briskly, or with such contempt. I would not dream of telephoning my garage and barking out the order 'Eight tomorrow morning, new engine, new tyres, polish, valet, spick and span. Pick it up at three o'clock!' Other matters of courtesy often lacking concern the time of the bookings and the numbers of people booked. Good food is not created by pulling rabbits out of a hat. A restaurant which asks you to telephone and confirm your reservation, especially if this was made quite a few days previously, is always a good restaurant. There is very little point in the woman at the other end of the telephone adopting a superior attitude and protesting 'But I am Lady So-and-So'. The reason why restaurants want to ensure that a booking on any particular night, say for four people, does not go by default, is because they wish to survive, to flourish, to produce better and greater food. When a restaurant has 36 seats, a table of four not honouring their reservation can mean the difference between profit or loss, and a restaurateur with any conscience wants to ensure that as many people as possible who wish to eat at his restaurant can do so. A good restaurant will not be good for long if 36 or 40 people all want to arrive at eight-thirty, all want to sit down at eight-fifty, and all want their starter at nine o'clock. It will not remain a good restaurant for long if for every table booked for four only two people arrive, or if every table of two arrives as a table for four: these people would not get into many theatres with two tickets. 'Can't you squeeze another one in?' The answer may very well be 'No'. Often three people turn up at a restaurant, having booked for two, and within minutes are complaining that there are no peanuts or olives or Perrier water. Lateness can cause real problems for us and we were recently involved in some acrimonious correspondence with customers who wrote to us after a dinner one evening saying what a delicious meal they had had, how good the service was, but how rude I had been. They thought nothing of booking a table for six at seven-thirty, having two members of the party arrive ten minutes early, two some 25 minutes later with the news that they would now only be five, and the final member of the party finally showing up at ten minutes past eight. They could not see that they had messed us around, did not understand that we had turned customers away because we were full and could not accept our annoyance at their lack of consideration.

Expectations

Anticipation and habit are another matter. These expectations cause a lot of problems. People do not necessarily expect good food, they expect to see and experience certain things. When these expectations are not fulfilled because a restaurant is a cut above the rest, the trouble starts. Steak diane, scampi Provençale, Melba toast, canard à l'orange, Irish coffee. When I see menus featuring these clichés, my mind clicks like a camera and before me the following scene unfolds: low ceilings, exposed beams painted black, little table lamps, red table cloths, smoke-covered yellowing white walls, violently patterned carpets, brass objects placed here and there and the stale smell of deep-frying. Such a dining room will inevitably be presided over by an experienced, continental waiter in an ill-fitting, shiny black coat, his épaulettes covered with dandruff. It is sometimes difficult to compete with such an emporium! Imagine the disappointment in going out on a Saturday evening to what is supposedly a good restaurant and not finding the prawn cocktail, the tournedos Rossini, the Black Forest gâteau? How *can* this be a good restaurant? Where is the flambé lamp?

Time, of course, has marched on and we now have seen the appearance of a new cliché. Enter the travesty of *nouvelle cuisine*, with its bland vegetable terrine, sliced duck breast, or a whole duck breast filled with lobster and deposited on a sauce of pawpaw or mango. Graduates from such restaurants are immediately confused when they encounter the real thing. They see no familiar dishes and wonder whether, because of the lack of them, the restaurant can possibly be a good one.

We were pleasantly surprised when Conservative politician Edwina Currie came for lunch at Simply Nico, but here was a perfect example of inverted snobbery. Her first question to us was 'Don't you have something simple like avocado pear or tomato soup?' Much of the food we serve *is* simple and much thought goes into its presentation. So we were quite dismayed firstly by her initial question and then by the way she mashed up her food on her plate with the fork. It seems that even quite sophisticated people simply do not know what to expect. Instead of being secure in the knowledge that they are in the hands of a good restaurateur and allowing themselves to be guided, the barriers immediately go up, aggression begins to creep in, insecurity appears and they are on the defensive. Out come supposedly innocent phrases such as 'We thought we would come and give you a try as you were recommended to us' – a sentence which in the past made my blood boil. My instinctive reaction was to say 'Thank you very much, whilst you are giving me a try, I'm going to give you a try'. I have, in fact, said this on several occasions but that attitude doesn't seem to bother me very much any longer. If the mentality, the attitude, the instincts, the whole ethic is wrong, how can I, as an individual, change them overnight? Maybe one hundred years from now people will stop saying to those who come after me, 'But you must educate them'. Frankly, I have very little inclination to educate anybody at this stage. I educated in the 1970s during the days when we were in Dulwich and was indeed educated myself by my wonderful customers.

Ordering food

We were always being asked, 'What do you recommend?' 'What is good tonight?' This particular sentence is one which annoys my wife intensely.

Frankly, it's one of the most asinine enquiries anybody can make of us. Surely, the answer is that if you have come to eat in a restaurant of our class, 'Tonight everything is good – and every night and every lunchtime, and if it wasn't good, it wouldn't be on the menu', Dinah-Jane eventually tells them. It really depends on you, what *you* want to eat. Do you want fish, meat, game, offal? If they want specific advice, she may mention the sweetbreads or the kidneys. But more often than not, in such circumstances, the reaction is, 'Oh I don't like sweetbreads'.

The dialogue between a good restaurateur and a customer must necessarily be on a different level. It has to assume certain things; perhaps that the restaurant is a good one; perhaps that the customer wants to be helped and assisted and guided: certainly that ingredients are fresh and perfect. A relaxed, easy, polite dialogue between customer and restaurateur leads to better standards, higher standards, more effort from the part of the restaurateur, a greater happiness and desire to serve from the waiters and a warm, bubbling atmosphere all round.

Criticisms, suggestions, advice – these are all things which help. Surprisingly as it might seem, we do not only accept and encourage, but positively invite them. But criticism can be constructive or destructive, it may be merited or it may not. When it is not, I say so – we always say so – because after all, having for years attempted to educate the customers, the time may now be right to start educating the educators and the critics. Our quarrels have mostly been with them. The instances where we have had strong disagreements with the customers are not as common as some might think. I must, however, mention a couple of these occasions. The first was in Dulwich – a witness who can corroborate this particular story, since the occasion went beyond the realm of serious gastronomy to pure comedy – is the comedian Hugh Lloyd. A husband and wife brought along with them a visitor from Africa. He must have been of some importance to them. When they ordered and the guest decided to have the fillet, it was clearly pointed out to him that it would arrive rare. The host insisted that we should cook it more and my wife equally insisted that he should choose something else. The English couple insisted and persisted and having been warned once more clearly, the steak duly arrived nice and rare. Under no circumstances (and especially for these two!) was I prepared to cook it more. The steak was sent back twice, both times returned in the same state and by this time getting colder. They finally decided to order chicken for their guest who was getting hugely embarrassed by their fuss. When the time finally came to pay the bill where both steak and chicken were charged, the inevitable commotion took place. I came out of the kitchen, took the man's money (from which had been deducted the price of the steak) tore it up before his very eyes into little pieces and threw them under the table. I spun around and left the scene. We withdrew to a corner and following the eyes of everybody else in the restaurant we beheld the spectacle of a grown man on hands and knees under the table collecting torn pieces of £5 notes!

On another occasion, years later, when we first opened in Reading, we served a dinner for 40 people to the managing director of a local company and his staff and customers. There was to be a starter, a main course and a pudding. At the end of the evening we were thanked very warmly and my wife was congratulated and fêted by all the senior men there. Two days later, a letter arrived with two serious complaints. One, that we did not offer a sorbet between the starter and the main course, and two, that the chef did not appear after dinner to circulate among the diners to show himself. I honestly thought that we had landed on a different planet and we were dealing with very odd people indeed who didn't understand that you cannot serve a sorbet when only two savoury courses are offered and that they had expected one to appear automatically and within the price even when the subject had not even been mentioned. I also deliberately did not appear in the dining room as there was an enormous volume of animated conversation and my impression was that they were eating and drinking and were so preoccupied with their own conversations and affairs that I did not wish to intrude. When I replied to this gentleman in these terms his reaction was that I had a supercilious attitude.

It was a bad omen and it clearly gave a pointer to what we had let ourselves in for. Sure enough, we were not disappointed. Our decision to open in Reading, in our experience of a year there, was, with hindsight, a most catastrophic one. It rained the whole year we were there. I was in a permanent daze of amazement at the expectations of certain customers. My appreciation of my colleagues running restaurants elsewhere in the country rose considerably. Now that we are back in London, it is a pleasure to take orders again and few of these problems occur. We have, none the less, certainly noticed the difference between the behaviour and expectations of out-of-town customers – the 'Shinfield types' we call them – and our more regular customers. They tend to display a kind of inverted snobbery and try to assert themselves in foolish ways.

The myth of the food revolution

Over the years, I suppose the thing that made us come to the attention of the culinary world was our insistence that because we served the very finest beef available, it was pointless to cook all the life, the flavour, the juices and the taste out of it. Thus it followed that because we always insisted on serving our beef rare, our 'difficult' image and our notoriety developed. The same thing could be said about the cooking of a lovely piece of fresh, wild, Scottish salmon. In the last ten years, as we all believe, there has been a revolution in the eating habits of the English speaking world. I find this very cynical. Tell it, perhaps, to chefs working in the provinces, to people in England such as Ian MacAndrew in Canterbury, or Steven Bull in Richmond or Sean Hill. If they don't laugh at you it's out of pure politeness. The truth is that I think all these lovely articles about food, the mouth-watering pictures in the glossies, the beautiful television programmes and the rise of the Foodie are all in the realms of fantasy. Beneath this sophisticated façade, the age-old habits of the average person in the street might change a little towards the Big Mac or Kentucky Fried Chicken, but the true food revolution is yet to come. When the sales of the *Guide Michelin* reach a quarter of a million copies, then perhaps, maybe the revolution will have arrived at last and you could open a restaurant in Wigan, a bistro in Newbury, or a serious establishment in Reading and be full every night. As for the Foodie, this phenomenon eats with its eyes closed and analyses every mouthful. Out come the clever sentences we overhear all the time, 'Perhaps a bay leaf too many in the stock', or 'Twenty seconds too long!' He or she is often found in the company of the wine snob, somebody often on the fringes of the trade whose knowledge of wine enables him to pronounce on it with great authority. The decanting of the house wine is an essential ceremony for this type and his analysis of the wine list and the remarks apertaining to it are always hilarious in their superficiality. The revolution in eating habits, I feel, has left some restaurants generations ahead of their customers.

Dress codes

When it comes to choosing a restaurant, economics play the key role in people's decisions about whether to go out and where to go. Prestige and location of the restaurant are also important – not all that many people like to go slumming. Décor comes next and the type and quality of the food comes last. I am quite sure that certain restaurants have dress codes because in the minds of their customers this means it must be a good restaurant. A tie does not make a good man. I wonder if Shakespeare was alluding to a man's heart or his bank account when he wrote you can tell a man from his apparel. Nor does the insistence by an establishment that ties be worn mean that it is a good restaurant. Furthermore it does not mean that if you wear a tie you automatically know about food or that you are a person of sensibility and taste. One day, two fatuous women took one look at our dining room in Reading, put their heads down, lifted their eyes and whispered loud enough for us to hear 'The food is alright, but you've got to shut your eyes because the décor is

223

so awful'. Another lady entered the dining room, saw a tieless diner, turned to her husband and remarked loudly, 'I think we're overdressed for this place, darling'. Our restaurant had obviously gone down in her estimation.

Continuing the theme of dress, a recent magazine article criticised the 'designer-dressed' wives of prominent chefs. Because we are in a service industry, it is taken for granted that restaurateurs, their wives, their children and their staff are not expected to look smart or to dress well – certainly we should appear no smarter than our customers. We have noticed that our staff receive more tips when they are rather plainly dressed and that the customers prefer them to speak with a French or at least a foreign accent (if their accent is a good English one, there is a danger, apparently, that customer and servant might be deemed to be on similar levels) – that way, they cannot look down on them. Customers in England, especially in the provinces, love to be in the presence of somebody they can feel superior to – this does not apply so much in London, of course. In France and elsewhere in Europe, this phenomenon does not apply at all.

Of course, it is not all one way. The staff must always look clean and well turned out. They should always smile, they should always be keen to serve and to make people feel comfortable. They must be there to advise and help, but not to intrude. They should always recognize a customer who has been to the restaurant before as this creates a certain rapport. They should remember their wine, any drinks they had, their favourite dishes, what they ate last time they came and where they like to sit. That is pleasant service, that is good service, and it goes to emphasise what restaurant critic Fay Maschler likes to reply when people ask her, 'Which is the best restaurant?' The best restaurant is where the proprietor and the staff know you best and following on from this, customers always feel much more at home when they see familiar faces and a restaurant where the staff does not continuously change. A 'regular customer' in a restaurant in the English countryside is somebody who eats out on his or her birthday, or their anniversary, regularly every second or third year. On the last day of our year-long sojourn in Reading, when the removal van was parked outside the front door and when in a couple of hours' time we were due to hand over the keys of the restaurant to the new owners, a young man walked in carrying a baby. He came, he said, to have a look at the menu, because he had had a very good meal there five years ago and was seriously thinking about whether he should come again. He had not even noticed the striking change of décor and clearly didn't know whether he was in a Berni Inn or the Moulin de Mougins. That same day, completion day, Dinah took two telephone calls enquiring if we were the previous restaurant. These gastronomes were about to leapfrog from one owner to the next but one. In the same day, three different names were bandied about referring all to the same premises. It is quite a shock how uninterested people really are.

However, the fact does not escape me that when all is said and done, as restaurants go, we probably have the most faithful clientele of all. Every time we have moved, we had letters and flowers and cards of encouragement and hope. Many have followed our progress since 1973, growing up with us in the process. Some have become personal friends and even directors of our newly formed company. These were the people who could see beyond well-done steaks, who understood what we were trying to achieve, the anguish we went through, who followed our ups and downs and watched our standards and their expectations grow higher. There never actually has been a time when we have not had gin and tonic on the aperitif list. We have always served gin and tonics, but we expect people to go beyond what that represents. Salt and pepper pots are not put on the tables but will always be offered if requested, with a very mild suggestion to try the food first. Without the constant inspiration, attendance, and encouragement we have had from our regular customers we would not be where we are today. With people like these, we are very generous with our secrets, enquiring about their criticisms and anxious to remedy the slightest blemish.

A measure of our strong following is the fact that when we opened our restaurant in Rochester Row just before Christmas in 1986, we were very quickly fully booked for both lunch and dinner three weeks in advance. The warmth of our reception back to London both from critics and from old and new customers genuinely astounded and overwhelmed us.

I have never set out to be controversial, but I have never hesitated to say what I feel. The picture of me as an ogre does not stand up, either where it concerns my behaviour with customers, or indeed with my staff.

CHAPTER NINE

My Basic Recipes

'*Sauces interest me*
almost more than anything else
for this is one area of the kitchen
where you can constantly improve.
You can make a sauce lighter, glossier.
The muslin cloth and the chinois sieve
are all-important tools for making
good sauces.'

Colour, clarity, taste and texture. This is what you should look for in a good veal stock. Three vital requirements are freshness of the veal bones, size of the veal bones, systematic and persistent skimming and cleaning – and, of course, a long and careful simmer. Bones must be chopped very small in order to allow all the flavour to escape into the liquid. If you do go to the trouble of making a good veal stock, which is the basis of serious French cuisine, you will end up with brilliant sauces. You can, of course, freeze it in recipe-sized batches.

Fond de Veau
Veal Stock

The colour of the stock will come from the roasting of the bones and the tomatoes. You could accentuate colour by individually painting your bones very lightly with honey. Otherwise, colour can be controlled by the addition of tomatoes. It follows, therefore, the redder and riper the tomatoes, the better the colour. Since red tomatoes are not readily available all the time, I use whole tinned Italian tomatoes and strain off the juice. The tomatoes are then finely chopped.

MAKES 1 litre (1¾ pints)
30 ml (2 tbsp) pure groundnut oil
100 g (4 oz) carrots, coarsely chopped
100 g (4 oz) onion, coarsely chopped
1 small leek, white part only, cut in ½ and
  washed thoroughly
2 shallots, finely chopped
2 garlic cloves, finely sliced
225 g (8 oz) tin of whole Italian tomatoes,
  washed (pour them into a strainer and
wash under cold water to remove all
  the pips and juices, leaving just the
  tomatoes) and finely chopped
200 ml (7 fl oz) clarified butter (page 241)
30 ml (2 tbsp) clear honey
1 kg (2¼ lb) fresh veal bones, knuckles and
  marrow bones are best, finely chopped
1 thyme sprig
1 parsley sprig
1 bay leaf

Place the oil in a heavy stainless steel pan and fry the vegetables very lightly. This should be done very carefully so that the vegetables begin to caramelise but do not burn.

Brush the veal bones lightly with the clarified butter and honey. Roast them in a hot 220°C (425°F) mark 7 oven for about 45 minutes until the bones are nice and brown.

Tip them into the vegetable pan and deglaze with water. Add more water until it covers the bones well and reaches 10–12.5 cm (4–5 inches) above them. Bring to the boil and skim well.

Simmer for 4–5 hours, adding the herbs halfway through. Skim all the time and top up with cold water as necessary.

When cooked, strain the veal stock, ladle by ladle, through a tammy-cloth. Never tip the liquid out because by agitating the contents in the bottom of the pan, you will inevitably end up with a less clear stock.

Demi-Glace

Basic Brown Sauce

A demi-glace is not simply the arbitrary reduction of veal stock. A good demi-glace should be full of flavour, and should not be dominated by the strong meaty flavour of beef. In order to achieve this, reduction has to take place very carefully and a good balance of flavours from fresh, very finely chopped vegetables should be imparted to the demi-glace. My experience has shown me that extravagant use of vegetables at this stage arrests the strong meat flavour of reduced veal stock and adds sweetness from the natural sugars from the vegetables. If you add to this a careful balance of red wine, port, cognac and Madeira, you should get the kind of demi-glace which will make your sauce stand out.

MAKES 350 ml (12 fl oz)

1 litre (1¾ pints) veal stock	75 g (3 oz) dried Provençal herbs
175 g (6 oz) shallots, finely chopped	50 g (2 oz) mignonette pepper
225 g (8 oz) carrots, finely chopped	150 ml (¼ pint) port
175 g (6 oz) onions, finely chopped	150 ml (¼ pint) red wine
175 g (6 oz) celery, finely chopped	75 ml (3 fl oz) Madeira

First reduce the veal stock by one third, skimming carefully all the time.

Next, add all the vegetables, herbs, pepper, port, wine and Madeira. Simmer carefully and reduce by a further third. Your reduction at this stage must be very slow and very careful.

When the liquid has reached about one-third of its original volume and the sauce looks bright and sparkling, strain through 2 or 3 layers of wet muslin, cool and refrigerate. Next day you will have a lovely loose jelly.

Fond de Volaille

Chicken Stock

With the advance of science and the requirements of health laws, certain giblets no longer accompany the chickens one buys in a market or supermarket. My own personal conviction is that the gizzard of the chicken has so much flavour, it is almost necessary for a really good chicken stock. Of course, the most ideal way to make a chicken stock is to boil a whole chicken and this is the basis for the recipe which I am giving below. The juice from the chicken is both delicious and extremely nourishing.

MAKES 2 litres (3½ pints)

1 large maize-fed chicken about
  1.6–1.8 kg (3½–4 lb), with the gizzard
  and the neck
1 medium onion, peeled and stuck with
  1 clove
1 large leek, white part only, trimmed,
  split in half, then chopped

leaves and inner stems of a head of celery
1 garlic clove, finely chopped
125 g (4 oz) carrots, washed and finely
  chopped
thyme sprig
parsley sprig
1 bay leaf

Place all the ingredients in a large pan, add 2.8 litres (5 pints) of water and bring to the boil. Turn down and simmer.

Cook the chicken for 1½ hours, skimming thoroughly throughout the cooking time. Remove from the heat.

Pass the stock carefully through wet muslin. Eat the chicken cold with a salad and mayonnaise.

Gelée

·

Meat Jelly

Meat jelly has always played a very important role in my cooking. I have had to get to grips with it because, since I can remember, I have always served a well-flavoured jelly with my various terrines and pâtés. Honey is very important when you make jelly. It gives colour and flavour and it builds up the quantities.

MAKES ½ litre (18 fl oz)

five 2.5 cm (1 inch) thick slices from the
  knuckle of veal
30 ml (2 tbsp) honey
45 ml (3 tbsp) groundnut oil
1 calf's foot, chopped in small pieces
1 thyme sprig
1 parsley sprig
1 bay leaf
15 ml (1 tbsp) finely chopped carrot
15 ml (1 tbsp) finely chopped white part of
  leek

for the clarification:

175 g (6 oz) meat from the knuckle of
  veal, minced
1 carrot, finely chopped
1 medium-size onion, finely chopped
1 white part of leek, finely chopped
1 tarragon sprig, chopped
15 ml (1 tbsp) dried Provençal herbs
1 egg white
salt and pepper

Brush the veal slices with honey, then lightly fry in the oil. Add the calf's foot, herbs and vegetables, plus 2 litres (3½ pints) of water. Simmer very slowly for about 10 hours, adding water as the level reduces, and at the same time skimming and cleaning the surface.

Strain through wet muslin and place in a large, clean pot.

Mix together all the ingredients for the clarification and moisten with a little water. Add this to the strained liquid and bring to the boil, then simmer carefully for 30 minutes. Strain through muslin and allow to cool.

If you wish to concentrate the flavour and make the jelly thicker, all you need to do is reduce it very carefully.

Gelée au Sauternes
Sauternes Jelly

500 ml (17 fl oz) Gelée (page 229)
150 ml ($\frac{1}{4}$ pint) Sauternes

Melt the jelly. Remove from the heat. Stir in the Sauternes (don't cook or it will lose flavour). Allow to cool. If the jelly doesn't set you may need to add gelatine.

Fond de Poisson
Fish Stock

My own experience has taught me that a good fish stock can only be made with sole bones. If you are making a fish stock for a soup, heads of cod are very good. However, whatever kind of fish stock you are making, especially if you want to use it for fish sauces, you must always thoroughly wash and trim the heads and bones well. Any traces of blood, veins or skin should be washed and trimmed. Also discard any roe. I have never been able to make a satisfactory fish stock with turbot or brill bones, but thoroughly washed and cleaned bones from a sea bass make a wonderful stock for fish soups. Remember, a fish stock must not be cooked for too long.

MAKES $\frac{1}{2}$ litre (18 fl oz)

1 kg (2$\frac{1}{2}$ lb) sole bones	15 ml (1 tbsp) chopped white part of leek
$\frac{1}{2}$ litre (18 fl oz) dry white wine	1 bay leaf
1 medium onion, roughly chopped	parsley sprig
15 ml (1 tbsp) chopped carrot	1 clove

Wash the sole bones thoroughly. Trim off all the skin, cut off the heads and with a pair of scissors cut them at the spine into 25 g (1 oz) pieces.

Place in a small stock pot and pour over the white wine plus $\frac{1}{2}$ litre (about 1 pint) of water.

Bring to the boil slowly, then skim thoroughly.

Add the vegetables, herbs and clove and cook for 30 minutes. You can reduce this fish stock to concentrate its flavour.

Strain through wet muslin for a finer filtration.

Wild mushrooms

Wild mushrooms have a very different taste from cultivated ones and I make extensive use of black truffles, morels, cèpes and girolles in my cooking.

Morels have a distinctive smokey flavour. Some come from Switzerland and as far as I know a lot of the dried morels on the market now also come from India.

Cèpes have a strong meaty taste. The ones I use are from France. The girolle is slightly musky, almost earthy in flavour. Again, mine are French. I use bottled black truffles for garnishes. The aroma and deep flavour of the black truffle is very earthy.

Few people have access to fresh wild mushrooms but I almost prefer to use the dried kinds which have good strong flavours and obviously will keep almost indefinitely.

Beurre de Cèpes

Cèpes Butter Sauce

This is a very unusual sauce. I have not come across it anywhere else and I would like to think that this, together with its brother, the Girolles Butter Sauce, are very much my own invention.

SERVES 4
250 g (9 oz) butter
15 ml (1 tbsp) finely chopped shallots
175 g (6 oz) dried cèpes, finely chopped
2.5 ml ($\frac{1}{2}$ tsp) mignonette pepper
15 ml (1 tbsp) chopped fresh chives

150 ml ($\frac{1}{4}$ pint) dry white wine
150 ml ($\frac{1}{4}$ pint) chicken stock
150 ml ($\frac{1}{4}$ pint) double cream
salt
squeeze of lemon
30–45 ml (2–3 tbsp) milk

In a stainless steel *sautoire* melt 50 g (2 oz) of the butter and put in the shallots.

Fry until transparent and add the cèpes, mignonette pepper and chives.

Cook well together and deglaze with the white wine and chicken stock.

Reduce carefully by two thirds, then slowly add the double cream and the remaining butter chopped into small pieces, as for a beurre blanc.

Cook a little, to a thick buttery coating consistency, then strain through a triple muslin making sure that all the sand and dust from the dried cèpes is left behind. Add salt to taste, a squeeze of lemon juice and the milk. Stir with a whisk and keep warm.

Beurre de Girolles

Girolles Butter Sauce

With cèpes butter sauce, this sauce has pride of place in my kitchen. It goes exceptionally well with vegetables and I use it freely to coat them. It is a little more delicate than cèpes butter sauce.

SERVES 4

250 g (9 oz) butter
15 ml (1 tbsp) finely chopped shallots
175 g (6 oz) dried girolles, finely chopped
5 ml (1 tsp) mignonette pepper
15 ml (1 tbsp) chopped fresh chives

150 ml ($\frac{1}{4}$ pint) dry white wine
150 ml ($\frac{1}{4}$ pint) chicken stock
150 ml ($\frac{1}{4}$ pint) double cream
salt
squeeze of lemon
30–45 ml (2–3 tbsp) milk

In a stainless steel *sautoire* melt the butter and add the shallots. Fry until transparent and add the girolles, mignonette pepper and chives.

Cook well together and deglaze with the white wine and chicken stock.

Reduce carefully by two thirds, then slowly add the double cream and the remaining butter chopped into small pieces, as for beurre blanc.

Cook a little, to a thick buttery coating consistency, then strain through a triple muslin making sure that all the sand and dust from the dried girolles is left behind. Add salt to taste, a squeeze of lemon juice and the milk. Stir with a whisk and keep warm.

Fumet de Cèpes

Brown Sauce Flavoured with Cèpes

I love this brown sauce more than any other. The flavour of the very pungent wild mushroom comes through in a most determined manner. The dried cèpes themselves release some very bright brown juices which give the sauce a lovely sparkle. In looks, smell and taste, this is a truly wonderful sauce and so very simple to make. After many elaborate attempts to do it in different, complicated ways, I found that the very best way to do it was also the simplest.

SERVES 4–6

1 litre (1$\frac{3}{4}$ pints) Demi-Glace (page 228)

350 g (12 oz) dried cèpes
300 ml ($\frac{1}{2}$ pint) Madeira

Bring the demi-glace to the boil in a large pan, throw in the dried cèpes, add the Madeira and simmer for 20 minutes only, pressing the dried cèpes into the liquid.

Strain the cooked cèpes into the bowl of a blender, add 300 ml ($\frac{1}{2}$ pint) of the demi-glace and blend thoroughly.

Tip the contents back into the remaining demi-glace and cook for a further 15 minutes.

Strain through a *chinois* or conical stainless steel sieve, pressing really hard to release all the juices. Pass through a wet, double layer of muslin and let the sauce settle and any froth disappear.

After about 30 minutes, skim off any remaining froth and the sauce will be ready to use.

Beurre de Truffes
Truffle Butter Sauce

This is the famous salad dressing which we first encountered in Vergé's restaurant at Mougins. The flavour of this dressing is so delicate, it needs the purest of ingredients to make it succeed well. The most important ingredient is unsalted butter, preferably French, from the Charentes. The black specks and flakes of the truffle against the yellowish white fluffy butter sauce is another added bonus.

SERVES 4

30 ml (2 tbsp) finely chopped truffle peelings with their juices
150 ml (¼ pint) Noilly Prat
juice of 1 lemon

30 ml (2 tbsp) double cream
225 g (8 oz) good-quality unsalted butter, sliced
pinch of salt
pinch of sugar

Finely chop the truffle peelings and place in a stainless steel *sautoire*. Pour over the Noilly Prat and reduce to 15 ml (1 tbsp) of liquid.

Squeeze in some lemon juice and add the cream.

Bring to the boil and add the sliced butter in a steady stream, as for a beurre blanc.

Whisk well to amalgamate. Adjust the salt, add a pinch of sugar and a little more lemon juice to taste.

Crème de Girolles
Girolles Cream Sauce

When it happens to be your day and this sauce works well, it is the most delicious cream sauce to accompany chicken or veal you are ever likely to come across. There is no point in trying to make this sauce from fresh girolles. It is just not the same. I am finding it increasingly more difficult to acquire dried girolles, so sadly it is a sauce which is gradually dropping from my repertoire.

Whenever I come across dried girolles, my mind automatically goes to this sauce. It goes very well with chicken, veal and sweetbreads.

SERVES 4–6
225 g (8 oz) dried girolles, chopped
15 ml (1 tbsp) chopped shallots

15 ml (1 tbsp) fresh chopped chives
900 ml (1½ pints) chicken stock
900 ml (1½ pints) double cream

Place the girolles, shallots, chives and chicken stock into a stainless steel pan. Bring to the boil and simmer for 1 hour.

Pass through muslin into a glass bowl and allow all the sediment from the girolles to settle. After an hour, carefully tip the liquid into a stainless steel pan, discarding the sediment. Add the double cream and cook until you obtain a slightly syrupy consistency and the sauce has acquired an absolutely heavenly flavour.

Beurre Blanc
·
Butter Sauce

People have a great fear of making beurre blanc, and certainly when I first started cooking I became very apprehensive over the preparation of this magnificent sauce. But I instinctively added almost all the butter at the same time, in pieces, instead of adding the butter little by little which most recipes tell you to do. If you are not going to use the beurre blanc for fish, you should of course exclude the fish stock and replace it with reduced, concentrated chicken stock. Instead of fish stock you can flavour beurre blanc with reduced, strained fresh orange juice or with cream and the water from fresh tomatoes.

MAKES 600 ml (1 pint)
6 small shallots, finely chopped
300 g (11 oz) butter, cut into 25 g (1 oz)
    slices
5 ml (1 tsp) mignonette pepper
75 ml (3 fl oz) white wine vinegar
150 ml (¼ pint) dry white wine

25 ml (1 fl oz) double cream
75 ml (3 fl oz) fish stock
salt
pinch of sugar
juice of 1 lemon (optional)
25 ml (1 fl oz) milk (optional)

Cook the shallots slowly in 25 g (1 oz) of the butter so that they are well cooked and transparent without browning or caramelising.

Sprinkle the mignonette pepper over the shallots and add the vinegar and the white wine. Reduce this very slowly, stirring constantly.

When all the liquids have very nearly evaporated, add the double cream and the fish stock and cook together for a very short time. Add the pieces of butter in rapid succession, one after the other, stirring constantly all the time. When the butter has been well incorporated, bring to the boil quickly and season with salt, sugar and lemon. Whisk in the milk to thin the sauce, if you wish.

If you prefer the sauce to be sharper, adjust the salt and add some lemon juice.

If like me you prefer your Beurre Blanc to be slightly runny and a little whiter, add the milk, whisk well and strain through wet muslin.

Beurre Blanc au Romarin

Rosemary-flavoured Butter Sauce

This is a variation on the traditional beurre blanc. When you add garlic and rosemary, the flavour becomes a lot more interesting. It goes particularly well with a grilled or fried fillet of red mullet.

SERVES 8

2 bunches of rosemary, leaves only
16 black peppercorns, crushed
100 g (4 oz) chopped garlic
350 g (12 oz) butter
225 g (8 oz) chopped shallots
250 ml (8 fl oz) white wine

175 ml (6 fl oz) white wine vinegar
85 ml (3½ fl oz) white fish stock
45–60 ml (3–4 tbsp) double cream
60 ml (4 tbsp) milk
salt
lemon juice (optional)

Fry the rosemary, crushed peppercorns and garlic in 25 g (1 oz) of the butter.

Add the shallots and cook well, then the white wine and white wine vinegar, and reduce by boiling to a syrupy consistency. Strain through a tammy-cloth and squeeze through every drop of the liquid.

Place in a clean pan, add the white fish stock and cook until reduced to nearly a glaze.

Add the double cream. Slice the remaining butter and add, one piece at a time. Stir and whisk to amalgamate. Add the milk, adjust the seasoning and add a squeeze of lemon juice if you wish.

Sauce Crème de Ciboulette

White Wine Sauce with Chives

This is my standard white fish sauce and it is always available in my kitchen. I almost invariably serve it with chives, but if you wish you can mix a chiffonade of sorrel or watercress leaves.

MAKES 600–900 ml (1–1½ pints)

200 ml (7 fl oz) white fish stock
75 ml (3 fl oz) Noilly Prat
50 ml (2 fl oz) good white burgundy
100 g (4 oz) finely chopped shallots
100 g (4 oz) white part of leeks, finely
 chopped

500 ml (17 fl oz) double cream
50 ml (2 fl oz) Sauternes
30 ml (2 tbsp) chopped fresh chives
50 g (2 oz) butter, sliced
salt and pepper

Put the fish stock, Noilly Prat, white burgundy and shallots in a stainless steel pan and reduce over a moderate heat to 60 ml (4 tbsp).

Place the chopped leeks and 150 ml ($\frac{1}{4}$ pint) of water in another pan and reduce to 15–30 ml (1–2 tbsp) of liquid. Pass this mixture through a fine sieve and add to the first reduction.

Add the cream, the Sauternes and 25 ml (1$\frac{1}{2}$ tbsp) of chives and bring to a boil. Beat in the sliced butter, stir and whisk lightly until it melts entirely.

Adjust the seasoning and strain carefully through a wet tammy-cloth. Sprinkle over the remaining chives just before serving.

Sauce Béarnaise
Béarnaise Sauce

Perhaps the best accompaniment for Sauce Béarnaise is a beautiful piece of tender Scotch fillet, charcoal grilled, sprinkled with butter and lemon. In the kitchen each one of my brigade takes turns to make this sauce when it is on the menu, and I personally classify it as one of the six great sauces of French cuisine.

SERVES 4–6

225 g (8 oz) butter
4 shallots, finely chopped
5 ml (1 tsp) mignonette pepper
1 large tarragon sprig, finely chopped,
    including the stalks, plus a
    small bunch of tarragon leaves,
    chopped

90 ml (6 tbsp) dry white wine
90 ml (6 tbsp) white wine vinegar
6 egg yolks
salt
juice of $\frac{1}{2}$ lemon
cayenne pepper

Melt 200 g (7 oz) of the butter in a stainless steel pan. Set aside.

In another stainless steel pan fry the finely chopped shallots in the remaining 25 g (1 oz) of butter. Sprinkle over the mignonette pepper and the chopped tarragon sprig and mix together.

Deglaze with the wine and vinegar and stir together.

Reduce to 45 ml (3 tbsp) and strain everything through a tammy-cloth, squeezing well to release all the juices. Place in a stainless steel sabayon pan and set aside.

Place the eggs in the warmed bowl of a mixer. Sprinkle 15 ml (1 tbsp) of warm water over them and beat to double their size. Scrape the contents into the sabayon bowl and whisk well over a low heat.

Bring the melted butter to the boil and dribble over the egg mixture, whisking thoroughly all the time.

Season to taste with salt, lemon juice, cayenne pepper and the chopped fresh tarragon leaves.

Sauce Hollandaise
Hollandaise Sauce

Hollandaise is a sauce which we prepare in my kitchen twice a day without fail – once for the lunch service and once for dinner. Although Hollandaise can be served very successfully with fish (it has a special affinity with steamed turbot), I prefer to use it as a sauce for vegetables or as a glaze for a tartelette filled with a mushroom purée.

SERVES 4–6

5 ml (1 tsp) mignonette pepper
5 ml (1 tsp) vinegar
4 egg yolks

200 g (7 oz) butter, melted and very hot
salt
juice of $\frac{1}{2}$ lemon
cayenne pepper

Mix together the mignonette pepper, vinegar and 45 ml (3 tbsp) of water. Heat through well, strain through a cloth and tip into the warmed bowl of a mixer. Add the egg yolks and beat thoroughly until they have doubled in size. Tip this into a stainless steel sabayon bowl.

Bring the hot butter to the boil and tip it slowly onto the frothy egg mass, whisking all the time. By doing this, your Hollandaise will be made very quickly and will also be very fluffy. Add salt, lemon juice and cayenne pepper to taste.

Coulis de Tomates
A Light Tomato Coulis

This is the best tasting *tomato coulis* I have yet encountered. It is really fresh and clean and so full of flavour.

You can serve this sauce hot or cold. To serve hot, warm the *coulis* very carefully, whisking all the time to avoid the mixture separating.

SERVES 8–10

450 g (1 lb) very red tomatoes, skinned
   and deseeded
1–2 large bunches of basil
1–2 large bunches of tarragon
10 ml (2 tsp) sugar

10 ml (2 tsp) cayenne pepper
100 ml (4 fl oz) pure olive oil
100 ml (4 fl oz) Vinaigrette de Légumes
   (page 239)
salt and pepper

Chop the tomatoes and place them in a large bowl. Add the basil, tarragon, sugar and cayenne pepper. Mix well together.

Add the olive oil and the cooked vinaigrette and stir together.

Cover the bowl with a cloth and leave to one side to infuse for 4 hours.

Pass the mixture through a mouli-légumes, or blender.

Line a sieve with muslin, pour in the pulp and drain off all the thin, insipid tomato water. Pass through a conical stainless steel sieve. Adjust seasoning to taste.

Aïoli
Garlic Mayonnaise

Stricly speaking, aïoli is the Provençal sauce which is traditionally served once a year all over Provence. Various villages serve this on different festive occasions. In the village of Provence where we live, it is usually served up on the occasion of the *fête aux olives*. The actual mayonnaise is made with heavily scented olive oil and lots and lots of garlic. It has a green tinge and is eaten with boiled, salted cod, boiled vegetables and boiled eggs.

SERVES 10
8 garlic cloves
3 egg yolks
12.5 ml (2½ tsp) mustard
salt

cayenne pepper
800 ml (1¼ pints) groundnut oil
90 ml (6 tbsp) white wine vinegar
    (optional)

Trim the 8 cloves of garlic and blanch in boiling water for about 1 minute. Crush with a garlic crusher in the bottom of a glass bowl, and stir into the eggs, mustard, salt and cayenne pepper. Then add the oil and adjust the seasoning with the salt and cayenne pepper, following the method in the previous recipe. Pass through a sieve.

Mayonnaise aux Fines Herbes
Herb-flavoured Mayonnaise

Mayonnaise-based emulsion sauces provide a good base for the use of fresh herbs, or other green fruits or leaves. For example, a mayonnaise lends itself ideally to a marriage with chives, chervil, tarragon, watercress or avocado and parsley. You can make a green mayonnaise with any one of these herbs, or all of them.

There are two reasons why mayonnaise separates: either the egg yolk is too cold or if you pour the oil in too fast. In order to rectify this, remove from the bowl, place 30 ml (2 tbsp) of very hot water into the bowl, whisk a little of the separated mayonnaise into it, then dribble in the rest gradually.

Green mayonnaise is an ideal accompaniment for cold fish mousses, pâtés and terrines.

MAKES ABOUT 300 ml (½ pint)
1 egg yolk
300 ml (½ pint) groundnut oil
5 ml (1 tsp) mustard
salt

cayenne pepper
45 ml (3 tbsp) white wine vinegar
    (optional)
1 egg white (optional)

Make sure that the egg yolk, oil and mustard are all at the same temperature. This means you will have to collect these ingredients and leave them at room temperature for 30 minutes. In a large glass bowl, place your egg yolk, mustard, salt and pepper. Start to whisk with a good round whisk, or make your mayonnaise with an electric whisk.

When the egg, mustard, salt and pepper are thoroughly mixed, start pouring your oil in, a little at a time. Whisk carefully to the point where the mayonnaise is thick and cannot absorb any more oil. Adjust the seasoning with the salt and cayenne pepper.

If you want your mayonnaise to have a very white, glossy and creamy look, you can either bring the vinegar to the boil and pour over the mayonnaise, mixing carefully with a spatula, or, if you want to make the mayonnaise even lighter, whisk the egg white until stiff and fold into the mayonnaise. Add the herbs of your choice.

Vinaigrette de Légumes

Cooked Vinaigrette

There was a time when this formed the basis for all salad dressings at my restaurant. It is, however, a vital ingredient in the preparation of tomato coulis (page 237). I came across this vinaigrette by accident. I used to lightly cook and pickle a variety of vegetables in white wine, oil, vinegar and herbs. When the vegetables were eaten, there remained behind this very delicious liquid.

For salads use a combination of 2 parts cooked vinaigrette to 1 part hazelnut oil and a drop of lemon juice. If you want to make an orange sauce (to serve with fillets of Dover sole) reduce some orange juice, add the cooked vinaigrette and thicken with butter.

MAKES 1 litre (1¾ pints)

1.5 litres (2¾ pints) good olive oil
150 ml (¼ pint) white wine
85 ml (3 fl oz) white wine vinegar
75 g (3 oz) carrots, finely chopped
75 g (3 oz) celery, finely chopped
75 g (3 oz) onions, finely chopped
50 g (2 oz) leeks, finely chopped
50 g (2 oz) fennel, finely chopped
50 g (2 oz) red peppers, finely chopped

1 sliver of orange peel
12 black peppercorns
1 bay leaf
2 rosemary sprigs
2 thyme sprigs
2 parsley sprigs
2 tarragon sprigs
15 ml (1 tbsp) sugar
5 garlic cloves, finely sliced

Mix the olive oil, wine and vinegar in a cast iron enamel pot.

Add the rest of the ingredients, bring to the boil and cook over a very low heat for 45 minutes.

Remove from the heat, cover with a cloth and allow to infuse for another hour.

Strain the mixture through muslin, cool and then store in the refrigerator, preferably in bottles with a squirt top to aid sprinkling, or in screwtop bottles.

Purée d'Ail Doux

Light Garlic Cream Sauce

This sauce, or purée, has been my standard accompaniment for roast, best end of lamb. Again, as is often the practice, having attempted to do it in many different ways, I have discovered that the best way is also the simplest.

SERVES 6–8

large bunch of thyme

600 ml (1 pint) double cream

45 ml (3 tbsp) clarified butter (page 241)

10 medium shallots, cleaned

10 garlic cloves

salt

squeeze of lemon

Tie up the bunch of thyme and wrap it in muslin.

Tip the cream into a stainless steel pan and add the thyme. Bring to the boil very carefully, then remove from the heat and place to one side. Allow the thyme to infuse for about 1 hour.

Meanwhile, warm the clarified butter and sprinkle it over the shallots and garlic. Place in foil, wrap up carefully and roast at 180°C (350°F) mark 4 for 1 hour, until the shallots and garlic are very soft. Remove from the oven and pour the contents into the cream, discarding the clarified butter and the thyme.

Tip into the bowl of a blender. Purée thoroughly and pass through a chinois or conical stainless steel sieve. Adjust the seasoning and add a squeeze of lemon juice to sharpen the taste.

Sauce Madère au Truffes

Madeira and Truffle Sauce

I have never really much cared for the distinctive classifications given to the truffle-flavoured brown sauces. Is it a sauce Périgeux or a sauce Périgourdine? Does it have sliced truffles or chopped truffles? Does it contain foie gras, or does it not? For the purists and the theorists these are wonderful exercises in sauce making. I make a Madeira sauce from a demi-glace, I add cognac, Madeira, truffle juice and finely diced truffle peelings. Thickened with a little butter and spiked with a few drops of Madeira, this is my Madeira sauce.

It is important to note that the brilliance and clarity of this sauce will depend on your demi-glace.

SERVES 2

150 ml ($\frac{1}{4}$ pint) Demi-Glace

25 ml ($1\frac{1}{2}$ tbsp) cognac

25 ml ($1\frac{1}{2}$ tbsp), plus a few extra drops of
    Madeira

30 ml (2 tbsp) truffle juice

15 ml (1 tbsp) truffle peelings, finely diced

25 g (1 oz) butter

squeeze of lemon

salt

DRAMATRIX PRODUCTIONS IN ASSOCIATION WITH
THE DRILL HALL ARTS CENTRE PRESENTS

CINDERELLA
THE REAL TRUE STORY

BY CHERYL MOCH
MUSIC BY HOLLY GEWANDTER
FROM AN ORIGINAL IDEA BY HOLLY GEWANDTER & CHERYL MOCH
DIRECTED BY NONA SHEPPHARD
DESIGNED BY AMANDA FISK
LIGHTING DESIGN BY KATE OWEN

OVEMBER 26 – DECEMBER 19 • TUESDAY – SATURDAY 8PM

HE DRILL HALL ARTS CENTRE

6 CHENIES STREET • LONDON WC1 • 01-637 8270

  LBGS

CINDERELLA
THE REAL TRUE STORY

THRILL TO THE **ROYAL GOSSIP** YOU WOULD **REALLY LOVE TO HEAR**

'The story I want to tell you is about a time when the streams ran as clear as crystal and the sky was the colour of your dreams and the fish and the animals still spoke to us – oh, they can speak to us, they just don't want to anymore. Can you blame them? In any case, this is a story that is still being passed on, from parent to child, from generation to generation, but in the years of the telling, through the prism of prejudice, it's been altered. I want to set the record straight. I want to tell you the real true story of Cinderella . . . '

PRINCES KISSES GIRL

RUMPUS AT PALACE OVER ALL-GIRL LOVE MATCH!

the New York Critics said:
'AN ABSOLUTELY HILARIOUS SHOW'
'INSPIRED . . . SPECTACULAR'
'FIZZING WITH ELECTRICITY BETWEEN AUDIENCE AND PERFORMERS'

ARCHDUKE IN LOVE TANGLE WITH ARCHDUKE!

with **KATE CORKERY, GILLIAN HANNA, NICOLA KATHRENS, BRYONY LAVERY, DALLAS LINGHAM, MARY McCUSKER, ADÈLE SALEEM, FAITH TINGLE**

Tickets:
Tuesday – Thursday £4.50
Friday & Saturday £5.00
Concessions (UNWAGED, CAMDEN RESIDENT, STUDENT, NURSE, SENIOR CITIZEN) £3.00
ONE FREE TICKET IN EVERY TEN BOOKED

Performances:
Thurs 26 Nov – Sat 28 Nov
Thurs 3 Dec – Sat 5 Dec
Tues 8 Dec – Sat 12 Dec
Tues 15 Dec – Sat 19 Dec

8PM

BAR & RESTAURANT · FREE CHILDMINDING FOR UNDER 5s on FRI & SAT EVES

THE DRILL HALL ARTS CENTRE · 16 CHENIES STREET · LONDON WC1E 7EX · 01 637 8270

Printed by Spider Web, 14-16 Sussex Way, London N7

Place the demi-glace in a small stainless steel pan. Bring to the boil, add the cognac and Madeira, simmer and skim for 10 minutes. Add the truffle juice and diced truffle peelings, then add the butter, a squeeze of lemon juice and a little salt. Remove from the heat, stir and add a few drops of Madeira.

Jus de Carottes et de Sauternes

Carrot Sauce flavoured with Sauternes

This is a lovely new sauce which goes well with sweetbreads, white meats or indeed with fish. The best accompaniment for it is puff pastry, or sweetbreads, or both. I could forgive you for thinking that carrot and Sauternes (two sweet things) would be overwhelming. They are not. They go very well together and the carrot somehow brings the flavour of the sweet wine and its aroma prominently to the fore.

SERVES 8
450 g (1 lb) carrots
300 ml (½ pint) aromatic chicken stock
fresh thyme sprigs enclosed in muslin
1 garlic clove, finely sliced

salt
cayenne pepper
300 ml (½ pint) double cream
75 ml (5 tbsp) Sauternes
few drops of lemon juice (optional)

Dice 350 g (12 oz) of the carrots and place in a pan with the stock, thyme, garlic, salt and cayenne pepper. Simmer for over 1 hour. Remove the thyme and add the cream. Return to the heat and cook very, very slowly for 20 minutes. Add the Sauternes and cook for a further 5 minutes.

Tip the contents of the pan into the bowl of a blender. Liquidise well and strain through a *chinois* or conical stainless steel sieve.

Dice the remaining 100 g (4 oz) of carrot into a very fine *brunoise*. Blanch and add to the sauce. Adjust the seasoning by adding either salt or a squeeze of lemon. Discard the pulp of the carrot, or make a purée out of it by placing it in a muslin cloth to drain well.

This sauce keeps very well in the refrigerator for a number of days. Reheat it slowly and serve.

Beurre Clarifié

Clarified Butter

Clarified butter is often used as an ingredient in a dish or for frying food. By clarifying the butter you will prevent it burning when frying food at high heat.

Heat the butter until it melts and all bubbling stops. Remove the pan from the heat and let it stand until the salt and sediment have sunk to the bottom. Gently pour off the fat, straining it through muslin. Clarified butter keeps well, tightly covered, in the refrigerator.

Beurre Clarifié à l'Ail

Garlic-flavoured Clarified Butter

If you like the taste of garlic and you want to make garlic-flavoured clarified butter, all you do is cut several cloves of garlic in half and simmer them carefully in clarified butter for 30 minutes. Let them steep and infuse for another 30 minutes, then strain.

Sauce Langoustine

Dublin Bay Prawn Sauce

Of all crustaceans, Dublin Bay prawns, in my opinion, make the loveliest sauce. A sauce made from crustaceans will always be better when the shells are from live shellfish rather than from cooked ones. Though you can make quite a good sauce from cooked shells, for an authentic flavour and strong aroma, the shells need to be uncooked.

MAKES 600 ml (1 pint)

450 g (1 lb) uncooked Dublin Bay prawn shells
475 g (1 lb 1 oz) good quality butter
1 bottle of dry white wine
100 ml (4 fl oz) good olive oil
45 ml (3 tbsp) finely diced onions
15 ml (1 tbsp) finely diced carrots
15 ml (1 tbsp) finely diced leeks
15 ml (1 tbsp) finely diced celery
5 ml (1 tsp) fennel seeds, crushed
5 ml (1 tsp) fresh tarragon

2 star anise, crushed
15 ml (1 tbsp) finely chopped shallots
2–3 cloves garlic, sliced
5 ml (1 tsp) dried tarragon
175 g (6 oz) concentrated tomato purée
200 ml (7 fl oz) cognac and dry white wine mixed in equal quantities
250 ml (8 fl oz) double cream
cayenne pepper
salt and pepper
a few drops of Pernod

Clean the langoustine heads thoroughly, discarding all the substances inside the head. Crush the heads and shells well, taking care to break the claws into small pieces.

Allow 450 g (1 lb) of butter to soften slightly, then slice finely. Pour 150 ml ($\frac{1}{4}$ pint) of white wine into a blender. Add small quantities of butter, followed by crushed langoustine shells, then butter, then langoustine shells, alternating until everything is finished. Blend very carefully to get a very smooth, homogenous mass. Remember to keep all the ingredients which go into the blender at the same temperature, and warm up the blender slightly to avoid the butter splitting. Put this mixture aside.

In a large stainless steel pan, warm up the olive oil and add the onions, carrots, leeks, celery, fennel seeds, fresh tarragon and the crushed star anise. Cook carefully for 5 minutes, then add the langoustine mixture. Reduce the heat, spread the langoustine mixture evenly over the bottom of the pan, reduce the heat still further, do not stir, and leave to cook.

After about 10–15 minutes, carefully pour in all the remaining white wine, bring to the boil and simmer for 25 minutes.

Meanwhile, in another pan, melt the remaining 25 g (1 oz) of butter, add the shallots, garlic and the dried tarragon, cook well together, then add the tomato purée. Stir well, then pour in the cognac and white wine mixture. Simmer for 10 minutes. Remove and strain through a muslin cloth. You need to keep the red juices only and discard the tomato pulp. Reserve.

Strain the langoustine mixture through a *chinois* or conical stainless steel sieve, pressing thoroughly. Pass through a muslin cloth. Let it cool, then place in the refrigerator.

After 3 hours, remove it from the refrigerator and lift off the langoustine butter which will have set on the top and reserve. Below you will find the langoustine liquid.

Place the liquid in a pan and return to the heat. Add the liquid from the tomatoes, the double cream, a little cayenne pepper and reduce.

Skim the sauce and add to it the langoustine butter, a little at a time. Stir, whisk, skim and cleanse as you go along until you reach the right consistency. Do not allow the liquid to become too concentrated and strong. It should have a light creamy consistency.

Strain through a muslin cloth, adjust the seasoning and sprinkle over a few drops of Pernod.

As the sauce cools, keep on stirring until it gets thick and well mixed.

You can keep it in the refrigerator for 2 days.

Sauce à l'Estragon

Tarragon and Red Wine Vinegar Sauce

This sauce was one of the first I encountered shortly after I began my cooking career. It is an excellent accompaniment to a roast chicken with roasted tomatoes and a little puff pastry. It has the added advantage in being a sauce which is very easy to make.

SERVES 4

2 shallots, finely chopped	75 ml (5 tbsp) Madeira
3 tarragon sprigs, finely chopped	75 ml (5 tbsp) double cream
30 ml (2 tbsp) red wine vinegar	salt and pepper
700 g (1½ lb) mushrooms, finely sliced	100 g (4 oz) unsalted butter

Put the shallots, tarragon and vinegar into a small heavy saucepan and reduce over low heat.

Add the mushrooms and Madeira and simmer for 5 minutes.

Stir in the cream, season to taste with salt and pepper and continue cooking over a very low heat, so that the surface of the sauce barely moves.

Beat in the butter. Line a sieve with muslin and strain.

Sirop aux Citrons Verts

Lime Syrup

This is one of my stock sauces, and comes straight out of my head. I have made it since the very start of my cooking career and, to this day, it forms the flavouring for the fruit arrangements which we serve either by themselves, or to accompany our sorbets. The aroma is sensational and the colour a very beautiful, vivid transparent lime green.

MAKES 300 ml ($\frac{1}{2}$ pint)

8 limes
200 g (7 oz) sugar

Remove the zest from the limes. Put the sugar, the zest and 300 ml ($\frac{1}{2}$ pint) of water into a pan. Bring to the boil and simmer for 30 minutes.

Take off the heat and leave for 1 hour to infuse. Squeeze the juice from 3 of the limes, strain and very carefully add to the syrup. Pass through wet muslin into a clean glass bowl. Sprinkle over fruit. It is delicious.

Coulis de Framboises

Raspberry Sauce

A very unfortunate victim of the perils of *nouvelle cuisine*. By now, unfortunately, it is a cliché. If you want your raspberry sauce to be in a class of its own, you have to use excellent, deep red, ripe fruit. Since raspberries are available only once a year, you can make an excellent sauce with frozen fruit. To give your sauce distinction, add a flavoured liqueur such as kirsch, or liqueur de framboise, or eau de vie de framboise.

MAKES ABOUT 450 ml ($\frac{3}{4}$ pint)

300 g (11 oz) sugar
650 g ($1\frac{1}{2}$ lb) raspberries

75 ml (5 tbsp) either kirsch, liqueur de framboise, or eau de vie de framboise (optional)

Make a sugar syrup with 150 ml ($\frac{1}{4}$ pint) of water and the sugar, and while still hot add the raspberries off the heat. Do not cook, but allow to infuse for 1 hour and blend well in a blender.

Strain through a very fine stainless steel or plastic strainer. Press thoroughly to extract all the juices.

If you wish, you may now add your chosen liqueur. Stir well, put in a clean bowl, and store in the refrigerator.

When first made, the raspberry sauce will be cloudy and whitish – these are air bubbles. When they have burst and the sauce has settled, it will become much darker in colour.

Sauce Caramel
·
Caramel Sauce

Another of our little sauces. This one accompanies either the thin apple tart, or the caramel ice cream.

MAKES ABOUT 450 ml ($\frac{3}{4}$ pint)

250 g (9 oz) cream   250 g (9 oz) sugar

Bring the cream to the boil.

In a separate, very clean pan, mix the sugar with 150 ml ($\frac{1}{4}$ pint) of water and boil together until it is a deep golden brown. (Be careful the sugar doesn't burn.)

The next process is tricky and a little dangerous. Add the caramel to the cream, exercising great care. It is likely to splutter, boil over (even away from the heat) and cause a thoroughly nasty mess. Whisk carefully and return to the heat until all the caramel has dissolved. Store in the refrigerator.

Sauce à l'Orange
·
Orange Sauce

This is a lovely little sauce to accompany chocolate.

MAKES ABOUT 450 ml ($\frac{3}{4}$ pint)

20 oranges

sugar to taste

15 ml (1 tbsp) flour

Squeeze the oranges and strain the juice into a saucepan. Add sugar to taste.

Dilute the flour in a little orange juice, then add it to the orange juice in the pan. Bring the liquid to the boil, stirring occasionally. Reduce the sauce, then cool.

Crème Anglaise Orangée
·
Orange-flavoured Crème Anglaise
Illustrated on page 208

Somehow, ever since I have made this sauce, I have instinctively flavoured it with orange so that I have reached the point when I only like it and find it complete if it is scented well with the oil from the skin of the orange.

MAKES ABOUT 600 ml (1 pint)

75 g (3 oz) sugar

8 egg yolks

600 ml (1 pint) milk

zest of 1 orange

1 vanilla pod

1 drop of orange essence

30 ml (2 tbsp) Grand Marnier

Whisk the sugar and egg together. Place the milk in a pan and add the orange zest and vanilla pod. Bring to the boil.

Add half the milk to the egg and sugar mixture, then return to the heat. Add the rest of the milk and cook until the mixture coats the back of a wooden spoon.

Strain through a clean, wet muslin. Add the orange essence and the Grand Marnier. Leave it to cool, then store in the refrigerator.

Save the vanilla pod for use in other dishes.

Crème Pâtissière

Confectioner's Custard

I use small quantities of this custard in my soufflés. You can always use it in home-made fruit flans if there is any left over. I find it gives a lighter texture and flavour than the traditional flour-based *panada*.

MAKES 300 ml ($\frac{1}{2}$ pint)
300 ml ($\frac{1}{2}$ pint) milk
$\frac{1}{2}$ vanilla pod

2 egg yolks
60 g ($2\frac{1}{2}$ oz) caster sugar
25 g (1 oz) plain flour

Bring the milk to the boil with the vanilla pod inside.

Mix well together the egg yolks, the sugar and the flour. Make a very well amalgamated paste.

Add half the boiled milk to the eggs, mixing and stirring all the time. Pour this mixture into the rest of the milk and cook stirring well until thick. Pour into a glass bowl to cool down.

Crème pâtissière is one of the pillars of French pastry making. The dangers to avoid and the points to look for are smoothness and the elimination of lumps. Invariably, a skin will form over it and if you cannot mix thoroughly well, you should pass it through a very fine sieve before using it.

Pâte Brisée

Sweet Flan Pastry

This pastry is mostly used in the preparation of delicious fruit flans. It is soft and crumbly and it matches perfectly the aroma of vanilla, or the flavour and taste of different fruit-based liqueurs. With a perfectly textured *crème pâtissière*, it forms one of the great marriages in French cuisine. It is not difficult to make.

MAKES ABOUT 450 g (1 lb)
300 g (11 oz) plain flour
1 large egg yolk and 2 small egg yolks
5 ml (1 tsp) sugar

$7\frac{1}{2}$ g ($\frac{1}{4}$ oz) good sea salt
175 g (6 oz) butter
25 ml ($1\frac{1}{2}$ tbsp) milk

Put the flour on your pastry board (preferably marble), make a well in the centre, and add the egg, the sugar and the salt. Cut the butter into small pieces and add this to the mixture.

Using your fingers, lightly rub all the ingredients together. With your left hand, you should be drawing in all the flour and with your right hand you should be amalgamating everything together.

Sprinkle in the milk and knead the dough two or three times only with the palm of your hand. By now it should be smooth and firm. Wrap in greaseproof paper and refrigerate until ready to use. It also freezes well and can be kept frozen for several weeks.

Pâte Feuilleté
Puff Pastry

The most important consideration in the making of puff pastry is a very cold ambient temperature. At the same time, you need to use very high-quality butter, preferably French. I prefer to use beurre Lescure from the Charentes. And you must handle the dough very lightly. The process of making puff pastry is a long one, because the resting time can extend to beyond 5 or 6 hours, though the actual preparation and cooking time is only about $1\frac{1}{2}$ hours. It is impractical to make this dough in small quantities or with any less than 450 g (1 lb) flour.

These days most non-professional cooks use high-quality bought pastry for convenience and this can be used wherever one of my recipes calls for puff pastry.

MAKES ABOUT $1\frac{1}{4}$ kilos (3 lb)
450 g (1 lb) plain flour, plus a little for sprinkling on working surface and while turning

225 ml (8 fl oz) milk
15 g ($\frac{1}{2}$ oz) fine sea salt
50 g (2 oz) melted butter
400 g (14 oz) well-chilled butter

First make your dough, and there is nothing difficult in this. Make a well in the centre of the flour, pour the milk, the salt and the melted butter and work together well with your fingers.

When all the ingredients are mixed together, start using the palms of your hands to knead the dough until it is smooth and the different elements are well amalgamated. It should not be too elastic. Shape it into a ball and make a cross on the top. Wrap in greaseproof paper and place in the refrigerator for 3 hours.

Remove the dough from the refrigerator and sprinkle flour on the work surface. Roll out by exerting light pressure with your palm on each of the edges. This way you are making 4 flaps which will envelop the chilled butter.

With a wooden rolling pin, beat the chilled butter down to make it a little more supple and shape it into a slab which will sit in the centre of the dough. Start folding the dough flaps over the butter; press the edges down lightly so there are no gaps. Wrap in greaseproof paper. Put back in the refrigerator for 30–45 minutes until the dough and the butter are the same temperature.

Sprinkle more flour on your work surface and roll the dough out to form a rectangle about 76 cm (30 inches) long by approx. 45.5 cm (18 inches) wide. Fold the bottom third up and the top third down over it. Keep the edges straight and seal them lightly. Wrap again in greaseproof paper and refrigerate again for another 45 minutes.

Remove from refrigerator and repeat the rolling and folding exercise again twice more. Place in the refrigerator for 1 hour. Remove and make two more folds, so that in total you have made six folds in total. The dough can now either be stored in your refrigerator for 48 hours or kept in the deep-freeze for several weeks until required.

A note on shaping and cooking
Puff pastry should be cut and shaped when very, very cold. Any pressing of the edges will prevent rising and will result in stodginess. Once you have cut the pastry into the required shape, do refrigerate the shapes for at least 25 minutes before baking. Puff pastry should be baked at medium to high temperatures.

Puff pastry cases
Cut the pastry to the required shape then refrigerate for at least 25 minutes. Place the shapes on a greased baking sheet and put in the oven. Arrange another baking sheet immediately above the one with the pastry, preferably no more than 2.5–5 cm (1–2 inches) above it. Bake the pastry in a preheated oven at 220°C (425°F) mark 7 oven for about 15 minutes or until lightly browned and well risen. The baking tray above the one with the pastry will prevent the shapes rising unevenly.

Pâte Sablée
Sweet Flan Pastry Cases

This is the pastry from which the lovely *sablés* are made for petits fours. It is the crumbliest of all pastries and the French word *sable* (sand) perfectly describes its fine, crumbly texture.

The secret of pâte sablée lies in the flour. You must always mix it in last of all and you must never overwork it. It should remain loose and crumbly and it must not become elastic. Try and avoid placing this pastry in the freezer. You may keep it 5 or 6 days in the refrigerator.

Try using tiny quantities, either of vanilla essence, rose water, Pernod, orange essence, lemon essence, or kümmel as flavourings.

MAKES ABOUT 700 g (1½ lb)
300 g (11 oz) plain flour
225 g (8 oz) butter

100 g (4 oz) icing sugar
pinch of salt
2 large egg yolks, or 3 small ones, beaten

Tip the flour on your pastry board (preferably marble) and make a well in the middle.

Cut the butter into little pieces, place them in the centre of the well and work the two together with your fingers until soft.

Mix the icing sugar and the salt and sift both over the mixture. Work together and add the beaten egg yolks.

Collect the mixture together and knead lightly for a few seconds. Add the flavouring, if wished, then finish it by kneading the dough lightly 2 or 3 times with the palm of your hand.

Tartelettes de Pâte Sablée

Tartelette Cases

MAKES ABOUT 4

37 g (1½ oz) soft flour	rind of ½ lemon
small pinch of salt	1 egg
25 g (1 oz) ground almonds	15 ml (1 tbsp) dark rum

Put all the dry ingredients into a food processor, then lightly whisk the egg and add it with the rum to the dry ingredients. Mix well.

Shape into a ball, wrap in cling film and leave in the fridge to cool and set. Once set, roll out and cut into tartlets. Bake at 190°C (375°F) mark 5 for about 10 minutes until golden brown.

Brioche

Brioche

Brioche is the king of all breads. It should be light and buttery, but not greasy. Toasted, it goes supremely well with a terrine of foie gras. Add to this a chilled glass of Muscat de Frontignan and you have a *ménage à trois* — blissful coexistence! Making brioche is a long, laborious process and you should allow 6–7 hours, most of which is resting and rising time. It is never necessary to make a brioche in the specially fluted brioche moulds. Try and make it in tiny little moulds, or in miniature loaf tins. It is different and it looks pretty.

MAKES ABOUT 1.4 kg (3 lb) dough

75 ml (5 tbsp) warm milk	600 g (1 lb 5 oz) plain flour
15 g (½ oz) fresh yeast	8 eggs
5 ml (1 tsp) salt	300 g (11 oz) butter, softened
	25 g (1 oz) caster sugar

In a bowl mix together the warm milk and the yeast until well amalgamated.

Put this liquid, the salt, flour and eggs into the bowl of a mixer or food processor and beat with a bread hook for 10 minutes.

Mix together the softened butter and the sugar, in another bowl and with the machine running at low speed, add to the bowl of the mixer, a little at a time. After about

4 minutes, the dough should be smooth, shiny and elastic. Leave in the mixer bowl, cover with a cloth and set aside somewhere warm, until the dough has doubled in size.

Turn out the dough to knock it back. Turn it over 2 or 3 times, then cover it with a cloth and refrigerate for 12–14 hours.

Remove the dough from the refrigerator. Shape it into a ball if you are going to use a traditional brioche mould (I invariably make brioche in miniature non-stick bread moulds or non-stick baking tins). Whatever you choose as a mould, make sure your dough is perfectly smooth and has no folds, creases, or cracks or the egg and milk glaze will stick or settle into cracks in the dough and prevent even rising.

Brush the dough with egg and milk and leave in a warm place to double in size and rise. If you are using miniature, non-stick bread moulds, bake them in a pre-heated 220°C (425°F) mark 7 oven for about 10 minutes.

Brioche dough can be frozen, but better still, bake all your little brioches, wrap them up well and then freeze them.

Cookery Notes

The recipes in this book were, of course, originally developed by a chef for use in professional kitchens. Nonetheless, they are, for the most part, eminently suitable for domestic use, though timings and temperatures will inevitably vary according to your oven (professional ovens are far hotter than their domestic counterparts).

All spoon measures are level, unless otherwise stated. Always preheat your oven in advance unless directed otherwise.

METRIC CONVERSION SCALE

LIQUID			SOLID		
Imperial	*Exact conversion*	*Recommended ml*	*Imperial*	*Exact conversion*	*Recommended g*
¼ pint	142 ml	150 ml	1 oz	28.35 g	25 g
½ pint	284 ml	300 ml	2 oz	56.7 g	50 g
1 pint	568 ml	600 ml	4 oz	113.4 g	100 g
1½ pints	851 ml	900 ml	8 oz	226.8 g	225 g
1¾ pints	992 ml	1 litre	12 oz	340.2 g	350 g
			14 oz	397.0 g	400 g
			16 oz (1 lb)	453.6 g	450 g

For quantities of 1¾ pints and over, litres and fractions of a litre have been used.

1 kilogram (kg) equals 2.2 lb.

OVEN TEMPERATURE SCALES

°Celsius Scale	Electric Scale °F	Gas Oven Marks	Temperature
110°C	225°F	¼	very cool
130	250	½	very cool
140	275	1	cool
150	300	2	cool
170	325	3	warm
180	350	4	moderate
190	375	5	fairly hot
200	400	6	fairly hot
220	425	7	hot
230	450	8	very hot
240	475	9	very hot

Recipe Index

General Index